Understanding Rock 'n' Roll

Popular Music in Britain

Understanding Rock 'n' Roll

Popular Music in Britain 1955–1964

Dick Bradley

Open University Press
Buckingham · Philadelphia

Open University Press
Celtic Court
22 Ballmoor
Buckingham
MK18 1XW

and
1900 Frost Road, Suite 101
Bristol, PA 19007, USA

First Published 1992

A catalogue record of this book is available from
the British Library

Library of Congress Cataloging-in-Publication Data

Bradley, Dick.
    Understanding rock 'n' roll: popular music in Britain 1955–1964 /
Dick Bradley.
      p. cm. – (Popular music in Britain)
    Includes bibliographical references and index.
    ISBN 0-335-09755-3   ISBN 0-335-09754-5 (pbk.)
    1. Rock music – Great Britain – To 1961 – History and criticism.
    2. Rock music – Great Britain – 1961–1970 – History and criticism.
    I. Title. II. Title: Understanding rock and roll. III. Series.
    ML3534.B688   1992
    781.66'0941'09045 – dc20   91-44925
                                                   CIP MN

Typeset by Best-set Typesetter Ltd., Hong Kong
Printed in Great Britain by St Edmundsbury Press,
Bury St Edmunds, Suffolk

Contents

Editorial Preface

What *is* British popular music? Does such a thing exist? What makes certain music and songs popular? And who made the musical cultures of these islands? What did Scots, Welsh, Irish and North American people have to do with the process? What part did people in the English regions play – the Geordies, Cockneys, Midlanders and all the rest? Where did the Empire fit in? How did European 'high' culture affect what most people played and sang? And how did all these factors vary in significance over time? In the end, just how much do we know about the history of musical culture on these tiny patches of land? The truth is that we know very little, and this realization led to this series.

The history of British people and culture has been dominated by capitalism for centuries; and capitalism helped polarize people into classes not only economically, but culturally too. Music was never *simply* music: songs were never *simply* songs. Both were produced and used by particular people in particular historical periods for particular reasons, and we have recognized this in the way in which we have put this series together.

Every book in this series aims to exemplify and to foster inter-disciplinary research. Each volume studies not only 'texts' and performances, but institutions and technology as well, and the culture practices and sets of social relationships through which music and songs were produced, disseminated and consumed. Ideas, values, attitudes and what is generally referred to as ideology are taken into account, as are factors such as gender, age, geography and traditions. Nor is our series above the struggle. We do not pretend to have helped produce an objective record. We are, unrepentantly, on the side of the majority, and our main perspective is from 'below', even though the whole musical field needs to be in view. We hope that by clarifying the history of popular musical culture we can help clear the ground for a genuinely democratic musical culture of the future.

Dave Harker and Richard Middleton

Preface

This book has taken more than 13 years to complete, albeit not all full-time study. I worked alone in the main, but several people gave me valuable help and encouragement. My wife Pippa prodded me on, and accepted a spell of reduced income while I worked part-time at my job in order to finish the text. Paul Willis gave me heart and a sympathetic hearing at an early stage of my work. Philip Tagg in Sweden was an inspiration and a friend and, in the later stages, Richard Johnson of the Department of Cultural Studies at Birmingham University read and criticized the thesis on which the book is based, in a most constructive spirit, reminding me of the value of collaboration and a second opinion after some years of struggling along alone. Thanks also to our dog Duke, sadly now dead, who accompanied me on long walks around Handsworth and Sandwell Valley during which the main ideas in this book were worked out. And thanks to Kathy Joiner for typing the manuscript.

Introduction: Taking Popular Music Seriously

Popular music is entertainment, art, release, status symbol, badge of resistance, and aural wallpaper. Nowadays, it can be some or all of these to everyone. It creeps into almost every life for part of almost every day, if only as the 'sound track' to a TV show, the advertising jingle or the piped 'mood music' of the supermarket. And it serves as the hobby, the collecting passion or the daily, necessary shot of important meaning, for a great many people – and not only the 'rebellious', 'gullible' young.

Yet we are repeatedly told – by those who do write or broadcast about music as well as those who do not – that it should not be analysed, studied too closely, 'dissected', that it will not stand up to such treatment, or that it cannot be so treated. Some say 'study classical music, yes, but popular music simply "is", don't spoil it'. To others it is so trivial it would be ridiculous to bother to study it. But what bizarre ideas these are! Of course there are those few who think all 'social' or 'human' studies are an expensive waste of time; only science and technology offer real, useful knowledge. But leaving this aside, what a monstrous self-limitation! We can study history, economics, social behaviour, language, literature, psychology, classical music, but not popular music! Even authors who produce histories *of* popular music, or biographies of singers, tend to avoid any analytical or close, detailed examination of songs, records, performances, and especially listening patterns, choosing instead to mix the 'hard facts' of dates, names and places with a vague, decontextualized, overwhelmingly adjectival, avowedly subjective type of description of the music. The same kind of writing is found in most popular music reviews in newspapers and magazines.

Of course musical meaning is not easy to pin down in words. In fact I believe there is an irreducible, specific, musical level or moment of meaning which quite simply *cannot* be translated. But this need not stop us from studying all sorts of aspects of music making or listening, any more than the fact that we cannot fully translate the taste of a beefsteak into words need prevent us from understanding a lot about cuisine, the chemistry of food and digestion, the role of eating and preservation in our culture, and so on.

The beefsteak is important because it *reproduces* the body, it has a lasting effect on the eater. Now this is in fact why music is important too, and why the search for an understanding of music is a valid task. Music is among the 'signifying practices' which *reproduce* people, their minds and their feelings, what modern sociologists and others call their *subjectivities*. Language, and visual signs (and mixtures like TV), play major parts of course, as do activities which may not directly use these (making things, eating, sleeping), but music, while admittedly often marginal, is definitely involved in its own right. Therefore, the justification for a close study of all aspects of music is the same as the justification for studying 'ideology', 'literature', 'the media', and so on. These things *reproduce* us, constantly, and if we want to do better, and *be* better, we need to drag into consciousness, and into the searchlight of investigation, *how* they do it. We can exert more control over them if we understand them better.

Popular music, in being a factor in the reproduction of society and its subjects, has *effects* – it does something to people. It would be the very liquidation of critical thought to realize this and yet not want to know *what* it does; it would also be to pretend that everything in society and one's own mind is acceptable and justifiable. But everything is very far from being acceptable, and the study of what popular music has done to us, can do and might do – as well as what we can do with it – is as justified by this as any other mental task.

There is, however, very little attention given to studying popular music in British universities, polytechnics and schools. It is no exaggeration that until about 1980, every person who set out on such an investigation in Britain – including myself – found him or herself alone, encouraged but only marginally assisted by any institutional support. None the less, a body of books and articles which do take popular music seriously is now developing and I shall refer to a few of these in due course. I will not try to summarize this book here. It is wide-ranging and full of argument. But I hope the complexities in it (which are plentiful) do not prevent the reader from following the argument right through. What I hope has been emerging in Britain and elsewhere in recent years (at first among handfuls of investigators, but now more widely) is a *culture* of popular music understanding, going decisively beyond what previously existed. If this book helps maintain and accelerate that development, I shall be very pleased.

1 *Prey to a Thousand Certainties*

When I began this study some 13 years ago, I had in mind the writing of a 'culturalist' history of rock 'n' roll. However, my reading since then has led me far and wide, through many fields and disciplines, and the whole project has taken on a more *theoretical* quality. For a time, therefore, I was wont to say it was not a *historical* project at all but a theoretical exploration which made use of a historical case study. This I now think is wrong. When one is trying to write in an interdisciplinary and theoretically self-conscious way about a 'cultural' field or object, one must always keep in sight the basic questions one is asking. And mine are: '*What brought about* the rock 'n' roll "explosion" in Britain?' and 'Why did music-use go from being very incidental to quite central and even crucial, in many young peoples' lives and priorities?' These are questions of *history*, not just of general social theory, and it was the infuriating shallowness and smugness of much existing history writing about rock 'n' roll that first motivated me to try to do better. And at the end of a long trek, it is still some of the elements of a cultural or culturalist *history* I am trying to present to the reader now. I now see what a huge task this is, and that this book can only be a contribution to what will probably have to be an ongoing collective project. To be precise, it is a contribution about *how to write that history*, the concepts that need to be employed and criticized. It does not contain any new store of empirical data, but rather draws together existing writings within a loose developing framework of critiques and constructive suggestions. It is about how we should understand what we already think we know.

And so I will begin by surveying some other history writing, and explain what I think is wrong with it. I begin by drawing a line at roughly 1980, and surveying the state of rock history writing before then. This sets up a rather bleak description, which I will gradually qualify in later chapters by remarking on the flowering of quite a number of better, more useful approaches in the 1980s, approaches largely compatible with, and in some cases influential on, my own.

Probably the chief histories of rock prior to 1980 were those by Gillett, Belz, Laing, Cohn, Shaw, Palmer and Grossman. Other books and articles can of course be added, including studies, biographies, and so on, which contributed to the general picture of rock history writing. My initial arguments here are based on these histories, studies and biographies. Since the late 1970s, a lot more analytical and serious writing has begun to be published, of which more in due course. Contributions in the older vein of course have continued also, and some of them are very useful.

The descriptive-evaluative mode

One of Gillett's books is entitled *The Sound of the City*.[1]* Already in this title, a case is argued, namely that rock 'n' roll is connected with city life in some way. This sort of procedure is found at other points in the book too: the title of Part One, 'They Got What They Wanted – Rock 'n' Roll 1954–58', itself argues a thesis within the 'mass culture'/commercial-exploitation-versus-'consumer-choice' problematic. From the outset, Gillett claims to *interpret* rock 'n' roll, not merely to describe it. Indeed, he writes in the Introduction that the book is a 'study of the music *and meaning* [my emphasis] of rock 'n' roll'. And yet there are really only a few remarks in the whole book which explicitly follow up this concern with 'meaning'. Much of the short Introduction is concerned with it, but after that only a few sentences here and there. In the Introduction he mentions 'adolescent freedom', changing attitudes to sex and love, the 'brutal and oppressive' nature of city sounds, and the changing relationship, in the USA, between black and white populations, and yet subsequently he has little to add on these themes. Certainly he does not make any attempt to systematically relate his discussions of particular records and artists, which constitute the great bulk of the book, to these general themes, except for the occasional brief comment, such as his claim that the 'mood' of rock 'n' roll was one of 'implied protest', or the statement that 'it seemed beyond the resources of white Americans to develop a nationally acceptable style that did not draw most of its inspiration from black music'. These hints are hardly the fulfilment of the Introduction's promise to study the 'meaning' of the music. But what, then, is the nature of the description, evaluation and enumeration of instances, the detailed 'history writing', which makes up the largest part of the book?

I propose to describe *this* writing, provisionally, as the *descriptive-evaluative mode*. It is a mode which we find throughout rock books and articles, and I will therefore dwell on it at some length here. It consists of accompanying 'facts' (usually assembled through an unexplained selection procedure) about particular artists, groups, records, labels, etc., with a type of description that is overwhelmingly adjectival, and uses mostly such terms as 'raw', 'wild', 'raunchy', 'heavy', 'light', 'sweet' and 'strong', terms that often fall into

* Superscript numerals refer to numbered notes at the end of the book.

contrastive couplets such as 'rough/smooth', 'light/heavy', 'authentic/ inauthentic'. A whole lexicon of such terms can be discovered in Gillett's text, while other authors, notably Cohn and Marcus,[2] make such incessant use of their equivalent lexicons that their prose often disintegrates grammatically, becoming a semi-poetic attempt to 'evoke' the impact of the music discussed. This descriptive-evaluative, adjectival mode is the most recurrent strategy resorted to by rock writers for dealing with the specifics of musical meaning. Apart from the history books mentioned, it can be readily found in almost every rock magazine, in the reviews, the features, even the interview questions and answers.

These terms, as descriptions of musical qualities (including qualities of vocal delivery, of recording, etc.) are used in a way which is at once vague and resonant. We often know, or feel we know, what Gillett means when he writes that Presley was 'impatient' or Little Richard was 'frantic'. Yet we cannot readily translate these descriptions into precise musicological or semiological ones. What Gillett is achieving, through this very fluid discourse, with its imagery, its associations and its fleeting analogies ('driving', 'thundering', etc.), is a verbal equivalent to musical meaning, which remains highly sub- jective and intuitive. Of course all descriptive writing and speaking does this to some degree, and I am not arguing that it is invalid as a procedure. But where this is *all* (or, as in Gillett's book, very nearly all) that the writer offers on the question of musical meaning, then it leaves off at the very point where my central questions begin. On the one hand, it more or less rejects or avoids the task of seeking the determinations of the social life out of which the music has sprung in the musical practices and artefacts themselves. On the other, as far as the effects the music might itself have in the world are concerned, it confines itself to a subjective rendering of the music's *affects* as registered by the individual author-as-listener. This writing, then, passes into deception when and where it claims to do more than it does. Such is the case if Gillett's well-researched and even encyclopaedic book is judged by its own claim to be a 'study of the meaning of rock 'n' roll'. And, unfortunately, Gillett's is one of the better rock books!

One paragraph from *The Sound of the City* will serve to illustrate the problems:

> At M.G.M. a more authentic singer, Hank Williams, recorded eleven songs that each sold a million copies or more between 1949 and 1953. Although most of his songs were at least as sentimental as other popular songs of the time, Williams's style of singing established a personal presence that suggested connections be- tween the feelings of the songs and his own experience. In his faster songs, such as 'Hey Good Lookin' and 'Lovesick Blues', he created a good feeling of urgency and excitement.[3]

What qualifies a song as 'sentimental'? Presumably, Gillett is referring to the lyrics, since he argues that Williams redeems them in some way by his style of singing. This style apparently has the ability to establish a 'personal presence', a mysterious statement if it implies that other singers have styles which establish 'impersonal' presence, or no presence at all. Gillett may well be right, but are we not being asked to grant all sorts of assumptions and connections which he does not spell out? To be taken in full seriousness, these claims would need to be made much more explicit, and shown to rest on a defensible view of the structures and elements of musical and lyrical meaning as a whole, something which neither Gillett nor any of the other rock writers have attempted, at least until the late 1970s. We are being asked to assimilate as unquestionable, as it were, his ways of thinking (and not thinking) about these complex problems, in the interstices of a prose which is superficially plain and simple.

When Gillett writes 'he created a good feeling of urgency and excitement', he is collapsing his own response to the songs into a sentence which appears to be a claim about their objective character. He manages this by resorting to the word 'feeling', which, in the discourses of music description at large, can be used to refer to either the emotion supposedly 'aroused' in the listener *or* to something encoded at the moment of composition. This too is a technique – if it is conscious enough on Gillett's part to be called a technique – which recurs throughout; and, incidentally, it demonstrates his relationship to the dominant academic discourse or discourses of music writing and talking. The most widely accepted contemporary academic views on musical meaning in general seem to be: (1) that which sees it as the expression of emotion (or the 'morphology of feeling') and (2) that which is reluctant to accept even this, and claims that music is merely sonorous design with no 'expressive' power.[4] (I will return to these views in Chapter 2.) In relation to these approaches, Gillett is clearly a supporter of the first view. Most of his adjectives for the description of musical effects and qualities are of a kind which suggest the arousal of emotion ('exciting', 'wild', 'sentimental', 'sad', 'merry'). Others are less precise but contain some such component ('earthy', 'raw', 'strong').

It would be interesting – but outside the scope of this book – to trace the stages of the process whereby a rock journalist like Gillett comes to reproduce the basic character of a discourse which is formed originally by scholarly investigations into 'classical' or 'serious' musics. It is indeed very easy to find plenty of examples of writing similar to Gillett's in books of 'serious music' criticism: I have chosen the following two examples at random by simply opening a book and reading a few pages:

> His urge towards contrapuntal line-drawing ... gave cohesion to his part-writing ... counteracted its purely instrumental exuberance, bringing to it an almost vocal simplicity and purity. ...

> His music may well strike the listener as evocative and deeply meaningful, in its solemn mystic beauty, its melodic richness, suppleness of rhythm and contrapuntal strength.[5]

Despite the technical terminology, these passages are, if anything, even more vague than the Gillett quotation, especially the second passage in which the terms could be switched around to give 'its supple melodies, the richness of the counterpoint, and rhythmic strength', with virtually no apparent change or loss of meaning at all! Clearly Gillett and other rock writers are in a long tradition, even if they do not know it.

Here is what Roland Barthes, the leading French semiologist and critic, has to say about the way 'language manages when it has to interpret music'. He points to the way writers always reach for an adjective, to attach to each musical element, and suggests a reason why this procedure is so common:

> If one looks at the normal practice of music criticism (or, which is often the same thing, of conversations 'on' music), it can readily be seen that a work (or its performance) is only ever translated into the poorest of linguistic categories: the adjective. Music, by natural bent, is that which at once receives an adjective. The adjective is inevitable: this music is *this*, this execution is that [his emphasis]. No doubt the moment we turn an art into a subject (for an article, for a conversation) there is nothing left but to give it predicates; in the case of music, however, such predication unfailingly takes the most facile and trivial form, that of the epithet. . . . The man who provides himself or is provided with an adjective is now hurt, now pleased but always *constituted* [his emphasis]. There is an imaginary in music whose function is to reassure, to constitute the subject hearing it (would it be that music is dangerous – the old platonic idea? that music is an access to jouissance, to loss, as numerous ethnographic and popular examples would tend to show?) and this imaginary immediately comes to language via the adjective.[6]

Barthes seems to suggest that language helps the listener become and remain 'constituted', a 'subject' during listening. Pinning an adjective to the tail of the musical phrase, rhythm or harmony sets up a mediation which *constitutes* the listening subject even as he or she does so. Without it, apparently, music might flood or take over the listener, so that he or she would lose him or herself in it. It seems to me that an unstated assumption behind this claim is that language is (always? necessarily?) the most important by far, the *central* practice in the constituting of social life and subjectivity, and that music is a threat to these things because it can signify or communicate somehow, something, *without* language. More of this in the next chapter and Chapter 8.

Returning now to Gillett's passage on Hank Williams, we might go on to ask what the 'authenticity' of the singing consists in, as well as the implied inauthenticity of other singers who are mentioned in the preceding few paragraphs – Frankie Laine, Guy Mitchell, Rosemary Clooney and Patti Page. Here the framework of assumptions and categories into which the reader is drawn, implicitly, is of course the folk art/popular art distinction, as well as the 'mass culture' debate. Once again Gillett fails to say what it is that is authentic about Hank Williams's singing, and what it is authentic *in relation to*. Let us assume that Gillett means that Williams is a representative of a white, rural, community-based type of singing which existed before, and exists outside of, the pop industry. In this case, how does his authenticity survive the choice of 'sentimental' songs which are apparently very definitely *of* that industry? Again, in what does it consist? Surely Gillett is once again assuming his own response to be an objective characteristic of the singing. He may be right, of course, but this approach will never be able to tell us. To put it more strongly, if Frankie Laine dressed up in cowboy clothes and drawled, as he sometimes did, and if this led many listeners to believe that *his* was authentic 'Country' singing, what could Gillett point to in the singing (or the accompaniment or the recording) to prove them wrong?

It is in such formulations as this that we can see most clearly a central characteristic of this mode of writing. Not only is it inexplicit in its terms for musical 'content' or meaning, but, by virtue of this inexplicitness, it elides evaluation and description, so that the former is able to pose as the latter. Once again, I am not accusing Gillett of perpetrating a conscious fraud, nor am I claiming that the two elements can be completely segregated. The problem is that such confusion of subjective response and supposed objective qualities contributes to the existence and the furthering of two overlapping illusions: first, that all responses to music are simply 'valid', and that neither musicology, nor semiology, nor a cultural study can alter this radical self-sufficiency of the individual listener (i.e. 'its all a matter of taste'); and, secondly, that other types or levels of meaning, (apart from the affective-emotional ones which Gillett concentrates on overwhelmingly), are in some way ineffable and indescribable if they exist at all. Both these illusions are more widespread in relation to modern popular music than perhaps anywhere else. And this book is directed against them. Suffice it to say here that this merging of an inexplicit description, and a subjective and narrow type of evaluation, and the posing of the resulting style as a full and 'informed' commentary, constitute the most fundamental and defining qualities of the greater part of all rock writing; hence my term 'the descriptive-evaluative mode'.

Many other books on rock music can be readily criticized along the same lines. However, I do not wish to imply that they contain little or nothing of value. Dave Laing's *The Sound of Our Time*[7] mixes some descriptive-evaluative writing, notably on Buddy Holly, The Beatles and Bob Dylan, with an intelligent overview of the differences between folk and popular musics, and some interesting insights about the role of electrical instruments and effects, the nature of dancing, etc. Likewise, Carl Belz[8] makes a number of similar points, and puts forward a (rather abstract and over-general) theory of rock 'n' roll as 'folk-art' as opposed to 'fine art'. A very different, and in many ways very extraordinary book, is Richard Middleton's *Pop Music and the Blues*.[9] Middleton, who has musicological training, offers a particularly rich lexicon of descriptive-evaluative terms and distinctions, incorporating some technical points about musical forms and structures. It still remains subjective and intuitive however, though, as with Gillett I often feel agreement with his intuitions. What Middleton does that is different is to survey a staggeringly large range of music from early blues right through to the 'progressive rock' of the late 1960s, and relate this survey to a set of ideas about the relationship between black and white culture in America, and the 'non-Western' or 'primitive', or 'pre-Renaissance', qualities of black American music-making and white rock 'n' roll. This is an important book certainly, and I shall later make some use of his arguments as a 'sounding board' for clarifying my own.

I will not continue to discuss books one by one any further, since it becomes pointless once my chief criticisms of the tendencies of rock writing as a whole have been made clear, which I hope they now have been. The most central criticism can be summarized as follows: the investigation of musical meaning slips through the net of almost all rock writing; in this respect, rock writers are partly following on from existing limitations in serious music criticism, and partly, no doubt, reflecting a general lessening of verbalization which characterizes the reactions of almost all rock listeners, in comparison with listeners to other types of music. I must now move on to examine more closely the 'content' of the various histories, the actual accounts they do offer of rock 'n' roll in general and the rock-to-Beat development in Britain, and the occasional hypotheses they put forward to explain these events. Out of my critique of *their* accounts, in the first place, the basic shape and limits of mine will be rough-hewn.

The composite account of rock 'n' roll

It is possible to construct a sort of standard composite account of the main events and developments known as 'rock 'n' roll', based on the main texts discussed above and other similar books. It consists of a list of factors on which they more or less all agree, and on which they confer major causal status in relation to the rise of rock 'n' roll and Beat music. It also involves a starting definition or delimitation of the body of musical artists, and records, radio and TV shows, which make up the phenomenon of rock 'n' roll and Beat music.

The USA

The following is a summary of what might be called the standard view, the agreed wisdom, or the prevalent *myth* about early American rock 'n' roll.

1 'Popular music' already exists in the early and mid-1950s as an industry, with its 'major' and 'independent' recording companies, publishing houses, radio stations, etc. 'Live' venues exist in most towns and cities, while for records a whole infrastructure of distribution and sales outlets, as well as large chains of juke boxes, are well established. Trade magazines, magazines for listeners, and the charts or hit parades all serve promotional functions. The popular music audience already includes almost the whole population. Profits are high and, consequently, plant and other investments are expanding; this is especially true of record production, which, having all but died during the Depression and the war years, is growing dramatically, on the basis of improved and still improving materials (vinyl replacing shellac) and technology (hi-fidelity and, later in the 1950s, transistorization of radios).[10]

2 'Popular music' also exists already as a *tradition* familar to virtually all

American listeners and musicians. Certain styles are nationally established as 'popular', others are more locally based (Country music), or are excluded, to some degree, from the national popular charts ('race' music, as gospel, blues and rhythm and blues were then called), though they are closely related to popular music, in being often catered for by the same companies, and in providing numerous popular artists. There are also several varieties of jazz, from 'traditional' to 'modern', each of which is less than fully familiar but by no means unknown to the 'mass' of the listening public. Both modern jazz and Country music enjoy 'booms' in the late 1940s and early 1950s, but these are not on the scale of the rock 'n' roll developments which follow.

The presence of a black, working-class population in every major city of the USA by 1950, a result of migrations mainly from the First World War onwards, means that local radio stations and record stores almost everywhere reflect, to a significant degree, the tastes of these communities. And since neither radio-dial-twiddling nor shopping-around can be censored, despite the industry's compulsive categorizing, young white people in ever-increasing numbers do listen to the music which is becoming known as 'rhythm 'n' blues' and 'rock and roll' (or rock 'n' roll) in these years. Those local DJs, juke-box operators and independent record store and record label owners who are close to this development take note, and begin to consciously promote this music for white listeners.[11]

Most of the authors agree, to some extent, that the 'boring', 'bland', 'sentimental' state of the nationally popular (among whites) music of the early 1950s, as a whole, contributes to the defection of these young white listeners, but they all argue this in a very generalized, sweeping way, and all argue for different exceptions. Their problems with regard to verbalizing musical meaning are clearly displayed in this difficulty or weakness which they all share.[12]

3 A 'post-war boom' in the USA is the economic background to a new scale of working-class and middle-class 'affluence' in the 1950s. Both pocket money and widely available part-time work swell the disposable income of 'teenagers' at high school, while wages are often relatively high in the first years of work, in comparison with the 1930s and 1940s. The overall effect is to create a large group, throughout the country, of independent young or 'teenage' consumers, of relatively high spending power, even despite the rise in numbers staying on longer at school.

Most of the rock histories use the term 'teenagers' uncritically, ignoring the fact that it was a neologism of the late 1940s or early 1950s, replete with many new connotations. The connotations which are clearly retained in the rock historians' appropriation of the term are (a) a style of *leisure*, and of *consumption*, found among 'kids' from the ages of 13–14 to the early 1920s, (b) a certain exuberance or rowdiness, which can become a threatening wildness, and which includes (c) a foregrounding of sexual practices (dating, going steady, courtship in general, and the 'threat' of 'sex before marriage'). Behind these implications of the term, we can also see clearly that the standard notion of 'the teenager' is usually of a boy, not a girl, and that the 'threat' of sex is a threat *of* boys *against* girls, as seen *by* parents, teachers, etc. These things, sadly, remain unsaid in the rock histories.[13]

4 The search for 'novelty', derived from the competitive economic character of the pop industry, and in particular from attempts by 'independent' record companies to outflank 'majors', leads to 'cover versions' of dance blues and vocal group successes from the 'race' market, being offered on the mainly white pop market as a whole. In a sense, this is merely the equivalent of the raids on jazz and on Country music of the same years, but partly it is also the result of an 'authentic' pressure from existing teenage audiences, as spotted by adventurous DJs and independent studio producers. These 'cover versions' are normally produced by 'acceptable' white artists, and involve some changes in musical style, and some cleaning up of lyrics on occasions, but none the less they have the side-effect, when successful, of arousing some interest in the originals, and the longer-term effect of familiarizing the white pop audiences with some of the conventions of the black styles. Some groups of white musicians actually begin to specialize in a 'half-way' style, notably Bill Haley and the Comets,[14] whose 'Shake Rattle and Roll' is a cover version of a rhythm 'n' blues hit, while 'Rock Around the Clock' is an original number modelled on the work of black artists to some extent.

5 A cluster of media events combines to shoot the Haley style, and that of some others, into national prominence, notably the use of the music in the sound track of 'Blackboard Jungle', a successful film about 'wild' adolescents, and subsequently the appearances of Elvis Presley on the Nashville TV show 'Grand Old Opry', and later on the nationally screened 'Ed Sullivan Show'. Later come other films, such as 'Rock Around the Clock' and 'The Girl Can't Help It'.

6 At this point, the competitive logic of the industry once again influences developments, producing a race to imitate the initial successes and to promote the music with all the resources available. In particular, again, the 'independents' see their chance to compete on more equal terms with the 'majors', since both are relatively new to the style, and neither is very sure at first of how to predict who and what will be successful. Literally dozens of young artists are signed up, especially by independent companies, to produce rock 'n' roll; others are converted overnight, from aspiring crooners or Country singers into imitation Elvises.

The very over-production and financial chaos which result help to ensure that this situation cannot last, and by about 1958–59 in the USA, the initial 'explosion' of production of, and enthusiasm for, rock 'n' roll is over. However, the consequences of this period of upheaval are that one or two independent companies do indeed establish themselves as small majors, that a new generation of producers, artists and song writers becomes established in the industry, and also that some black rhythm 'n' blues artists share in the explosion, singing their own music more or less as they would be doing anyway, but reaching young white audiences. Fats Domino, Little Richard,

Chuck Berry, Jackie Wilson, Lloyd Price, Larry Williams and The Coasters are among those who owe their wider success to this upheaval.[15]

Britain

Each of the rock histories devotes a section to Britain (though not normally to any other country), tracing the story of the impact of rock 'n' roll (and of the home-produced 'skiffle') and placing these events, usually, as 'background' to The Beatles and the 'Beat-boom' years of 1963–66. I would argue very strongly that the view which sees the period 1955–63 in Britain as a mere 'background' to later Beat, and other later styles, is heavily distorted by an almost fetishistic attention to the charts (i.e. the successes of The Beatles, etc.), and that, sales of records notwithstanding, the development of a 'youth culture' in Britain, and of a music *of* that youth culture, can only be understood by reversing that emphasis. In a very real sense, there is an element of *myth* in the way rock histories skip from one commercial peak to another, or from one 'great artist' to another, ignoring almost totally the social roots of both the music making and the listening, which ought to be among their objects of study. None the less, the main points of a composite account can again be enumerated, this time relying, however, on a slightly different list of books.[16]

1 The pop industry is already international. American music already features strongly in British record stores, and on Radio Luxemburg, while the BBC allows a little of it into the major popular radio shows. British artists 'cover' most big US hits themselves. Equally, and very importantly, American films are readily available at British cinemas. Any BBC resistance to 'American trash' is out-flanked by the rise of records and by films; and when ITV comes along, it exhibits no scruples in adding to this trend with its pop shows. In any event, pop music coverage on radio and TV is on a very small scale in these years, by 1990s standards, and young listeners rely heavily on record buying and jukeboxes.

2 The Teddy boys already exist, chiefly in London, before rock 'n' roll arrives in Britain. They probably originate (according to Hebdige[17]) in the traditional working-class areas of South and East London in the early 1950s. Their style of dress is, in part, an imitation of the Edwardian man about town, but in other respects, they imitate American models. The interest in unusual clothes itself is odd (and new?) among male, working-class Londoners, as is the responsiveness to rapid change in fashions of music which follows in the mid-1950s. Hebdige calls this style 'a focus for an illicit delinquent identity' and points out its connection to a fantasy of America. The phenomenon apparently needs only publicity to spread: only later does commercial exploitation of the style move in.

3 The absence of a large black community with its own musical life (though this was beginning to take shape in the major cities), and also the resistance to pop and rock in general, and American pop and rock in particular, which

is maintained by the BBC, combine to give the films which feature rock 'n' roll a greater importance in Britain than in the USA. The film 'Rock Around the Clock', and its title song, are adopted by Teds in particular and teenagers in general all over Britain in 1955–56: various 'riots', and the occasional destruction of cinema seats to make room for dancing, gain the music and the audiences much notoriety, orchestrated by the newspapers into a full-scale 'moral panic'. This reaction tends to make rock 'n' roll a sort of badge of defiant identity, rather than just another fad of taste, for the kids involved.

4 Skiffle, a musical style taken initially from traditional jazz bands, coincides with this early rock 'n' roll enthusiasm and, being slightly more respectable in origins, is accepted as a quaint offshoot of jazz or folk music, even by the BBC, who launch '6/5 Special' as a TV pop show specializing in skiffle. One of the important things about this style is that its great simplicity, and the cheapness of using home-made instruments, lead to a wave of amateur and semi-professional imitations by the kids themselves. (What almost every account omits to mention, but is none the less true, is that it is *boys*, specifically and almost exclusively, who take up playing skiffle.) This craze lasts from 1956 to 1958 or so, after which amateurism continues, but now mainly in imitation of American rock and post-rock musics.[18]

5 At the same time as amateurism becomes firmly established among teenagers, by about 1957 or 1958, the 'real' rock 'n' roll records from the USA dry up, and post-rock 'balladeers' and British artists exhibiting little or no rock influence come to dominate record sales and radio and TV shows, Tommy Steele, Marty Wilde and Cliff Richard perhaps being the most rock-influenced of these. Some of the new 'rock-pop' records lack the prominent beat of rock 'n' roll, and most are also highly 'arranged' pro- ducts; on both counts they are not seen as good models by the teenage amateurs, who aim chiefly for a lively dance music. The result is that young audiences seeking live dance music turn away from the charts, just as some American teenagers did in the early 1950s. A live dance music style which becomes known as 'the big beat', and later as 'Beat', develops, as does a standard group format of lead and bass guitars, sometimes a third ('rhythm') guitar, drums and vocalist(s), sometimes with a piano or organ, or a harmonica. This Beat music thrives most strongly in the provincial British cities where the hit-making, and indeed, record-making, machinery is virtually non-existent (Liverpool, Birmingham, Glasgow, Manchester, Newcastle).

6 A somewhat more self-conscious movement of rejection of the charts leads to the British 'rhythm and blues' movement, chiefly in the colleges and universities and their milieux. Though this has much in common with the earlier and later jazz booms, in being mainly middle class and often idealistically anti-commercial, it also resembles Beat and rock 'n' roll in many ways: it is performed by small groups (four or five members, with guitars and drums the chief instruments), it uses electrical amplification, and it includes a lot of dance music with a strong beat. The Rolling Stones,

The Animals and The Zombies are among many representatives of this movement who become pop successes, while other more 'uncompromising' groups have less success in the early and mid-1960s but strongly influence the later 'British blues', 'underground' and 'heavy' rock developments (John Mayall, Alexis Korner's Blues Incorporated, etc.)

Some problems

At this point, I think it is worthwhile to stop and to begin to point out some of the limitations of these accounts, both in what they include and in what is absent from them. I have already mentioned some of these in passing. First, the accounts of the USA rather dodge the problem of understanding and explaining the phenomenon of white kids responding to black styles. This phenomenon is, in a sense, all the more extraordinary in Britain where the proximity of the rhythm 'n' blues-creating communities and the availability of the original music on radio as well as on record, did not apply in the same way as in the USA. Even Gillett, who mentions this problem in the Introduction to his book,[19] and who discusses black styles and artists at great length, avoids the questions which this development necessarily raises.

There exists, of course, in literature and in history writing of various sorts, a hypothesis that claims that 'Afro-American' music (and culture in general) has a 'corporeal' quality which distinguishes it radically from 'European' – especially 'serious' – music and other culture. In the writings of Mellers, Middleton, Small and others, the rise of jazz and rock musics is taken to represent the incorporation of this element into white popular music, and may be part of an overall cultural movement, the return of the 'sensual' and the decline of the highly repressed and repressive post-Renaissance human type, a trend which is supposed to be equally discernible in the visual arts and literature of the twentieth century.[20] This is an important argument. However, the chief histories of rock 'n' roll adopt a somewhat odd attitude towards it, hardly referring to it explicitly yet relying on it, assuming it, in many of the descriptive terms they use. Thus the words 'rough', 'dirty', 'hard', 'earthy', 'raw sex', the 'blues feel', etc., all acquire their resonance as descriptions of rhythm 'n' blues, and of particular artists, in the first place from the notion that 'the Negro' is a repository of 'corporeal' qualities in a way in which (most or all) white people are not. Such usage is not far removed from talk of 'primitiveness' and 'natural rhythm', and the absence of justification and qualification of these usages in some rock books and articles surely amounts to racism by default. This is unfortunately compounded by the absence of discussion of the concrete processes by which, first, familiarity with, and later imitation of, 'blues', 'gospel' and 'soul' styles arise among young white audiences, and what changes and adaptations are made along the way. The questions can be posed quite simply: why, from the 1920s onwards, but on a new scale in the 1950s, did black musical styles, and styles overwhelmingly influenced by black-produced originals, achieve great success with white audiences, and, in particular, why did this success flow over into actual music making among those unlikely amateurs, white teenage boys? This is no more than the rock histories claim, or even take for granted. This general question suggests more particular ones: why certain groups of white Americans and British people (chiefly boys, mainly of the working and 'lower middle' classes) and not others? What differences were there between the American rock 'n' roll development, and the events in Britain, and what do these differences mean? I will return to all of these problems in later chapters.

A second area of importance which the histories glide over – noticing it and yet not noticing it as it were – is the development of the *group*. The small ensemble of instrumentalists and singers who, with the help of one or two others, often write, plan (or 'arrange', though this is often too formal a term for the planning) and execute every stage of their own songs, even on record, is a largely new development in the white music of the 1950s, its only close precedents being in (mainly black) jazz and urban blues and the (largely middle-class) white American jazz milieu of the 1930s and 1940s. The studio – a set of techniques and equipment, plus specialist personnel who enter into the collective creation, with the artist or group, of the recording – this too is really new to the 1950s; the earlier period of recording (which anyway sharply declined in scale in the 1940s) had involved very different techniques.

One of the most important and revealing absences in the composite account, as I have summarized it, is the failure of rock historians to even notice in some cases (Gillett, Laing's *The Sound of Our Time*), or to take seriously as a problem (Cohn, Belz), the overwhelming *maleness* of rock 'n' roll. There were very few female singers or instrumentalists associated with these styles, despite strong female representation in the audiences. Once again, this absence does not stop the offending historians from using references to this maleness *within* their descriptive and evaluative writing – singers are 'sexy', 'masculine', 'boyish', with 'cruelty' in their songs of desertion, 'leering' on their faces, and so on. Elvis Presley represented adult sexuality, we are told,[21] but nowhere is this explained or analysed. Even Laing, who brings some sophistication to his study of 'teenage' lyrics, manages to ignore this maleness problem, generalizing happily about the boys and girls among listeners without making any real distinctions. (In his later writings, Laing does address these questions.[22]) This, of course, is not merely a sexist absence, but also yet another symptom of the difficulty all of these writers encounter in trying to define and analyse musical meanings properly: in this case, they clearly cannot even formulate the question of how rock practices, songs, records, etc., can articulate 'sexuality', or gendered-ness, in any sense, or masculinity in particular.

Also important (and especially so when we consider Britain) is the investigation of amateurism itself: the conditions and causes of the phenomenon of music making among working- and middle-class boys which arises in the 1950s; the determinations involved in its particular character as a 'peer group' rather than a family-based amateurism; its place in the new youth 'sub-cultures'; the use of a black musical tradition as a major model for imitation;

the relationship between this new, collective, group-based music and the apparent tendency of the media of records and radio to domesticate and individualize listening, and to 'atomize' music consumption.

These problems are really only a few of the many which could be raised here. Each of them itself points to more, and it soon becomes clear that a comprehensive account of the rock 'n' roll explosion, even if we limit it to the USA or to Britain, and even before we have begun to analyse particular records or to make evaluative comparisons, will necessarily be a quite unmanageably massive undertaking. Therefore, I must say now that I will not offer fully satisfactory, thorough or detailed answers to all of these questions in this book. But they will all recur in later chapters.

Yet the very histories and commentaries which suffer from these obvious limitations and errors do actually contain – sometimes explicitly, at other times implicitly – the germs of hypotheses about musical meaning which might begin to suggest answers to these problems, or at least directions for investigation. The 'sound of the city', rock 'n' roll is 'implied protest' – these are hints from Gillett. Laing suggests, rather more explicitly, that the music of songs can be analysed functionally, i.e. in so far as it seems to complement, to contradict, or to overwhelm the lyrics in the listening experience. He also suggests a relationship between electrified ensemble music and a kind of new collectivism or communality of listeners and players, which is not found in, say, 'serious' European music. Thus we are not without starting points; both the descriptive-evaluative mode's choice of adjectives, and these suggestions of an explanatory nature, often point to hypotheses which might prove valuable. What is needed is a loose, developing framework for pursuing such notions, formulating questions which are capable of being answered and relating the various directions of enquiry to each other.

In a sense, most rock writers are prey not to doubts but to a thousand *certainties*. It comes all too naturally to them to describe musical meaning through word-painting, through the fluid and vague, but resonant, descriptive-evaluative mode. *They* know what *they* mean by 'rough' and 'smooth', 'rich' and 'sweet', and they discover a certain recognition of such usage among listeners and readers; then, perhaps believing that there can be no greater objectivity in matters of musical taste, they conclude that this is the only – or the only *legitimate* – way music can be written about or talked about at all. Thus their intuitive hypotheses receive no serious development.

In so far as I intend to avoid playing the 'how I rate Buddy Holly' game, in order to ask a different range of questions, my own 'thousand certainties' must be made problematical; that is, I cannot now employ the mode of writing I have identified, since it shows itself to be deceptive from the point of view of the *problems* I have discussed. On the other hand, it is very difficult to construct an investigation into a field like pop music in a way which owes little or nothing to my own judgements and preferences, and any such debt would of course also be a debt to wider discourses of musical value (and other things) which have influenced me. I am not free to start from scratch. My only recourse is to attempt to drag into consciousness, to formulate, and then to use, *as starting points, as hypotheses,* my own feelings about the music, as far as possible, in the same way as I find hints from Gillett or Middleton very useful despite everything. Of course, it is not quite the same, because the nature of music listening is such that there is always more to my feelings about a song or a singer than I can capture in such forms, and these residues of extra-linguistic affect (as I will later call it), are not, finally, to be denied.

Anyway, I will not express my own questions and hypotheses within the conventions of descriptive-evaluative rock writing. It is an *easy* and a deceptive mode that is extremely limited and limiting, since in seeming to describe musical meaning it actually forms an obstacle to real understanding. Where insights and potentially fruitful hypotheses are buried within it, they can only receive further development by being excavated, and placed in some very different framework or methodology. This is what I will now go on to discuss.

2 The Character of Music as a Cultural Practice

Some background

In this chapter, I set out some basic ideas about music and music use, which underpin everything that follows. I begin by considering the *tradition* of writing about music in a 'culturalist' or 'cultural studies-type' manner. Such a tradition is not readily to hand, but has to be *excavated* from large bodies of writings which deal with music in every conceivable way. I have begun to carry out this task elsewhere.[1]

There *is* a tradition within music history and even within musicology of what might be called 'music and society' approaches. The problem is that there are virtually no contributions on modern popular music of this kind, except those by Kerman, Mellers and Meyer. Likewise, there is a tendency within *sociology* to include music as a legitimate area of study, a tendency which actually begins with the 'great names' Dilthey, Simmel and Weber, but which has sadly not really borne the fruits they would have hoped. And there are *semiologists* of music, notably the formidable Nattiez, but they have so far contributed little on popular styles.

We find ourselves left with a number of radically minded, interdisciplinary, consciously innovative authors who have preceded me in tackling the subject of popular music in a broadly 'culturalist' way. The most famous is Adorno, the Frankfurt marxist and mass culture critic, who wrote several influential books and articles, condemning most if not all popular music as crass, 'regressive' mass-manipulation, and doing so at a level of sociological and musical understanding which cannot be lightly dismissed. Despite his elitist, over-abstract and ethnocentric failings, Adorno has been a major influence on my work, and especially on this chapter. Then there are those authors who have approached popular music history and/or musical analysis in a spirit similar to mine: the originators, I hope, of a 'cultural study of music' tradition. These include Philip Tagg, Wilfred Mellers, Richard Middleton, Ed Lee,

Christopher Small, John Shepherd and his collaborators, as well as (within the self-styled 'cultural studies' movement itself) Paul Willis, Dick Hebdige, Iain Chambers, Dave Laing and others. I hope I have not offended anyone by omitting them: the field is, thankfully, growing. Finally, there are a few authors on whom *I* have drawn because I have found something very relevant in them, even though they have written little or nothing *directly* about popular music: Roland Barthes and Julia Kristeva are the most notable examples.

These, then, are *my* tradition, and in bringing them together in this chapter and later ones I hope that this aspect of their work will also come to be more widely read and appreciated by those readers who are motivated to explore the field for themselves.

Basic concepts

The ideas I will now set out are at best only a beginning. None the less, I think it is important that I should spell out the general ideas which underlie my arguments in later chapters. Adorno has been a major influence on this section, but so have others: Shepherd, Tagg, Small, etc. I hope the next few years of popular music studies will bring not only better history writing, but also substantial progress in these theoretical areas: the two are really interdependent.

Music is a material practice, whose products and objects are material: even the sound waves in air as they strike the ear. Sound is invisible, and in a sense intangible, but we must not fall into the trap of ascribing to music a mystical or spiritual essence which is independent of the material basis. However, it is not like bread or guns: its *raison d'être* lies in some sort of *meaningfulness*, even though it lacks the capacity to meet a simple material need such as hunger or self-protection. This makes it one of the *signifying practices*, along with language, visual imagery and others. Musical works of all sorts are 'signs'. We could now go on to ask 'what, then, is the need which music does meet?' But I propose to leave this difficult question open for now, in order to approach it more obliquely later.

As a type of human sound production, music differs from other types (talking, coughing, making sounds incidentally while doing some task) by virtue of some organizing of the sounds and their sequence, i.e. some pattern (or studied lack of pattern which relies on the contrast with pattern for its effect) – some *work done* on sounds seems to be the precondition for realizing musical status and meaning. Also, it 'takes two' to realize this status and meaning, i.e. the listener recognizes the work done, and the *humanness* of the maker, and an identification is thus made between listener and maker.

Music has another material too, namely time. All music has duration, and it is partly through duration that its patterns are made: repetitions, rhythms, and the larger shapes of songs, orchestral movements, etc. This brings us again to the level of the most basic questions, however: 'Why these patterns and shapes?' 'What need or desire is being met?' Or, putting it in more familiar terms: 'What does music mean?'

I propose to set up a description of the simplest abstract cases of musical practice – the single music-maker and the single listener – and then to develop the argument from there.

The single music-maker and the possibility of ensembles

The first category we must posit is what Tagg calls the music-maker's 'store of symbols', and it refers to a *knowledge* or familiarity which is part of the maker's socialized subjectivity. In a given act of music-making, this figures as a *given*, and I will refer to it as the person's *given* from here on, since the word 'symbols' has implications I do not want to encourage. The given is a complex psychological phenomenon involving the memory, and some sort of semi-conscious comparison of music-heard, and *giving rise* to that even more complex process by which 'codal elements', definite and repeatable enough to acquire or constitute meanings, emerge, become recognizable and ultimately become *usable* in music-making. Thus the given functions for the music-maker are a resource, wholly individualized and internalized in relation to this person, yet socially derived in the sense that it is derived from music-heard.

The given is 'individualized' but everyone – not only makers but also listeners – has one. And it is an unspoken (usually) assumption of all descriptions of 'musical life' that since people experience music in common, (i.e. a single transmission can have several receivers), the predominance of certain music in the listening experience of certain people gives rise to large similarities in their givens. There is, in other words, a larger musical environment within which people are placed, in greater or lesser proximity to each other. It is such proximity that permits the two essential agreements among music listeners: (1) that a given object *is* music and (2) that it has a *meaning*. We can then go on to say that clusters of close proximity among listeners and makers form the social sites of 'codes', i.e. *congruences of givens in space and time*, which can be provisionally isolated and described. It may also be possible to posit a sort of musical fantasy, a music-making 'in the mind's ear', and to suggest that this, which would clearly develop along with, and out of, the given, has something to do with the transition from listening to music-making. Foot-tapping, whistling, humming, finger-snapping and so on are all interesting in this respect. There is a maker in every listener trying to get out.

We can now make one or two generalizations about *ensemble* playing and singing at the same level of abstraction as the comments above. It is evident that, to the extent to which each participant's music-making objectifies a different fantasy and project, arising out of a different given, the sound which an ensemble produces might be nothing other than chaotic and meaningless. A mutual limitation in pursuit of a group sound that can be considered a single musical message, is therefore inherent in ensemble music-making. The acceptance of a score, composed by one person, is one form of limitation by which such a development can be brought about, though only one among others. The following of a conductor, for both rhythmic and 'expressive' co-ordination, is another, related, device.

The co-ordination of several voices and instruments does of course open up possibilities of sound production which are impossible to the single music-maker and, in addition, there is the possibility of mutual dependence offering a new freedom to the participants, as with the singer or player who finds the 'beat' of the music handled by someone else, and is thus able to internalize that beat and relate his or her music-making to it, without actually producing it. The musician *is his or her own first listener*, and in ensembles is both listener to the sounds produced by the others *and* participant in the music-making.

Listening

This inclusion of a listening component in music-making, indeed the dependence of making on listening, is matched by an element in listening in general which is directly comparable with music-making. The listener *constructs* tunes, rhythms, progressions and so on by holding in mind the immediate and even the remote musical *past*, and anticipating the future, as well as by organizing sounds heard simultaneously, and thus creating in the mind a totality or unity which *is* musical experience. The resemblance of this mental product to some objectively defined sonic object, 'the music', is of course unmeasurable. Also, the musical experience will itself be part of a larger totality-of-apperception – including things seen, non-musical sounds (there is a car going past), thoughts or feelings which come to mind – during the duration of the listening act. Degrees of attentiveness vary too, while in some cases listening may be accompanied by another response to the music, dancing being the obvious example. The music and the dance will often seem inseparable in experience. This moment of music-heard, music-as-experienced by the active listener, is the moment which I believe to be untranslatable, irreducible and specific, as I stated in the Introduction. It is involved in all listening to music, and is present even when intricately intertwined with, for example, a dance response or a linguistic mediation.

Listening, as we have seen, is the co-production of musical events and of musical meaning. There is no doubt that music only exists when *decoded*. Thus listening is always, in a real sense, active, and any talk of 'purely passive' or 'merely passive' listening must be approached with great caution. If listening is the precondition of the development of the given, and hence also of code, then equally it is also the consequence of the given, and the activation of the 'code' as it exists. No-one can listen to music as music without the engagement of the given. This means *accepting the code*, as a *congruence among givens, the reproduction of such congruence over time and the grounding of musical meaningfulness in this congruence.*

This last point leads me nicely on to the question of particular musical meanings, the significance of the musical 'message' itself. The characterizations and distinctions made here necessarily have the very strictest of limitations, but I think it is valuable to present this sort of summary before attempting the description of living codes which follows. First, let us remind ourselves of the 'commonsense' discourse of musical meaning, and also of what the mainstream aestheticians have to say. The 'commonsense view' is summed up by Davies:

> . . . unlike other activities such as reading, talking or watching television, where the transmission of a more or less unambiguous message is readily apparent, music does not appear to pass on any message we can readily identify. Music does not really satisfy the requirements that would completely justify its being called a 'language', since we tend to use the word meaning rather differently in the context of music than in the context of language. In addition music seems to have something in common with simple forms of sensory experience like warmth, taste, or the smell of jacket-baked potatoes. For example, one can, in a sense, appreciate the taste of a good steak, although the question 'what does it mean?' is hard to answer. By the same token one can ask 'what does Beethoven's Fifth Symphony mean?' and again be at a loss for a satisfactory reply. Any answer we might attempt would be couched in terms of our own reactions and feelings, and these are not identical with another person's responses to the same piece of music. By contrast the message 'the cat sat on the mat' is fairly precise in its meaning, and relatively unambiguous. However it is not the kind of message most of us would become excited about.[2]

Davies is arguing, then, that music is non-referential, whereas language is referential; or better, that music cannot refer to precisely defined external objects or ideas, whereas language can. This is recognizable, it seems to me; it is how we are all likely to *feel* about music, it has the apparent self-evidence of common sense. It is therefore not very surprising that most of the philosophers, aestheticians and practising musicians who have tackled the problem in the recent past usually argue in the same direction, though with more terminological care and precision. Some, notably Hindemith and Stravinsky (both 'serious' composers from earlier in the century, as well as influential theorists), argue that music 'expresses' nothing, that any affective, ideational or ideological meanings attributed (in language) to a piece of music are unwarranted and unwarrantable intrusions at the receiver's end, pure projections arising from misunderstanding. I do not accept this view, which is contemptuous of the real, repeatable and pleasurable musical experiences of the mass of 'ordinary' people. But the majority, notably the influential Meyer and Langer, as well as Philip Tagg in his work on popular music, argue that music expresses emotions, or at least the 'morphology of feelings' (their ebb and flow etc.), and that this is accomplished, as Davies suggests, by the music's having an effect on the *listener's feelings* which the listener takes to be the meaning. Meyer, Tagg and others use the term 'affects' to refer to the whole range of psychological states and changes of state which can be stimulated by music – the term 'emotions' tends to have a rather narrower meaning. So, for example, music can be 'martial', or 'ethereal', or 'noble' – abstractions which are not exactly what we normally call emotions, but which certainly do have their *affective* aspect. Music, then, according to Meyer and Tagg, is in the first place *an affective stimulus*, and its meanings all develop on this basis. It does not *refer*, but it can affect. In essence, I shall accept this initial description, and I will return to some of its corollaries below.

Semiology

In the last 30 years, the science or field of *semiology* has developed: the study of signs of all types, including music. Unfortunately, semiological contributions on music, in English or translated into English, are few, sparse and often rather cryptic.[3] Also, they tend to analyse mainly 'serious' music. But I cover here some suggestions about musical meaning in a way which is influenced by semiology. I hope to see this area of enquiry develop greatly in the next few years.

Roland Barthes says music is an 'isologic' system, and defines this as one in which 'the signified has no materialization other than its typical signifier'.[4] This is no more than an attempt to restate music's 'non-referential' character in more precise terms. (Unfortunately, it is flawed: surely the signifier is – according to Saussure and most semiologists – arbitrary, and therefore not a 'materialization' of the signified in any real sense?) But I do not think the terms 'signifier' and 'signified' have much to offer at all in studying music. The former is supposed to be the word, image or tone (depending what type of signifying practice is involved), while the latter is the 'content' in some sense, that which is supposedly fixed, and communicated or expressed *by* the signifier. But in the case of a musical sequence, how do we separate out and point to the single signifier? And where does it end and the signified begin? The whole distinction breaks down, because it relies too heavily on an analogy between music and language (a referential system) which cannot really be sustained. If music has any relation to 'reality objects' at all, it lies not in *reference* to them but in its power to *produce real changes* of state in the listener, it is an affective sign as opposed to a referential one. For the same reason, I do not think it is helpful to see music as a 'connotation' system, as some authors do, because connotation is merely a type of reference, and one which does not normally exist without *denotation* alongside it.

A somewhat more useful distinction has been developed by Julia Kristeva in her work on language and poetry, namely that between the 'semiotic' and the 'symbolic'. The latter refers to the relation of language to referents or reality objects, however conceived, whereas the former – the 'semiotic realm' – refers to 'sound, rhythm and movement anterior to sense and linked closely to the impulses'. In other words, the sonic and temporal *materials* of both singing and speech, prior to any symbolic usage of them. Music once again poses a problem: whereas Kristeva envisages most signifying practice as a contradictory unity of the two realms, music seems to have a 'sense' which derives from an ordering of the semiotic realm only, and may symbolize nothing. None the less, I will return to, and make some use of, these categories in Chapters 7 and 8.

Before I move on, there is one more important idea I wish to introduce here. This is the idea of 'identification'. I have said that the listener recognizes the sound as music, and as meaningful, and that what particular listeners decode will vary, but will almost always display similarities or congruences which add up to code(s). I have also pointed out that the basis of the double recognition of the sound, as music (as opposed to natural sound) and as meaningful, lies in the process of identification which takes place in the listening subject. It is always a realization of 'sharing something', of 'being of a kind', of 'community', with the music-maker. The very word communication (cf. communion, commune, community) reminds us that this elementary *reaching out and finding that which is like the self* is involved in listening to music, as it is in listening to language, reading books and deciphering images, and even numbers. Code, then, is the specification of the something shared, and the building on to that of further meanings.

Now both Jacques Lacan and Kristeva posit identification – in the more rigorous psychoanalytical sense – as the precondition of *language*. By placing the self in a field of other people and things, close to one, far from another, etc. (the father-figure and mother-figure being, for these authors, the first objects of this identification), the infant sets up the possibility of *address*, that is of 'I' and 'You', and also of *reference* (the 'third person', he, she and it). These give an underlying structure to all further language development ('subject' and 'predicate'). In these terms, music is perhaps to be understood as a communication which does *not* develop such an address and reference system (syntax or *langue*). To be precise, music makes an *open* address, un-differentiated as between receivers. And it does not really *refer* at all. But it does still rest on identification, developing instead the different degrees and levels of it (self with other self, self with group, group with group) and placing it in different contexts, putting it at the service of different social functions, and thereby giving it different *imports*, in the various cultural formations of the world.

Because different degrees and levels of identity are involved, it is possible to hear music, recognize it as such by virtue of a first, virtually involuntary, identification (humans have made this), but refuse the further level(s) or degree(s) of identification available, thus becoming an *unsympathetic* listener. All music requires (for the more intense realizations of meaning, and the more intense *use* of it in a functional sense) *sympathetic* listening, an opening up to the available identification(s).

It might seem from what I have written here so far that I consider affective stimulus to be the whole and only *meaning* of music. In the sense in which the 'objective expressiveness', and the 'world-sense articulations' which I discuss below are themselves premised on the primary description of music as an affective sign, which I have given here, this is true. However, both of these categories, especially the latter, and also my discussion of 'linguistic mediation' below, actually take the category of affect *out of its original context*, as a borrowed psychological term (Meyer), and suggest further important dimensions of it.

Expressive and iconic meanings

Music is an affective stimulus. But we all know that we can sometimes grasp something about music-heard without feeling involved or changed by it. For example, the 'poignant Andante' and the 'merry Finale' of many a classical symphony are open to this 'cold' sort of decoding. We can find the 'emotional adjectives' to describe them without having to feel the emotions. Is this not denotation? Is this not symbolic meaning? It would certainly seem that, say, joy *as an objective idea* is 'expressed' in such music, when it is listened to by a listener who knows the code and its conventions. Is this objective idea not a reality object, a referent?

My reply would be to argue that in certain circumstances music can achieve what I call a sort of *iconicity*. This is not the same as simple 'reference' – as when words refer to 'things' – but it is a special kind of musical meaning none the less, namely that which is often called the 'expression of emotions'.

The idea of iconicity is taken from semiology, and I have explained in my thesis the precise way in which I have derived and defined it for my own use. Briefly, in Saussurean semiology,[5] three classes of signs are recognized: the index, the icon and the symbol. The *index* is a symptom or indicative sign, attesting to the existence of something else: clouds are a sign of rain, smoke of fire. *Symbols* proper are distinguished by the arbitrariness of the signifier in relation to the signified (and the exclusion of the 'reality object', if we grant the validity of such a term, from any effect within the system), so that any sign can mean 'any thing', as with the names of objects in different languages. The *icon* does not achieve this arbitrariness, there is a resemblance between sign and reality object, as with a photograph or portrait of a person. To be precise, the person precedes the photo, he or she is the true *reality object*, of whom a copy is made. But he or she is not the *signified*: this is an abstraction or concept of the person contingent wholly on the photograph.

Now the term icon, of course, has an ancient and more specific meaning than this very general one: the *icons* of religious art (e.g. Catholic, Byzantine, Russian, Greek). In these cases, it is hard to speak of a *resemblance* to the reality object *encoded* in the icon: the object may be God, or Angel, a long-dead saint, the Devil as a serpent, etc. In this sense, such icons might be thought nearer to the class of symbols, or a hybrid between the two classes. However, the difference between them and symbols proper is very clear if we consider not *encoding* but *decoding*. The icons have a power or magic stemming from the supernatural beings they are supposed to represent. They are objects of reverence, 'holy pictures', and sometimes they can effect cures or miracles. Always they are channels for prayer. This difference in *decoding* is what makes these icons different from other visual representations. They do indeed *resemble their objects*, as Saussure would have it, but it is a magical or metaphysical resemblance, an association and a fixing of the object's properties (in this case supernatural power) in physical form. In this sense, the passport photograph is one sort of icon, and the 'holy picture' a very different sort. I call it an 'icon of decoding'.

Music can function as such an icon, when makers and listeners agree the codal conventions of 'emotional expression'. Examples are the 'sadness' of Funeral Marches, or the 'romance' of Mantovani's 'shimmering strings'. The rhythms and minor chords of the former need not *resemble* sadness to 'stand for' it; they can, as it were magically, produce it in the listener. Similarly, the Mantovani sound can affect some listeners quite strongly, though I find myself in the camp of those who can decode it 'coldly' as 'romantic' without feeling romantic at all myself. In this case I am the non-believer. Some resemblance may sometimes exist at the *encode* end of the process – music with a slow pulse may be more likely to 'stand for' sadness than music of great speed – but essentially these meanings are *conventions*, albeit that they often possess, for sympathetic listeners, great affective power. But in the period of expressive 'serious' and 'light' music in Europe over the last few centuries, a point of saturation or over-production might be said to have been reached, where almost all the expressive conventions or icons have become so utterly familiar to most listeners that their *power* is felt less and less – the music becomes too obvious and requires no concentration, and as a result the distracted listener often gets little out of it.

Musical articulation of world-sense

Whereas the era of principally *expressive* (or iconic) music is only one among others, the *articulation, in musical practices and artefacts, of the world-sense of the (making and listening) cultural milieu is an inevitable and universal quality of all music.* It is not, however, a simple matter. I have taken the term 'world-sense' from John Shepherd, and specifically from his discussion of the 'musical coding of ideologies'.[6] By world-sense, Shepherd means something like 'world-view' in the broadest sense; he prefers the word 'sense' because he is trying to combat a visual bias in our culture as a whole. (He also uses 'world-sense' inter-changeably with 'ideology', more or less. I prefer to make a distinction, which is set out below.)

Basically, world-sense consists of the *common elements* in the way in which a whole group, or even society, of people sees, hears and feels the *socio-physical* environment: their shared assumptions about time, space, matter and motion, and about the nature of the self (body and mind), other people and the institutions around them. In particular for Shepherd and for me, because we are investigating *music*, it is the sense of *time* and of *sound*, since these are the basic materials of music. But we are not speaking here of 'natural' time and sound, but rather of the way the experience of them is socially and culturally mediated, so that different societies, different cultures and even different classes within a society can experience them very differently. It is because the experience of time and sound is always socially mediated that the work of the music-maker – *treating* time and sound in certain ways, adopting a certain attitude and relationship to them – will always have social implications and effects, thus opening up an area of potential musical meaningfulness which is very different from the 'expression of emotion', yet is there, as a *potential* for decoding, in even the most expressive or 'iconic' music. Furthermore, as we shall see, music can also articulate, *via* its treatment of sound and time, another aspect of world-sense, namely the sense of self and other people, in its deeper, often ignored aspects.

Here, however, I want to make a particular claim about how such world-sense is carried and transmitted in society, one which is left undeveloped in Shepherd's text. World-sense consists of a set of *feelings, assumptions* and *categories*, which is socially produced. However, it enters a person's subjectivity in many ways, of which language is only one among others. It is clear that I do not have to reflect consciously – and this means, in effect, *think in language* – on the nature of space, gravity, biology, etc., before getting up from my chair to cross the room. None the less, this capacity is not something I was born with. It has been passed on to me socially, and perfected by my own practice, perhaps on the basis of innate cerebral patterns, perhaps not. Yet it has entered deep into my mind, so that I do, precisely, take it for granted. Our senses of what is *me* and *mine* and what *not me* and *not mine*, what is threatening and what is comfortable in the socio-physical environment, of controlling or being controlled, of the socio-physical limits on what I can immediately *do* at a given time – all these enter deep into our subjectivities, and all of them *have and retain* dimensions other than the linguistic ways we use to refer to them. I believe that they have affective reality as experiences, and such affects register at a level of subjectivity which is not wholly dependent on (though condit-ioned and changed by) language. That is, the 'set' which Meyer calls affects, and which includes the smaller set 'emotions', must, I believe, also include the feelings, assumptions and categories of world-sense in their pre- or extra-linguistic dimensions. John Berger writes:

> Seeing comes before words. The child looks and recognises before it can speak.
>   But there is also another sense in which seeing comes before words. It is seeing which establishes our place in the surrounding world; we explain that world with words, but words can never undo the fact that we are surrounded by it.[7]

This is exactly what I mean, except that I believe that *hearing*, as well as seeing, is involved.

My argument here is that music can articulate aspects of world-sense *without benefit of* a conscious, analytical work ('words') by the listener's mind. A listener may indeed be unaware of, and may even *deny* (as a result of certain linguistic discourses *about* music), the articulation of world-sense, but it is always there. It is mainly in this way that music takes its rightful place among the practices whereby subjectivity itself is produced and reproduced, other than merely on its 'conscious' level. This becomes clearest when inter-cultural comparisons are made: music of great power to people of one culture is often perplexing or even simply 'noise' to people of another. However, the import-ance of the insight for my later argument lies in the fact that even within a single society, markedly different world-senses can exist, and major changes in world-sense can be wrought.

I have set out in my thesis at some length the meanings I give to the terms ideology and world-sense. Suffice it to say here that people relate to the real conditions of their existence through assumptions, categories and ideas, as well as through their actions. These assumptions are not all consciously used all the time, of course, and some of them are so deeply buried in the mind that they have to be excavated by analysis. 'Ideology' normally refers to the more conscious – or accessible to consciousness – of these, whereas I use 'world-sense' specifically to refer to the deeper and more subconscious ones. Shepherd uses the terms more or less interchangeably, but I prefer to keep this rough distinction. A person's sense of time, of sound, of the otherness or familiarity of other people, institutions, places, etc., all these are instances of world-sense. I believe that just as conflicts of ideology can exist in a society (and can often be broadly related to different social positions, whether of different classes, sexes or social groups), so there can be conflicts and differences of world-sense too.

But matters are not quite this simple. In order to function in the socio-physical world as it is, a person must accept and reproduce within him or herself certain basic patterns of world-sense, such as an awareness of clock-time, of certain causal sequences, of the limits on where he or she can go, and who and what can be influenced or changed in a given situation. But these *shared* assumptions – which working people and even the unemployed will be likely to have in common with capitalists and professionals – do not preclude further nuances and twists by which the different life-experiences of the former, for example, will be expressed. So the worker experiences the rigidity and alienness of the clock – 'my time is not my own' – as an oppressive condition of making a living. The banker or capitalist will be familiar with this rigidity, this sense of time as an enemy, but will also experience time as the means for realizing profit and interest. The two persons are likely to have very different time-senses in a certain sense, yet at the same time they will share enough to relate to each other and to their environments in a mutually acceptable and recognizable way. These are generalizations, of course, and over-simplified examples. But I think the point is clear. I believe music can articulate world-sense at these levels, including the responses to time, to sound, and even to other people and institutions, of people who feel these things to be oppressive, and who enjoy resisting them in various ways, from escape to transcendence.

Another area of world-sense (assumptions going deeper than 'ideology') concerns the subject's sense of his or her own body. A certain disciplining of the bodily functions, a 'drill' which gets us through the basic tasks of the day, is an indispensable concomitant of the individualism and control which characterize the subjectivity of the modern era, both within the bourgeoisie and in the rest of the population (albeit with differences). This situation means that music-use, which involves a certain lifting of repressions, an uninhibitedness, can articulate a resistant response to this, adding yet another dimension to musical meanings. I will discuss these matters at greater length in Chapters 7 and 8.

Communality

The audience hearing a piece of music can be seen as, in the first place, a 'series' of people with the music in common but no necessary intersubjective direct contacts among them. In reality of course, no audience ever is fully like this, though an audience of physically separated radio listeners, each in a different house or car, comes very close. The music, once heard, effects an affective change of state in the listeners, as we have seen. Assuming the existence of a unified code among them, this gives them 'something shared', apart from simply the presence of the musical sound. The 'something' is, as we have seen, an *identification* response. Music (though not only music, think of film or television programmes or rituals in a church before a 'congregation') thus has a unifying power. Now everyday language (normally one-to-one) or written language (the book, the newspaper) do not normally work this way, though they can. They address – and are intended to address – a differentiated, even a single receiver, and to distinguish him or her from other persons as well as objects referred to. Music does none of this. It unifies a multiplicity of listeners without distinguishing between them.

This unifying power may be realized in very different ways: in the 'expressive' music of the classical (and 'romantic') European traditions, the unifying effect on an audience is often submerged beneath the effort of decoding the individual expressivity of the musical sequence; the listeners in a concert hall may sit still, eyes shut, in silence, as though entirely unrelated to, and unaware of, the persons next to them, only for the unity of affective response to burst forth at the end in simultaneous applause. Conductors and critics often say the mark of a great success in performance is a pregnant pause between the end of the music and the eruption of applause, as the listeners each emerge back from their separate engrossments into a recognition that they have shared something good. The applause then, a few seconds later, grows, fed by the delight of hearing others applaud too, almost as though it were a surprise to find them there! Of course, this has become a ritual, carried out unspontaneously some of the time. But the shape of the ritual, its details, still point to its real meaning, derived from those cases where it has been, and is, spontaneous.

Another way in which music can unify is by the simple expedient of a strong emphasis on regularity of rhythm, whether this is done by drum beats or by repetitive chants, or whatever. This overtly synchronizes the responses of listeners, and may, in certain codes, and the styles within them, stimulate motor responses (clapping, swaying, foot-tapping, dancing). These possibilities are only very rarely involved in modern listening to classical music, as discussed above, where they would hardly be compatible with the 'effort' of decoding individual expressivity, but they are central to other types of music, and other meanings or functions music can have for listeners. One might say that the *submerged unity* of the classical concert audience, and the *advertised unity* of the crowd dancing and swaying at the climax of a rock performance, represent opposite types of realization of the unifying power of music, with much other music-use falling between them, or involving a bit of each.

Although it is obvious in the second 'type' I have described, and less than obvious in the first, we can, in fact, state that in both cases, and perhaps all cases, the musical element or parameter of *rhythm* is central to the realization of this unifying power. It involves the patterning of the duration of the sounds, which synchronizes the responses of listeners within earshot of it (even when this is not obvious or overt), and thus forms the basis for the 'something shared' of musical response. Furthermore, since, as I remarked above, collective music-making involves listening to the others and fitting one's music-making to theirs, the synchrony achieved by rhythmic patterning is probably essential to the making of all collectively made music in the first place. In a musical type where the unifying power is submerged beneath the aim of individual expressivity (though necessarily still present), the rhythmic parameter of music is normally submerged with it. Symphonies have regular rhythms, but they do not have a 'beat' in the way most rock music (and Beat, rhythm 'n' blues, etc.) does. In a musical type where unity is advertised, the rhythm is likely to be emphasized, foregrounded, and insisted on.

Linguistic mediation

I now move on from the question of types or levels of musical meaning and function, to the related problem of linguistic mediation. I leave aside here the question of lyrics – the words in a song – which will be examined briefly in a later chapter. In general, the relationship of musical meaning to the linguistic discourses used to describe and refer to it is a complex, dialectical one. If I listen to a 'blues' as 'the blues', knowing that this is what it is supposed to be, and with considerable reading and thought about 'the blues' behind me, I listen *for* and to a certain 'blues quality' in it. Even if I do not know what I am to hear, the recognition of this quality may enter my listening early in the experience and affect its development. Alternatively, I may stop attending to it because I 'already know I do not like the blues'. I believe that such discursive 'knowledge' enters into, and even merges with, the affective meanings of the music so that in terms of experience the two become inseparable, though they can be analytically distinguished.

If this is so, then the construction of musical styles, and developments in style, and even of codes as a whole, is itself crucially mediated by linguistic discourse. It does not arise out of mere congruences of extra-linguistic affect across different listeners, or from one time and place to another. Our view of the very nature of musical code is transformed by this realization. Codes (and also all the smaller congruences we call genres, styles, movements, trends, waves, schools, etc.) are not merely *given*, as self-evident affective congruences experienced directly by listeners; they are, in part, constructions arising out of discursive work which is done by both makers and listeners. This discursive work sets a context, a limit and a direction for listening itself, and the listening act thus becomes, simultaneously, a 'direct', extra-linguistic, musical decoding on the one hand, and a reproduction of the linguistically mediated aspects of code on the other. Equally, the music-*making* act is not independent of this linguistic-discursive work either, but conditioned and directed by it.

Thus when I criticized rock writers in Chapter 1 for their 'descriptive-evaluative' discourse, I was ignoring at that stage what is actually a major reason for my project of trying to transcend that mode, namely that they do not merely commentate from outside but actually help to *produce* and reproduce rock 'n' roll, its subdivisions, its beginning, middle and end. That is, the very constituting of rock as a body of musical practices is largely the work of writers, of talkers, of listeners reflecting discursively on the music and setting a context for their own and other people's listening (and making) processes. This, of course, is no less true of early rock, with its poverty of surrounding discourse, than it is of serious music with its embarrassing profusion of commentaries, though that is not to say that the level, degree or importance of linguistic mediation is the same in all cases. The 'immediate' or 'first' response to music is thus never natural or un-mediated. Certainly it is *prior to*, and not dependent on, the present, particular discursive work which accompanies listening, it is that on which the present, particular discursive work is done. But in itself, it results from the internalization, at the affective level, of responses (including discursive work) from past listening acts, as well as from the direct extra-linguistic presence in memory the past listening has necessarily achieved and never forfeits; the two elements are intimately interconnected.

In summary, musical meaning is dual, certainly, but it is also *fused*, so that its pre-linguistic element and its discursively produced element always merge and cannot be distilled out. The pre-linguistic foundation is only pre-linguistic in its given, already constituted presence in a particular listening act. In its history and genesis, this element itself proves to be discursively mediated. Thus we can now provide the fullest definition of code, the one which replaces all the provisional statements in this chapter with a synthetic and, for my purposes, a final one: *code* refers to *the multiple congruences of affective meaning and its representation in language, which exist in a given culture (with temporal-spatial limits), and also to the reproduction (in slowly changing form) of these congruences over time*. The definition of a culture is of course problematical, but broadly speaking I would argue that a set of techniques, practices and meanings which unite 'serious' and 'light' European musics of the last four centuries, and whose continuity can be musicologically established, constitutes the first 'code of the West', the hitherto dominant code of our culture. In this case, the various folk music traditions of the same period in Europe might perhaps be seen as subordinate codes, though their separateness from tonal-code music is something which has waxed and waned, and taken on different forms at different times. More importantly, however, the 'Afro-American' music of the black slaves and ex-slaves of North America certainly constitutes a different code (partly derived from European folk traditions), with an unquestionable history of separateness and 'autonomous' developments, even though a process of interrelationships between this and 'tonal-code' music can also be traced. I will develop these claims in the next chapter.

3   *Codes of the West*

The tonal-European code

In this chapter, I will compare and contrast the two great musical codes which form the basis of modern Western popular music, and which can be said to meet, and perhaps to fuse, in rock 'n' roll and Beat music. I will not spend too long on tonal-European music, which I have described at some length in my thesis. As a result, these comments will be highly generalized and should not be taken to refer equally to all tonal-European practice on all occasions, or to imply that it does not itself evolve.

By tonal-European music I mean the 'serious' or 'classical' music of Europe (and now worldwide) as well as various 'light' and popular styles of the nineteenth and twentieth centuries such as 'parlour music', 'Music Hall' and many Hollywood musicals. 'Tonal' refers to the harmonic system that unites more or less all this music, while 'European' refers to its origins and main lines of development in Europe.

Tonal-European music is characterized by (1) a certain *hierarchy* of musical parameters and (2) the great importance and even ascendancy of the (almost always individual) composer.[1]

The hierarchy of parameters

This music has a system of *harmony* based on triadic chords which centre around and normally return to (at the end of a sequence, movement or song) a 'tonic' chord. For example, a simple tonal-European tune, such as 'God Save the Queen', 'moves', by a sequence of conventional chordal steps, to the tonic chord at the end. If the melody line moved to its appointed end but the chords did not, they would be felt to 'clash'. And if the whole thing simply stopped on its penultimate chord and tone (at 'the'), it would leave the listener expectant. Such harmonic progressions and the completion thereof are the basis of virtually all musical sequences in this kind of music. They are put together in larger patterns, from song-forms of 16 or 32 bars in length to great symphonies which may last for an hour or more. The rhythms and metres of such music are kept regular and not too complex, so that players and singers can execute the harmonic steps together, or the solo pianist or other instrumentalist can co-ordinate his or her fingers. Rhythm is thus subordinate, though vital, in the structure of the music. Melody, too, is structurally subordinate, being required to conform to the harmonic sequences, and not clash too much or too often with them. Many of the 'parts' of an ensemble piece or a keyboard piece do not really amount to melodies at all, but are merely constituents of the chordal movement. And, finally, 'timbre' (of instruments and voices) and 'dynamics' (loud, soft, etc.) are important, but secondary: if the famous motif of Beethoven's Fifth is played a little louder or faster on one occasion than another this is permissible (up to a point); but if a note is changed it is sacrilege!

Of course, such parameters as timbre, and such values as a 'catchy' melody, can be very central to how listeners listen, much to the chagrin of some 'serious' critics and musicians.[2] This demand has been met, during the nineteenth and twentieth centuries, by 'light music' of various types. Such music has tended to be treated as marginal by music historians – and from the point of view of the development of the code and its possibilities for expressive and other meanings it may indeed be marginal – but in terms of the *scale* of listening practices, light music has probably reached larger audiences than serious, by and large. It prepared the ground for the boom in popular listening which has taken place in this century and, especially since 1945, in Europe and America.

The ascendancy of the composer

Tonal-European music is almost invariably composed by an individual, usually a man. He prepares a master score for performance, whether by one performer or many. The traditions of performance dictate that the musicians and singers change nothing, though a little freedom to vary volume and speed is usually left. But never a note, and above all never a chord, is to be changed or omitted. Where an old score is in bad condition, scholars labour prodigiously to produce a version which they believe to be true to the 'idea', the composer's intention. Even dead composers are still the 'boss' in relation to performers. Conductors, critics and teachers all act as 'policemen' of the composer's intentions.

Furthermore, improvisation is almost non-existent except in some operatic singing and the cadenzas of concertos: both of these are essentially survivals of older styles, and both are limited mainly to melody. Harmonic improvisation, and rhythmic improvisation in ensemble playing, are virtually unknown, and indeed are almost impossible within the conventions of tonal-European performance.

The listener to this music is expected to be respectful and silent, passive and contemplative. With serious music he or she is expected to concentrate, so as to grasp the movement, or structure-in-time, of the music. Ordinary listeners are credited with little musicality: enough to enjoy listening and perhaps to try a little amateur singing or playing. Performers are a step up, but composers are held to be gifted in a rare and special way. This, of course, fits together with the respect for the *score*, which in turn enables and sustains the priority of harmonic sequence among the parameters of the music. A gulf develops between amateur and professional, with extensive training and social dis-location involved in becoming professional. Simplified scores are composed or arranged for mere amateurs to perform. And, finally, reams of criticism, history, biography and 'appreciation' are written, ostensibly to support listen-ing but also with the effect of making listeners feel humble before the com-plexity, longevity and majesty of the great tonal tradition.

The extensional principle

The mode of compositional activity, and the chief types of musical 'form' which develop from these practices of the tonal code, can be called *extensional*.[3] Large structures are created by the movement from harmonic key to key, on the basis of quite small amounts of original harmonic and melodic 'materials', which are repeated, in identical or slightly altered form, again and again. Variations of instrumentation and dynamics are used, of course, to lend a sort of definition to different sections. An example of an extensional movement *par excellence* is the famous first movement of Beethoven's Fifth Symphony. The principle is the extension through time, by means of varied repetition of the small amount of harmonic and melodic material which is 'stated' at or near the very beginning. All the variety and even 'drama' is achieved by the 'modulations' to and through different keys, and by the 'vitalizing' effects of timbre and dynamics.[4]

If the symphony and the sonata are the classical forms of such music, the influence of the same principles and priorities is felt within all the other 'forms' of the tonal code, both serious and light – the concerto, opera, song, dance-music, sacred music, etc. In the work of the famous serious composers, even dance-forms like the waltz become fully-fledged extensional movements full of modulations, 'bridge-passages', 'second-subjects' and 'recapitulations' (Chopin, Brahms), while concertos become virtually full-scale symphonies with the added interest of the clash or alternation between soloist and orches-tra (from Mozart onwards), and whole operas finally acquire a unified tonal-harmonic structure (Wagner).

The meanings of tonal music

I now move on to the task of showing the sorts of meanings which are involved in tonal-code music-making and listening and, in particular, of relating the more or less explicit levels of meaning to the articulations of more unconscious and semi-conscious world-sense, which can also be discovered there.

First, the 'ascendancy of the composer'. This ascendancy is realized through the relative completeness of the performance instructions encoded in the score, and through the performers' acceptance of them. As such, it is dependent on the score, or on some other technique of storage. It has become more and more central to European tonal music as its period of hegemony has proceeded through to the early part of the present century, and it corresponds, in time, very broadly, to the liberation of composers from the ties of feudal service, their success as entrepreneurs or partners in enterprises reaching a paying public, and, in the later stages, the stubborn unrationalizability of compositional labour in the face of the capitalist tendency to 'proletarianize' producers. Eventually, a sort of pragmatic acceptance of this problem inspires part of the music industry to cloak itself in the dignity of an ideology of artistic freedom, so that a market for 'difficult' and 'radical' music is created largely on the basis of its difficulty and radicalism – the *avant-garde*.

I would argue that the real root and the significance of the discourse of the composer-genius-who-demands-recognition-and-acceptance, a discourse employed by composers themselves, critics and listeners, lie in the more generalized individualism of the bourgeois class in the period of its growth and ascendancy. It is indeed an (idealized) image of Man-the-transformer-of-Nature, a discourse which helped inspire all the bourgeois revolutions, and has entered into the self-conceptions of the politicians, traders, manufacturers, engineers, architects, artists and scientists of at least four centuries.

One man – virtually always a man – constructs a world of sound for the listener, in which it is possible to submerge the consciousness so totally that all the other senses fade away and hearing takes over. The whole (conscious) mental life is directed upon one object, the musical sound. On the other hand, this object cannot be seen, touched or dissected, because it *is* sound, arriving as if by magic in the ear and in the mind. Thus the 'world' of the attentive listener, for the duration of the music, *is* this internal–external unity of music. The listener's own consciousness and the external world become, for as long as the exclusivity of listening keeps the data of all the other senses at bay, unified. This is not just an identity, however, but a sense of mastering of the external, the feeling of containing it within oneself. The knowledge of the origin of the music in the 'inspiration' of one man, the identification with that man which the listener experiences, underlines this sense of human mastery, and individual mastery at that. It is probably no accident that almost all the highly regarded tonal composers *are* men, since in the traditional bourgeois as well as the Christian conception of mastery (of self as well as nature) women are normally considered fundamentally impaired and inferior, slaves both to their bodily rhythms (and the function of child-bearing) and also to their 'emotions'.[5]

This sound-world has a form – a temporal structure – that can be 'followed', grasped and, finally, anticipated. The laws of the 'world' are thus made manifest, and even simple, to the listener. The more complex and unexpected the twists and turns of harmony, the more total the listener's feeling of mastery when the anticipated return is triumphantly confirmed. Thus the structure of almost all serious tonal music, as the denial and postponement of harmonic expectations followed by their fulfilment, is seen to be related to the discourse of the individual, striving with and eventually controlling 'his' world. Such music – the symphonies of Haydn, Mozart, Beethoven, Brahms, Bruckner, Mahler, and many more, the unified operas of Wagner and Strauss, the 'symphonic poems' of Liszt, etc. – presents to the listener, through its composition by one man, and performance, if necessary, by thousands, a sort of microcosm–macrocosm of a world which brings the 'exterior' world of experience within the span of the single human subject, giving the listener the sense not just of belonging, but specifically of controlling, of being at the helm of the world. The music even becomes, for some, an image of the bourgeois individual, marshalling both natural and human resources in the conscious pursuit of an enterprise.

Now these meanings (individualism, triumphalism) are normally only implicit, which means they are hardly verbalized at all by most listeners. However, alongside them, and interlocking with them, are the relatively clear, and frequently verbalized, expressive meanings which I call 'icons', and which I have already discussed. It is in fact by virtue of the identification with the composer, 'at the helm' of the sound-experience, and ultimately triumphant, that the decoding of 'emotional expression' in this music is possible. We say Mozart's Fortieth Symphony is 'sad' not because it is a living sad person, nor because violins are being played sadly, but because in the context of the unity imposed on the orchestra by Mozart's score, listeners grasp what they take to be *his* expression or depiction of sadness, by virtue of *his* use of certain conventions (of minor key, pitch, melodic shapes, etc.). Thus the grasping of the conventions and the overarching individual mastery go hand in hand, and are interdependent.

This iconic order of meanings is, for many contemporary listeners, the main and perhaps the only order they decode, in a way which they can bring to consciousness, as either emotional reaction (crying, cheering) or description (this is martial music, this is sad music). And it is possible to construct a virtual catalogue of icons and quasi-icons which have passed into modern popular music, most though not all originating in light or serious tonal music of the past. Whole collections of 'mood music' exist for TV programme and film makers to browse through and choose the one they want for any given dramatic or documentary purpose.[6] This situation carries the danger, however, that much listening becomes very casual and distracted, since the music is so *obvious* in its explicit meanings. And a reaction against this occurs among composers and some listeners, who avoid the 'hackneyed' at all costs, producing and preferring esoteric and *avant-garde* works instead.

Sound-sense

I will now look further into the area of *implicit* meanings, to examine the articulations of 'world-sense' in tonal-code music. The invisibility and, in a sense, intangibility of sound has led many authors to consider it, and music in particular, as 'immaterial', or essentially spiritual. Ancient (Pythagorean and other) associations between sound and magic have undoubtedly lingered as traces in later discourse, adding weight to this view. Then, in the late Middle Ages of Europe, the great expansion of written language that followed the printing-press, and the general expansion of the natural sciences, especially physics and astronomy, during the Renaissance period, created and fixed decisively the discourses by which 'reality' and 'objectivity' are defined visually. The relative passivity, and inability to focus, of the ear as opposed to the eye, not only reinforced this but created a favourable condition for the survival and development of another conventional association – that between sound and human *interiority*.[7] Sounds arrive in the mind uninvited, mysteriously and as if by magic, and can work affective changes deep inside the mental process; they have a 'power' over the mind. But paradoxically perhaps, there developed, out of the sacred music, song and dance-music of Medieval Europe, a set of styles which consisted of big 'architectural' structures based on a technical rationalization of the physical qualities of sound. These are perhaps to be seen as an attempt to triumph over its mystery, and put it to use. Sound itself became a building block, a raw material, in structures whose logic and justification, incidentally, could often only be linguistically expressed by visual analogy: think of terms like 'tonal architecture', 'arch-form', 'horizontal and vertical lines', 'threads' of development, 'background and foreground', 'inner' and 'outer' movements, etc.

This 'raw material' approach to sound is of course consistent with the extensional principle. The harmonically based construction of long sequences or 'movements' requires fixed pitches and certain strict rules about the playing of each instrument, and about singing. This necessarily excludes, as incorrect, much possible sound production, and, in the case of singing, it largely cuts off the rules of correct singing from the expressive resources, and the evolution, of everyday speech. We can see clearly in all this the rationalism of the bourgeois 'conquest-of-Nature' project.

Musical practice always takes place in a context both of worked matter and of other practices, a physical and social environment. In terms of sound, we can posit the category *soundscape*[8] to denote the environment-of-sound at a given time and place. There is no doubt that the tonal code originated, and, for a long period, developed within a soundscape overwhelmingly dominated by (a) natural sound, (b) human speech and shout, and (c) the sounds of pre-Industrial Revolution labour. Of these, the third is the most significant for my argument here. The sounds made by 'labour' are, in almost all cases, incidental to the production process. The clink of hammers, the whir of the wheel, etc. They can of course acquire the status of 'signs' for the labour concerned, and can also acquire connotations – the buzz of the marketplace is conventionally taken to connote a bustling vitality and good humour, for example. But sounds are not actually *means* to a productive end, except very occasionally, as when the quality of the sound made by metal or gems when struck tells the worker something useful about the task. Most often, sounds are mere by-products.

This incidental aspect of labour-sounds reinforces the apparent uselessness of music, since if sounds are only ever by-products, never the actual materials or instruments of production, the production of sound 'for its own sake' cannot but seem an idle, non-utilitarian pursuit. However, it is not this interesting relationship that I am centrally concerned with here, but rather the change in soundscape which has occurred with, and since, the Industrial Revolution. There is now, in the cities and towns of all the world, a permanent, unceasing backdrop of sounds, and these sounds are labour-sounds (including machinery and transportation). Furthermore, continuous blocks and surges of sound, lasting many seconds, minutes or hours, form a large part of this permanent backdrop. The silence of modern, urban existence itself comprises a hum of innumerable engines and machines. Almost without exception, these new sounds are again incidental to the production and transportation processes which produce them. The overwhelming connotation which comes to attach itself to them is that of unnecessary, irrational intrusion; they speak of a grand social co-ordination but also of its irrationality, its uncontrolledness. This connotation is produced by a combination of (a) the manifest incidentality of the sounds, (b) the greatly increased volume which has made their incidentality more manifest, (c) the consequent discursive distinction, more and more characteristic of our culture, between 'sound' and 'noise', and (d) the continuing discourses of nature, the silent night and the silent countryside, the latter two having some self-evident, contrastive truth.

A soundscape which 'alienates', and which intrudes – both physically, at certain painful levels of noise (volume or intensity), and discursively, on account of the discourses enumerated above – is thus characteristic of urban life for the mass of people in the twentieth century. I would argue that these changes in soundscape, together with the rise of amplification, radio and records, have in a sense 'outflanked' tonal-European music. Music is no longer a rare experience, and great volume is no longer exceptional. The sheer impressiveness and the triumphalism of symphonies, grand opera, church music, etc., lose a lot of impact when a guitarist can fill a concert hall with sound by using a single finger. However, a new type of music that uses the new technology to produce a message against the alienation and oppressiveness of the environment has great potential, in this new context. This will form a part of my attempt to explain rock music in Chapter 6.

Time-sense

The 'world of sound', which I described as being produced by tonal music's takeover of the mind, has another crucial dimension – that of *time*, the temporal duration of the music. When the composer writes a score, complete with bar lines and tempo directions, it implies a certain span of time. This span is not the real duration of the writing of the music, nor is it any one performance-duration. A 'virtual' time is created. Furthermore, though the score provides a clear fixing of this virtual time, a moment's thought suffices to prove to us that it exists within non-scored music also, to the extent that any piece is held to be at all 'repeatable'. Suzanne Langer writes:

> Musical duration is an *image* [my emphasis] of what might be termed 'lived' or 'experienced' time – the passage of life that we feel, as expectations become 'now' and 'now' turns into unalterable fact. Such passage is measurable only in terms of sensibilities, tensions and emotions; and it has not merely a different measure but altogether a different structure from practical or scientific time. The experience of this vital, experiential time is the primary illusion of music. All music creates an order of virtual time, in which its sonorous forms move in relation to each other – always and only to each other, for nothing else exists there.

She goes on:

> In the first place it is entirely perceptible through the agency of a single sense – hearing. There is no supplementing of one sort of experience by another. This alone makes it something quite different from our 'commonsense' version of time, which is even more composite, heterogeneous and fragmentary than our similar sense of space . . . we co-ordinate . . . [it] . . . for practical purposes by letting the clock predominate. But music spreads out time for our direct and complete apprehension, by letting our hearing monopolise it, – organise, fill it and shape it all alone . . . the second, radical divergence of virtual time from actual lies in its very structure, its logical pattern, which is not the one-dimensional order we assume for practical purposes (including all historical and scientific purposes). . . . The direct experience of passage is the model for the virtual time created in music.[9]

Langer explains that 'passage' has *volume* as well as length, and that it is filled with 'tensions and their resolutions', whether physical, emotional or intellectual. 'Life is always a dense fabric of concurrent tensions.' She also points out that this subjective time experience, of which musical virtual time is an 'image', is actually identical to Bergson's *la duree reelle*, and like him she contrasts it utterly with the 'ingenious time concept' which is assumed by the clock and by scientific reasoning. She continues:

> . . . for all its logical virtues . . . [clock time] . . . is an abstraction from direct experiences of time and . . . not the only possible one. Its . . . advantages are bought at the price of many interesting phases of our time perception that have to be completely ignored.[10]

Now this is a very important passage, and most of it can be accepted without qualification. However, it describes only one side of the relationship between virtual and actual time. Langer is absolutely correct to stress the completely separate character of the virtual time of music in relation to the actual time of everyday life. Musical virtual time is not even that experiential *duree reelle* which defies the clock, but an 'image' of it. On the other hand, she takes the incommensurability of the two further than can be logically sustained, by totally ignoring the other side of the experience of music, namely the span of listening time. As so often in her frequently excellent study, she presumes the full concentration of an ideal listener, who understands totally the code. Of course, Langer knows that in reality not even the composer in person can give to a performance of 'his' work the fully adequate listening she is assuming. No two listening contexts are ever the same, competence varies from one instance to another, and there is always interference. Indeed, Langer considers some of these problems in very general terms in her subsequent chapter on 'The Living Work'. But she clearly feels justified in simplifying matters by making this assumption none the less. With this decision she takes aesthetics out of culture at a stroke.

It is no accident that she feels justified in decontextualizing musical experience so radically. For as she half admits, she is really describing only the music of the tonal code, only that music which does require, which seems indeed to imperiously *demand* of the listener, that attention, that acceptance of sound-filling-the-consciousness, which enables it to articulate individualist aspirations of mastery. Langer's argument is thus circular – she begins by excluding music which might differ from the description she is aiming towards. But of course this is by no means the only relationship that can exist between virtual and actual time, and herein lies Langer's omission. The very 'marginal' forms of tonal music – song, opera and dance, which preserve the association of musical listening with listening to the words of songs, attention to the drama of an opera, visual enjoyment of the spectacle, or, in the case of dance, a physical activity that may be very much 'uppermost' in the dancers' minds, and which in terms of listening practices are far from marginal as we have seen – themselves offer evidence of the complexities of real listening practices, and they point also beyond the tonal code to other musics of the world, in which other types of listening practice are indeed prominent.

The listener does not cease to apperceive (i.e. to receive, sift and composite a range of sense-data) during listening, unless by a conscious effort he or she chooses to at least come close to such active exclusion. Even then it is never total. Thus the virtual time of the music always comes into a relationship with the *duree reelle* of the listener: within the limits of the music's 'objective' (measurable) duration they might be said to 'interlock' to form a composite listening time, within which the listening subject 'moves', as it were, concentrating now more and now less on the sounds, though they would cease to be heard as music at all if there were not a semi- or unconscious activity of ordering them into rhythms and harmonic and melodic continuities going on all the time. To put it differently, the *duree reelle is entered by* music, whose flows and tensions/resolutions, etc., become part of the composite experience of passage, in which other elements (sights, smells, sounds other than music, thoughts and feelings aroused or incidentally present) occupy their places too. Only a certain type of effort will concentrate the 'whole' of the mind, more or less, on the music-heard.

The great majority of music listeners since the spread of radio (1920s and 1930s) and later modern record-players (late 1940s/1950s) and TV (late 1950s/1960s) must be assumed to listen primarily to 'light' and 'popular' music. Indeed, surveys have tended to confirm this,[11] as do sales of records. Therefore, despite the retrenchment of 'classical music' practice over the last few decades, the majority of listeners of the post-war period, in Britain, the

USA and no doubt much of Western Europe, Japan and large parts of the rest of the world, probably do not habitually listen 'properly', in the sense demanded by both the mode of composition and the critical-aesthetic discourses of serious, tonal music. Even performers of that music, in so far as they are unrepentantly inadequate listeners themselves, may render the score in ways which undermine the further survival of the code.

Light music (made up of song, dance, operetta, 'parlour music', the 'musical', etc.) was that part of tonal-code music which did, to some extent, reach the new class of the nineteenth and twentieth centuries, the workers and their families.[12] A mode of listening which was not honed by substantial amounts of musical education, but which was certainly not necessarily less enthusiastic for being less 'cultured', came to sustain a mode of composition and performance in which the harmonic-structural limits of the tonal code, at a given time, were taken more or less for granted. The interest of the listener was directed not towards these limits, as in the great symphonic structures of Brahms or Mahler, or the operas of Wagner, but towards melody, lyrics-in-performance, the tone of a singer's voice and touches of exotic or original instrumental sound such as the 'Irish', 'Scotch' or 'Nigger' elements of American parlour songs.[13] In the course of the twentieth century, a quite new type of music was to appear, and eventually to inherit this mass audience. But before I turn to that development, I must look at the other great code which became involved in it, namely the Afro-American.

The Afro-American code

If 'light' music as a whole remained within the *tonal*-European code, there developed none the less within it styles of 'popular' music that were, as it were, only tonal by default of other possibilities. The music-hall song of Britain was so distinctive a variant of tonal music (at any rate in performance), that it is instantly recognizable to most British listeners even today. But despite the success of this distinctive appropriation of tonal resources by predominantly working-class artists and audiences, the styles remained parasitical upon the tonal code as a whole, a code whose most basic articulations (individual mastery, etc.) were of limited relevance to these people. A contradictory situation thus developed, and, in so far as the old tonal code continues to provide the resources of much light and popular music practice, this contradiction has remained ever since.

I would qualify this account slightly by referring to a 'folk song' (and dance-music) tradition in Britain[14] which, though it was influenced by tonal-European music, and though it did itself feed into music-hall styles, none the less retained a certain distinctiveness in those areas where it survived (rural areas, and some areas of old established village-based industry). This music contained some features which are not normally regarded as tonal-European – such as unusual untempered instrument tunings, pentatonically (and modally) influenced melodies, 'coarse' singing tones, some improvisation, unusual harmonies and resolutions – and which are perhaps sufficient to justify its being designated a separate code, or a remnant of one. But it had dwindled to a very small-scale and localized existence by the early part of the twentieth century. Its revival since has been the work of collectors and antiquarians, followed by a mainly middle-class folk singing current since the 1950s. (This is less true of Ireland, and perhaps Britain's 'Celtic fringes'.) This music *has* had a little influence on popular music since the 1950s: there was a certain *rapprochement* between folk groups and skiffle and early Merseybeat, exemplified by groups like The Spinners, there was the 'folk-rock' or 'electric folk' movement of the late 1960s and early 1970s, and there is another cross-fertilization going on in the 1980s and 1990s, as in the work of The Pogues, Van Morrison, Elvis Costello and others.

The case of the USA, however, is strikingly different. During the long period of agrarian expansion, the difficulties of distance, the underdevelopment of the market economy and its failure to take on a nationally unified form, for many commodities, until late in the mineteenth century – these conditions provided a long gestation period for rural folk musics to survive and develop away from their European and African roots. Both white 'Country music' and black 'hollers', 'spirituals' and 'blues' thus retained their full vitality and contemporary relevance into the period of mechanical and electrical sound reproduction. It is true that mass production of both scores and instruments began early in the nineteenth century in the USA, but it co-existed with the survival of large, remote, rural areas populated thinly by white farmers, and of virtually 'sealed' black slave and ex-slave communities.[15] This unique conjuncture was to produce, eventually, a music that would be able to articulate in some way the world-sense, that is, the affective relationship to the social and physical environment, of industrial working-class people, something which American parlour music and British music-hall songs could never do satisfactorily.

Basic characteristics of the Afro-American code

Here I wish to present the thesis that 'Afro-American music' constitutes a quite distinct and separate code. Later I will argue that virtually all popular music since about 1930 exhibits, exemplifies and promotes a process of 'codal fusion' between this code and the tonal-European, which is still proceeding. And I will place 'rock 'n' roll' (itself a category that is predominantly discursively produced, and which embraces several separate styles) within this framework.

I begin with some historical and descriptive synthesis. A code is itself always more or less of a fusion. The musical elements, and the practices and discourses of making and listening, which together constitute a code, do not spring from nowhere, or out of some contextless transformation in the minds of creative artists alone. They are assembled by borrowings, and transformations, of given objects and ideas, and nothing else. Thus there is no pure Africanism at the fountainhead of everything which is different about Afro-

American music, no old wisdom or flame of truth. Like styles within codes, codes themselves are only ever 'relatively' distinct, and their development through time is only ever 'relatively' uninfluenced by other codes. Generally speaking, to delineate a code is something like the task of defining and distinguishing a community or a culture: the last word is never spoken. None the less, if conditions existed in Europe which permitted the flourishing, in the same societies, of both serious and light tonal musics *and* folk musics, from, say, the seventeenth to the nineteenth centuries, then it should not surprise us unduly that the rigidly separated and 'sealed' communities of blacks within the white-ruled society of the southern part of the USA, and later throughout, provided the basis for a divergence of code of at least comparable degree.

The reader is entitled to ask at this point, can it be said that all Afro-American music constitutes a separate code from tonal-European, or is it not more accurate and useful to see *African* music as the different code, and Afro-American as already in every respect a music of codal fusion?[16] The argument is persuasive up to a point, in the sense that no Afro-American musician can be entirely unaware of, or uninfluenced by, European tonal music in the form of hymns, pop and folk songs, the national anthem, etc. But I am not arguing that codes must have no meeting points or overlaps of material (certain chords, instruments, even songs), but that two radically different principles are at work, which affect and transform every parameter of the music made. (Of course, few musicians will embody the essence of one principle, unsullied by the other.) I hope I shall be able to demonstrate the usefulness of my chosen approach, even though I would not wish to close the door entirely on any other way of organizing the field.

Like other folk musics, Afro-American music does not characteristically display a great deal of dependence on formal training, institutionalization or critical-exegetic discourse. More so than the tonal code, its *site*, and the central requisite of its survival and development, is in the minds of its makers and listeners, and in their immediate musical life. This in no way diminishes its status as an independent code, however, for as I explained in Chapter 2, the final guarantee and site of *any* code lie in the interactive musical 'givens' of the makers and listeners. Merely the practices of the Afro-American code are different, and the linguistic-discursive mediations of its development less central.

The rural and urban black communities of the USA have existed in considerable separateness from whites, for the whole of the period since Emancipation. This has waxed and waned of course, with a particularly intense period of urban ghettoization taking place from the First World War through to the 1950s, and especially in the 1930s and 1940s. This separateness has allowed periods of relatively autonomous musical change, as well as an amount of borrowing and altering of white musical materials. There has, of course, also been white borrowing, exploitation and altering of black music throughout the period.[17]

What then was different about the black folk musics, blues and jazz, which made of them a separate musical code? The answer is really quite simple. The music of the white rural communities ('Country' music of various sorts) is continuous with European folk musics of the past, and, like them, exhibits 'modal' melody, tone bending, improvisation and some rhythmic freedom not found in most tonal music. And this music undoubtedly influenced that of black Americans. But it is in the music of the black Americans that so many and such considerable differences of technique and approach are to be discovered that many whites in the nineteenth and early twentieth centuries found them incomprehensible except as errors and naiveties. The prehistory of jazz, Gospel and blues has become a happy hunting ground for musicologists and historians, and the picture one gets by compositing their work is far from clear.[18] But it is clear that a different melodic principle is involved, that polyrhythms are frequent, and the rhythmic parameter in general is more prominent than in most tonal-European music, while the *harmonic* parameter is less so, that techniques of vocal production outlawed from most tonal music are prominent, and that extensive improvisation is central in all this music, from 'field hollers' to early New Orleans jazz.

The precise degree to which any of these can be described as African survivals will probably always remain conjectural (though I think enough evidence exists to be sure that they *are*, in part, African in origin), but the sense in which they add up to the existence of a distinct code is very much more easily specified. The evidence is clear: the hierarchy of musical parameters is wholly different, the ascendancy of the composer and the reverence for 'his' score are absent, and the composer–performer division is largely healed in the sense that no two performances of a blues or jazz-tune need ever be, or try to be, the same. Improvisation – the performer composing – is basic. Formal training, the abundance of necessary discourse and the use of scores are all normally absent, though *informal* training, and the use of various mnemonics, as well as a 'slang' in which music can be described and evaluated, do accompany the music-making process. The appropriations of the guitar, the European drums, and the harmonica all bring changes to the very making and tuning of the instruments (and accessories, like a 'bottleneck' for playing sliding-tones on guitar), as well as to their basic character when played – the guitar becoming more of a percussion instrument and the drums an integral rather than an incidental part of most ensembles. At every level, the Afro-American approach and techniques are so significantly different from the European-tonal that a qualitative 'break' must be involved.

The intensional principle

The structural principle in Afro-American music can be called *intensional*, as opposed to the extensional principle discussed above.[19] That is, the variation of melody, rhythm, dynamics and timbre *within* relatively small-scale and simple structures and sequences replaces the construction of large, complex structures out of small amounts of strictly controlled, rhythmically simple 'material'. Intensionality is clearly and intimately related to improvisation, and a good sense of the differentness of the tonal code can be obtained by considering just how central collective improvisation is/can be to jazz and ensemble-blues, while it is next to impossible to conceive of within the tonal-harmonic 'language' of, say, Mozart or Beethoven, except in the most rudimentary forms.

In describing and analysing Afro-American music, it is of great importance to understand the resources of intensionality, namely rhythmic variation and polyrhythm, 'blue' notes and tone-bending, 'rough' and falsetto vocal production, and the use of timbres and other possibilities of instruments not used in tonal music, *in their own right* and in relation to the practices and discourses which closely surround Afro-American music-making and listening, rather than as departures from European 'norms' or as mere additional resources which can be grafted on to tonal practice. Ultimately, they must be found to have their own *meanings*, to articulate their own social origins as well as to produce certain social and individual effects, and these meanings will reside in a whole more or less unified mode of musical life.

I do not propose to examine the social and cultural history of the blues and jazz milieux at length, except for the immediate pre-rock 'n' roll period. Suffice it to say that blues and jazz styles came into existence in the late nineteenth and early twentieth centuries, in black, working-class America, which exhibited all the qualities of the Afro-American code as I have described them but which (especially jazz) contrived to become very widely listened to among, and influential on, white listeners and musicians as well as black. The period of the Depression and the Second World War saw a retrenchment of the social separation of blacks from whites, in the form of numerous urban ghettos. And within these, some relatively autonomous black musical styles developed, out of earlier blues and jazz, which came to be known as 'urban blues' and 'rhythm 'n' blues'. These styles are central to the later development of rock music in all its forms, and I will consider them in some detail.

There is no doubt that the centrality of dance halls and dancing to leisure in the ghettos forms a major part of the explanation of these styles. The solo, self-accompanying 'blues-shouter' more or less (never totally) disappeared in the 1940s and 1950s as duos, small guitar and drums-based groups and also large dance bands with a full complement of horns emerged, playing for the most part variations on fast dance-designed blues – from piano-led or guitar-led 'boogie-woogie' and 'dance blues' to the blues-based jazz of Louis Jordan, Jay McShann, etc. By the late 1940s, this range of music was well established throughout the USA, and widely available on records, often under the label of 'race' music. Although the development of this music was largely uninfluenced by music outside the ghettos, it was not itself uninfluential: 'boogie' in particular (especially in its guitar adaptation) was very influential in white Country music of the 1930s and 1940s.[20]

What virtually all the urban blues bands shared was a basic conception of format: the players were divided into a rhythm section and 'leads', following jazz practice of the 1920s and 1930s, but greatly simplifying it. This simple duality of sound was used as the springboard for a complex improvisatory and semi-improvisatory practice by lead instruments and voice(s), taking turns and sometimes playing ensembles together. The most usual song form was the 'twelve-bar blues' played fairly or very fast; singing played a minor part or no part at all in some of the big band blues, and normally was hardly central to the 'jump' or 'dance' blues either. But in the small 'hard' and 'cry' blues bands the songs were often slower, the singer was very prominent, and his or her (usually his) vocal style was the most important distinguishing element, along with, in many cases, the 'lead' guitar, which might or might not be played by the lead singer. Of course, some groups covered several different styles.

The rhythm sections of these bands played a very strong 'beat' (i.e. prominent to the listeners and important to the rest of the band), regular and with little variation except for little drum flourishes to mark the end of sections. This permitted the lead instrumentalist(s) and singer(s) (or 'foreground artists', as I call them) to phrase their playing, *across* or *against* the beat, rather than themselves realizing that beat, and also to vary this phrasing at each repeat, building on the techniques of older blues singing, and guitar, harmonica and jazz-horn playing. Thus the functional demand of loud dance music was reconciled with the maintenance and development of some of the intonational and rhythmic practices of earlier jazz and blues.

Of course there were many different styles here: some using light and complex rhythmic patterns, others relying on an insistent thump, some exhibiting extravagant 'foreground artistry' by singers and instrumentalists, others much subtler and more restrained. Some of the music has a sonic middle ground, as it were, in which one or more instruments or voices repeats a pattern of harmonies and simple melodies, perhaps even with slight variations, and this pattern gives the piece much of its individuality. Patterns for 'boogie' piano or for bass guitar, sometimes called 'riffs' (though this term is imprecise, referring to repetitions in the foreground too), are examples of this, as are the horn patterns in 1950s 'city blues' such as that of The B.B. King Orchestra, and in much early soul.

The meanings of Afro-American music

So far I have not really begun to interrogate these practices of the 1940s and 1950s for their meanings, and functions. In order to now do so, it is first necessary to look back to the earlier history of black people in America, in order to see the importance which music-making, listening and dance had already assumed in their cultural life. In the years of slavery and the decades immediately after abolition, the black population of the USA had been divided into small, separate communities, and forcibly deprived of most of its African languages and religions. Often they were even prevented, by the buying and selling of individuals, from falling back on the supportive role of the family. The religions and other beliefs and customs of the slave owners were haphazardly introduced into these communities, for reasons in which a sort of racist altruism and the desire to discipline the workforce were mixed together. This process intensified as slavery neared its end, and in the decades immediately after 1865. In these conditions, of which we may surmise that the loss of language, and the fact that life was literally totally at an owner's disposal, were the most extreme, only those practices which could not be policed fully, and those which were approved of but not fully controlled by the owners, could retain or acquire a degree of autonomy without being suppressed. Music and (Christian) religion were the chief practices which could be so transformed. 'Worksongs' in particular were probably tolerated by slave owners because they actually facilitated labour, while the direct suppression of other black secular music died out in the second half of the nineteenth century.[21] The styles which gradually became known as jazz, gospel and blues developed: jazz in the cities, especially New Orleans, and gospel and blues in both the rural and the urban black communities.

In the 1930s and 1940s, when blues and jazz musicians began to adjust to the microphone, to dance-blues styles, and to being members of bands rather than solo artists or members of duos, they inevitably carried over into their new musical practices the vocal styles, the rhythms, and the very tunes and songs which they had always employed. Equally inevitably, these elements were subtly transformed, by both conscious and unconscious processes, by the encounter with the new conditions and demands. This took place in both technical and aesthetic senses. For example, Joe Turner, who sang for many years with the pianist Pete Johnson, recalled in an interview the encounter with the microphone:

> I used to have a powerful voice before the mikes came in. But they was really a fascinating thing. I figured it would give me a nice little riff and save me a while so's I could last out longer. But then I found that it really made me sing harder. I'd get to singing and it'd sound so good that I'd just keep on. I'd sing three, four hours and never sing the same verse.... And I'd get the people all stirred up just like a preacher. Stir 'em up![22]

Again B.B. King has recalled the trouble he had as a young singer and guitarist in the late 1940s, in controlling his playing and singing within the twelve-bar form, being inclined to merely internalize the beat and improvise:

> I had a saxophone, drums and me. I'd start to sing a song and at that time I didn't know any better – or I did know, but I didn't seem to care about it actually – I didn't know about how many bars you sing. I had a good beat, and the people liked that because they could dance to it.
>
> Long as you got your beat, they don't care about the bars – but the musicians who were trying to play with me, they would be crying murder. I'd start to sing a 12-bar thing, and I'd sing the first line like seven or eight bars, then when I made the change from the one chord to the four chord, the 12 bars is gone already. Even today, 30 years later, I still need a guide-line to follow...[23]

Such quotes give us an idea of the *openness*, the *fluidity* which continued to characterize the urban blues, then and later, the way in which the improvisatory essence of the music was not just a routine set of tricks for varying standard rhythms and phrases but a constant rediscovering of all the elements involved, and of their interrelations: the singer discovering a new, stronger role, the singer/guitarist simultaneously attuned to the dancing audience yet improvising dangerously on the edge of chaos. Excellent recorded instances of this are to be heard throughout the output of these and other leading bluesmen of the 1930s, 1940s, 1950s and even later such as John Lee Hooker, Big Bill Broonzy, Elmore James and Muddy Waters. The functional aspect of much of the music, as dance music, in no way inhibited the improvisatory essence, though of course we should remember that a highly 'free-form', improvised and often *solo* style of dancing accompanied such sounds. The slicker, streamlined 'band blues' of larger ensembles like that of Louis Jordan, of course, did inevitably sacrifice some of this fluidity, especially when performed for recording.

Time-sense

The setting up of a regular, more or less homogeneous rhythmic 'background' and a partly or wholly improvised foreground of one or more instruments and/ or voices, set against the background, offers what might be described for the present as an *image* (in the broadest sense, as used by Langer[24]) of 'individual' actions in the context of the shared experience of externalized, alienating time. By 'externalized time' I refer to the acceptance of the mediation of the clock, with its 'objective' mensuration of the passage of time across a whole society, as the authoritative expression of time's passage in the personal life also. This acceptance is of course a precondition for the economic system of capitalism – from the calculation of credit and interest to the quantification of labour power in terms of hours and minutes. The development of a modern urban industrial society adds more elements to this tyranny of the clock – timetables for transport, the social co-ordination of leisure time involved in the production of music for profit (starting times for concerts, 'getting one's money's worth', etc.), the entry of the media, designed to receive messages whose duration and timing are exactly pre-planned by producers, i.e. radio and television, into the homes of the mass of the people, in short a whole web of appointments, deadlines and time limits stretched across social life.

By 'alienating time' I refer to the way in which the otherness of clock-time in relation to subjective time-experience becomes a threat, a limitation, a constriction at every turn: 'My time is not my own.' To be at the mercy of work-time, of payday, of transport times, appointment times, the timing of leisure and the necessity of sleeping time, is to lose the *disposal* of the passage of time, to experience time almost exclusively as unfreedom.

Furthermore, it becomes charged with meanings, even symbolisms – the tolling bell, the ticking clock – and little victories won over time acquire great significance; for example, shortening the working day slightly, or apparently shortening it, by starting five minutes late, taking a few extra minutes before and after each break, spending a quarter of an hour in the toilet. The pleasurability of doing nothing at all in the morning, on Saturday or on holidays, the joys of not having to hurry – all of these speak eloquently of the tyranny of clock-time in urban industrial society. Time is like a rigid, tight-stretched, unyielding necessity which closes in on the individual and yet is always *external to* the individual, always a limitation, almost always a threat. I believe that urban blues and jazz do not merely imitate the experience of living with this externalized, alienating time-sense, but *respond to it* and offer, in a real sense, its antithesis or its symbolic transcendence.

Against a stretched-out, unyielding temporal background – the beat – the singer, guitarist, horn-player or whoever, uses the resources of *rhythmic intensionality* (anticipations of the beat, delays, accelerations), of melodic improvisation (even when singing/playing a known tune) and of freely varied timbre/sound production, to detach his or her (usually his) sound from the beat, cutting across or against the beat, and even, in jazz especially, attempting to destroy the listener's sense of that beat altogether. To 'fly', to 'soar', to 'free foreground from background', to 'bend, tease and subvert the regularity of the beat'[25] – these are the sort of phrases music writers use to attempt to describe what I mean. Stravinsky, of all people (?), wrote in 1942:

> Who of us, on hearing jazz music, has not felt an amusing sensation approaching giddiness when a dancer or a solo musician, trying persistently to stress irregular accents, cannot succeed in turning our ear away from the regular pulsation of the meter drummed out by the percussion?[26]

Whether Stravinsky was referring to the 'hottest' jazz of the time or to the 'swing' of the popular big bands only (probably the latter, hence the reference to tap-dancers), he was certainly right to point to the contrast of pulse and leads – or to be exact, of the pulse versus the realized rhythms of the foreground – and to show this to be a central quality of the music. But to say that the soloist's irregularity 'cannot succeed in turning our ear away' from the pulse is to miss the point in quite an important way. It is the judgement of a European who can only hear the realized foreground rhythms as 'irregular', i.e. departing from a norm. Stravinsky's conception of rhythmic adventurousness may be deduced from the changing metres and irregular accents of his famous 'The Rite of Spring'. When he listens to the rhythmic variety of jazz he *consciously* or unconsciously resolves all the anticipations, delays, accelerations, etc., which he hears into patterns which he already knows a name for – syncopations and shifting accents. In fact, of course, any attempt to *score*, say, 'hot jazz' from the performance would find that it did not deal merely in the half-pulses, quarter-pulses and 'triplets' of tonal music but that the rhythmic variety was little short of infinite. A permanent, pervasive polyrhythm involving all, or almost all, the instruments and voices (but with one or more 'leads' doing more rhythmically than the rest), is the new norm. Of course, many big bands and popular vocalists of the 1920s, 1930s and 1940s *did* reduce the richness of rhythmic variety to a few tricks – a standardized way of 'swinging' or 'jazzing' any given tune – and it was not long before this simplification was preserved in ink in the form of some new scoring conventions. To be fair, Stravinsky may have been thinking only of this limited quality.

It is of no importance, finally, whether Stravinsky, or anyone else, can still hear the pulse through all the foreground variety, if he or she is *trying* to. The victory which is won, in such music, over the alienating temporal environment consists not in 'abolishing' it but in being able to enter into a potentially infinite variety of rhythmic relationships with it. When there is nothing it can stop you doing, it is no longer oppressive and alienating. Indeed, the pulse then becomes a resource, permitting a rhythmic freedom which could in all likelihood not be attained without relating itself to, or bouncing itself off, some such background of regularity. The 'style' with which the player or singer – let us call him or her the *foreground artist* – differentiates her or his playing or singing, and imprints his or her 'personality' on the sound as a whole, including background, is thus the key to this aspect of the music. Hence the adulation paid to the great jazz and blues soloist/improvisers (Louis Armstrong, Charlie Parker, Lester Young, Miles Davis), the star blues and soul musicians (B.B. King, T-Bone Walker) and shouters/singers (Joe Turner, Jimmy Witherspoon, James Brown).

It is very important that I do not give the impression that only a frantic complexity of many improvised lines really deserves the name jazz, or blues, or Afro-American music. In the same interview which I quoted above, B.B. King put his finger on this:

> There was something to me in common which the way Johnny Hodges played. We phrase. Same thing with Lester Young and Bobby Hackett. These three people, they could take any song, never had to ad lib anything, just played it straight down – and the way they phrased it! Oh my God! They said everything to me.[27]

This is exactly the point: through *phrasing*, which means, first and foremost, rhythmic differentiation, they *individualized* everything they played. This quality of jazz has not only survived, but in many ways it has been intensified in later urban blues and in soul – often simple songs, simple melodies, often even very little improvisation of new melodic material at all, but the style with which the foreground artists shape the songs and the melodies, based mainly in rhythmic phrasing, makes each version unique.

I now want to point out another, somewhat different articulation, still rooted in the appropriation of time and time-sense. The principal interest in almost all jazz tends to be in the instrumental playing of the foreground artists, of whom there are usually several, while the urban blues is more often dominated by a single singer or shouter (who may also play an instrument), and in some styles that singer monopolizes to so great an extent the resources of pulse subversion and individualized sound production that he (and occasionally she) reduces the rest of the group to the status of accompanists, who do very little intensional variation themselves, except occasionally for short solos. None the less, the improvisatory and fluid essence of earlier Afro-American styles is retained in this music, sometimes even more so than in the more 'arranged' jazz styles; merely it is combined with the strong pulse (for dancing to) and monopolized somewhat by a single star performer.

In all urban blues and jazz, then, except the most 'arranged' styles, the image of individual action in an alienating (temporal) environment is overlaid by, and to a certain extent contradicted by, the way in which the whole of the music declares, in performance and even on recordings, its communal, collectively created character. Most of the rhythmic and timbric nuances of jazz and blues are effectively unscoreable, and thus cannot be wholly, objectively, pre-planned. Pre-planning therefore plays a much smaller (though usually still significant) part in determining the finished sound that in tonal-European music: the composer–performer division is largely healed, as all performers (though not all equally) partake of the compositional function more fully than any of the orchestral or chamber-group players of tonal-European music. The group *collectively creates* the virtual and the actual duration of the music, often deciding the tempo, the number of repeats, 'breaks' or 'solos', and so on, either just before starting, or even as the performance proceeds. Thus both the pulse and its transcendence are collectively created, the music is wholly mutual. The soloist or lead singer relies wholly on the rhythm section; without its regular pulse the foreground artistry which creates the image of individual action within, and even struggle against, an alienating temporal environment, could probably not exist, and would certainly be very difficult for listeners to follow. The pulse is, at one and the same time, a limit and a resource. This mutuality can often be a central value, both to the music-makers and the listeners.

There are two aspects, then, to the relationship to *time* which is realized in urban blues music: first, the creation of an image, even a quasi-symbol, of individual struggle against alienating time (foreground artists against rhythm section) and, secondly, the control, by the whole collective, over the actual and virtual duration of the musical event. The former is dependent, to a great degree, on the latter. These two aspects, bound together in this way, enable the music to articulate not just a sense of 'what time is like' but a resistant response to it, which becomes *quasi-symbolic* (even though not often decoded consciously in these terms) and also becomes *celebratory*. It is always to be borne in mind that performances of this music in its heyday were generally before an audience who shared the ghetto experience, and who were 'stirred up' by, and became highly involved in, the music. The experience took on a ritual character. What is resisted, then, by both aspects, but in the first place by the individual foreground artistry, is the alienation of living with un-yielding, external time. And what is symbolized and celebrated is, on the one hand, the individual struggle against heavy socio-physical odds (represented by the temporal), and on the other the value of communal togetherness, in coping with such an environment. The individual wins, in music, a glorious victory, expanding and fulfilling him or herself, in a way which is never possible in the rest of the social life. And the group (musicians and audience) enjoys a virtual apotheosis of what togetherness can do: the taking and keeping of control over time.

The reader may baulk at my use of the term 'quasi-symbolic', here, es-pecially in the light of my discussion of musical meanings in Chapter 2. The quasi-symbolic quality in urban blues is in fact a particular realization of the articulation of world-sense. The musical performance, for both makers and listeners, becomes, by contrast with the rest of social life, a representation of how time might be lived, of a better way of relating to it, and to other people.

This kind of 'quasi-symbolism' in this music may not ever be brought to the level of conscious verbalization by the listener, yet I think it is there, as a *potential* for decoding. Of course, there is an equivalent in the tonal-European code: the articulation of 'triumph' is a world-sense articulation which can acquire a sort of quasi-symbolic definiteness in the shape of, say, a symphonic movement.

Thus an overall antithetical image of a free and harmonious society is constructed. The autarchy of tonal-European composed music is countered not by a mere escapist individualism, such as foreground-artistry alone might articulate, but also by a powerful, serious, collective work, the music-making as a whole, in which the individual contributions and the totality are potentially wholly interdependent, and no (unresolved) conflict remains. Thus these are unmistakably the musics of oppressed people, but of oppressed people fighting back, and certainly retaining and cherishing the hopes and aspirations of freedom.

To complete the argument, let me add a word about the audience *identifications* involved in the music-use which sustains this type of music. These identifications are with first the 'collective' or group and, secondly, the foreground artist(s). Also, by virtue of the communalizing effect of the music on its listeners (with its synchronizing dance beat and the strong appeal generated by its time-sense articulations), the listeners also identify with each other, so that a sense of communal togetherness – in the teeth of a hostile wider world – is created. Contrast this with the identification of the tonal-European listener, with the single *composer* before all else. This hardly exists at all in urban blues, where the very idea of a 'composer' has limited relevance, since the music's extensional 'form' is usually utterly standardized.

It is also worth remembering that in the early development of both jazz and urban blues, and in their continued presence in dance halls all over the USA in the 1940s and 1950s, the mass media of records and radio intervened between makers and listeners much less than they do today. These were first and foremost *live* musics, and the listeners and dancers were present at the performance. Identification with the foreground artists and the rest of the group was easy, being favoured by an existing closeness, physical and cultural, between the musicians and listeners. However, it was realized with enough strength to survive mediation by record, radio and juke-box, once these things began to feature in ghetto music-use. And in this strength, the success of rock 'n' roll and Beat music in achieving identification responses through records and radio – and yet still reserving their greatest impact for the 'live' occasion – was foreshadowed, and the means by which it could be done were forged.

Is not this account *too* neat to be true? Undoubtedly. There must be more meanings, nuances and dimensions to these matters and I have no desire to close down the richness and openness of the music, to strait-jacket it with that arrogant and crudely normative criticism which sets up its supposed insights as tests of authenticity. I will move on now to another level of meaning in urban blues, namely the importance of *masculinity* in the music, i.e. in the singing, the lyrics and the stage-acts of many of the artists.

The great majority of urban blues artists, from the older ones who forged the styles out of jazz, ragtime and Country blues to the later rhythm 'n' blues singers and players, were men. There were quite a few women involved in the music, of course, and indeed some of the biggest early stars of blues, on records as well as in live shows, were the female 'classic blues' singers of the 1920s and 1930s, such as Bessie Smith and Victoria Spivey. But it is noticeable that the black artists who achieved some success with whites on the rock 'n' roll bandwagon, as it were, in the first few years after 1955 (Chuck Berry, Little Richard, Jackie Wilson, Lloyd Price, Larry Williams, Ray Charles, Sam Cooke, The Drifters) were almost all men. The black input into the early rock 'n' roll 'canon' was a male one. And also the black influences on the British (and American) rhythm 'n' blues movement of the early and mid-1960s were mostly male too (Jimmy Reed, John Lee Hooker, B.B. King). (Female jazz singers simply did not appeal, apparently, to the white rock 'n' roll, Beat or rhythm 'n' blues fans, while well-known female blues singers were by then very few in number.) Black women then staged a comeback in young peoples' pop music in the vocal groups who had a lot of hits around the early 1960s, and then in the related soul-as-pop movement led by the Tamla Motown label.

The masculine articulation is achieved by the combined effects of the lyrics, the singing, the stage act and the visual impact of the male blues singer, and to a lesser extent, other players. I will not cite long strings of lyrics here to prove the point: the books of Oliver and Haralambos, among others, contain lots of illustrations, and the recordings of leading 1950s blues artists such as Muddy Waters or B.B. King are full of sexist, aggressively masculine boasting (to other men), songs insulting women, songs of angst supposedly caused by faithless women and, indeed, very little else. The singing of these and similar artists (including the soul singers from the late 1950s onwards, such as James Brown and Jackie Wilson) achieves strong reverberations of a certain type of masculinity by a very particular means: it uses the sounds and rhythms of everyday masculine speech which already exist in the ghetto community. To be precise, it uses what I will call the 'heightened speech' of the boast, the plea, the exhortation, the shout of joy and scream of pain, as they already sound in the milieu the singer springs from. The singers or 'shouters' take these sounds to greater intensity than is common in speech, louder shouts, longer more agonized screams, and so on. This approach, which allows for a huge variety of sounds and rhythms, then individualizes, and makes powerful the singing.

This point raises the question of the *nature* of singing, the relationship of music to speech in different singing styles. I will deal with these matters again in Chapter 7. But the importance of this powerfully masculine singing for my argument here is that from 1955 onwards, it offered a sort of *bridge* from black ghetto to white male youth culture, even when they had no immediate social contact with each other, as white boys found something to identify with in the extravagantly advertised masculine swagger, and/or angst of the blues-men, and copied it. The early repertoires of British bands and singers of the 1960s, such as The Animals, The Rolling Stones, John Mayall, Rod Stewart and so on, offer many instances of their imitating the singing styles of the black artists, and choosing to perform and record some fairly sexist and 'explicit' songs. The same had of course been true of Presley and other American rock 'n' rollers of a few years previously.

I have not given any attention in this chapter to sound-sense articulations, or to iconic meanings, in respect of jazz and urban blues styles. This is not to say that they do not feature there, but merely that I would be repeating myself unnecessarily later, if I introduced them in any detail now. What I will now do is to move on to the events and artists of rock 'n' roll and Beat music themselves; the relevance of my arguments here will then gradually re-emerge.

4   *A Fusion of Codes:*
The Pop Music of 1955–1964

Rock 'n' roll and skiffle

A succession of Bill Haley and the Comets records entered the British 'Top Twenty' in 1955, 1956 and 1957, and many of them stayed there for long periods: 'Rock Around the Clock', on its first re-entry (October 1955), stayed in the Top Twenty for 17 weeks, in addition to its initial 2 weeks, and on its second re-entry stayed 11 weeks more. 'Saints Rock and Roll' lasted 22 weeks, 'Rockin' through the Rye' 19 weeks, etc.[1] These records established a first style, a preliminary definition and presence, of rock 'n' roll in Britain. They were records made by a group, smaller than most dance bands of the time but definitely a group rather than a singer with some hired backing musicians. Such groups were not unknown – indeed dance bands had been declining in average size since the Second World War[2] – but the music the Comets were playing *was* very unusual, and rather unfamiliar to the British pop audience as a whole. Most of the songs were constructed in 'twelve-bar blues' form, itself a rarity in pop at the time, and the speed and attack with which the whole performance was delivered contrasted sharply with most familiar pop, including much dance music. This was very much more true of Britain, where such artists as Eddie Calvert and The Ted Heath Orchestra were the leading purveyors of dance music in the early 1950s, than of the USA, where such 'wild' and 'raunchy' music as Louis Jordan's 'Caldonia' or Roy Milton's 'Hucklebuck' had been very successful with white audiences, especially in the dance halls, in the late 1940s and early 1950s.

The loud guitar and drum-led sound, with the use of a lot of amplification in concerts, was quite new to most British audiences, especially the younger ones, and it polarized the reactions of listeners quite dramatically. They either loved it or hated it. Those who loved it responded to it chiefly, even solely, as dance music. The 'beat' was very prominent on these records – indeed, in comparison with most dance music of the period, it was as though the rhythm section was playing loudly and crudely, for most of the time without any leads, except the voice – and the dancing which was done to them was necessarily fast, energetic and simple. The dance style which resulted was a development of the 'jiving' that often accompanied faster dance music in general, and had done since the 1930s. I shall discuss dancing again below; here, however, I wish only to point out that, as dance music, this music reached boys *and* girls, men *and* women, from the start, and was popular with both sexes.

The association of Haley's music with dancing, and also with teenagers, became spectacular, and was confirmed and guaranteed its impact everywhere in Britain, by virtue of the cinema 'riots' that took place at showings of the 'Rock Around the Clock' film. Though there was certainly a tendency to self-fulfilling prophecies (by the Press and radio/TV coverage), these occurrences do appear to have been largely spontaneous, and testify to the quite startling effect of the Comets' music on teenagers, something which it is all too easy to belittle a quarter of a century later, when these records sound very 'dated' to most listeners. I think it is necessary to examine this impact very closely.

The teenage or youth culture was already in existence, and already strong and (locally, at least) conscious of itself, when this music quite suddenly came along. In the USA, the events which led up to the successes of Haley and Elvis Presley were dramatic, certainly, but they were rather less concentrated in time. It was in 1952 that the DJ Alan Freed was first invited to a Cleveland record store to observe white adolescents dancing enthusiastically to records by Red Prysock the blues sax-player, and Ivory Joe Hunter the pianist-singer, while David Riesman observed some of the characteristics of a teenage sub-culture centred on music-use in a minority of young pop fans as early as 1950.[3] Thus although the subsequent rise of Presley was indeed meteoric, the development of white interest in rock 'n' roll music in America was actually a steady, long-term growth, which accelerated into a 'craze' in 1955.

By contrast, as Gillett rightly states:

> Lacking any regular access to the sound of Hank Ballard, Amos Milburn, Wynonie Harris and Muddy Waters during the early fifties, most people ... [in Britain] ... were taken by surprise when Bill Haley's 'Shake, Rattle and Roll' and 'Rock Around the Clock' were issued in late 54.[4]

The development of the Teddy Boy style, in clothes, slang, and leisure pursuits, preceded rock 'n' roll by 4–5 years, while the development of 'teenagers' in the more generalized sense was an even more long-term and gradual process dating back in some respects even to the 1920s and 1930s and beyond. None the less, rock music-use rapidly became one of the central characteristics of the youth culture, and has remained so ever since. It was as though teenagers had been waiting for it, and they now embraced it with joyful recognition.

If the cinema riots *fixed* the association of rock 'n' roll with teenagers, they also fixed another association, in the eyes of the parent culture – namely, that between rock 'n' roll and 'juvenile delinquency'. Gillett[5] suggests that this happened because the new, exciting music drew the existing street gangs and 'vandals' into the dance halls and juke-box cafes. This is a debate I cannot resolve here, but I am inclined to accept Colin Fletcher's view,[6] based as it is on first-hand experience, that the development of the amateur, and later semi-professional, *Beat groups* out of the existing gangs actually rechannelled the frustrations of the participants and caused a decline of violent and destructive acts.

Haley and the Comets, then, set a new pattern of music-use among British teenagers: music became much more central to their leisure style than previously. But Haley did not inspire the sort of identification from boys, or adoration from girls, which Presley and others were to inspire. Thus the music, and the dancing it encouraged, were even *more* central in this early phase of rock than a little later. It was the excitement of an encounter with a startling new style, and also of the rejection of the principal pop styles of the immediate past – and of their continuation at the hands of such artists as Dickie Valentine, Vera Lynn, David Whitfield and Ted Heath. This excitement, shown by the 'cinema riots' and recalled so vividly by Fletcher and many others, was clearly something which has rarely if ever been repeated in the subsequent 30 years and more.

These fast, loud, 'energetic' and highly rhythmic twelve-bar songs (except for 'Saints') accomplished a new breakthrough in the century-long process of *codal fusion* in British popular music. They became part of the 'given', for countless young British listeners, extending the stock of the musically familiar for these listeners in a quite fundamental way. It is true that the structural, melodic and rhythmic qualities which were prominent in them were all already to be heard interspersed through the dance-music and pop songs of the preceding period, but now these elements were brought together and presented on their own, without being any longer employed alongside elements which pointed back always like a compass needle to the light-tonal code. The type of beat, the pace, the twelve-bar form, the instrumental resources, the (limited) improvisations, the rhythmicization of the singing and use of the 'speaking voice', shouts, coarse tones, etc., at the expense of 'melody' in the old sense – all of these could be found here and there in 'dance-band jazz', 'Country and Western' pop, or in the 'bluesier' ballads. Here, however, they were employed not as spices or novelties, nor as iconic *references* to black or rural cultures, but for themselves, in a style which consisted of virtually nothing else. All of these elements are, of course, Afro-American. The only things *white* about the Comets were Haley's rather Country-ish vocal delivery on some records and the fact that they were not terribly good at the music they played, they did not always sound completely at ease, especially to listeners with some knowledge of blues and jazz. Gillett, however, does single out the sax solos of Rudi Pompilli as being pretty good.[7]

To be precise, Haley's music (of this period) was an imitation of 'Northern' or 'city' dance-blues of the kind which had been popular at black, and some white, dance venues in the 1940s and early 1950s, and which Haley had been mixing with his Country music repertoire ever since about 1947. This was not unique among white musicians; Hank Williams and Jimmy Rodgers were among many Country artists from the 1930s onwards who performed up-tempo blues-influenced songs. There were also lesser known artists very like Haley and the Comets, such as Freddy Bell and the Bellboys ('Giddy-up-a Ding-Dong'). Indeed, a whole small genre of somewhat similar music existed in the 1940s and 1950s in the southwestern states under the name 'Western Swing', appealing mainly to a 'Country and Western'-orientated white American audience; its most notable performers were Bob Wills and his Texas Playboys.

Haley himself was no musicologist and we do not need to take his own bewildering accounts of the Comets' style too seriously. In one interview, he said it was 'all jazz', whereas on another occasion he said:

> I felt that if I could take, say, a Dixieland tune, and drop the first and third beats, and accentuate the second and fourth, and add a beat the listeners could clap to, as well as dance, this would be what they were after.[8]

His confusing terms and classifications here are less interesting than the overall impression which the quotes unmistakably offer, that for a working dance-band musician, the barriers between different styles, and between white and black origins, were already, and as a matter of course, virtually non-existent. There is no sense of anything extraordinary having been achieved in these quotes, and that is because, despite the later impact on Britain, it was not such a big step in the USA of the 1950-or-so period to mix rhythm 'n' blues elements (often thought of largely as 'jazz') and Country and Western elements together. The other thing which is significant in these comments is that Haley was following his (white) audience – he saw their enthusiasm for 'dance-blues' and gave them more. And we have no reason to suppose that this audience was solely of teenagers; indeed, we know that a mixed audience of all ages *except* younger teenagers would have been typical, in the dance halls of the USA in the early 1950s. High school 'hops' and most coffee bar juke-boxes were conquered by rock 'n' roll artists and records only after the breakthroughs of 1954–1955.

In the second interview cited above, Haley went on immediately to say:

> From that the rest was easy ... take everyday sayings like 'Crazy Man Crazy', 'See You Later, Alligator', 'Shake Rattle and Roll', and apply to what I have just said.[9]

It is clear that he did not attach very much importance to the lyrics, and I think he was correct. Far more important than the lyrics, or even Haley's singing of them, was the rhythmic character of the music as a whole. I described it above as guitar and drum-led, and mentioned saxophone solos, but it would be more accurate, in a sense, to say that although these instruments are most prominent, the drums and *bass* are the dominant, and most essential members of the ensemble. In their steady, slightly variegated but basically homogeneous pulse lies the central, indispensable quality of the music, both as dance music and as music of a basically collectively created character.

This pulse became known as the 'beat', and I will discuss it at greater length, as befits its importance, in Chapter 6. The sax, guitars and voice all depend on this pulse, and on the marking of chord-changes by little flourishes in the rhythm section in exactly the manner of black urban-blues groups. The sax and guitar solos are, in a real sense, optional by comparison, 'Shake, Rattle and Roll' would be 'the same song' without the solo 'breaks' on Haley's version, and has been performed by hundreds of groups in different ways ever since. Thus it is not only an easy way of describing a felt difference but actually says something very apposite about rock 'n' roll to say that it sounds like a dance-blues or blues-jazz band's *rhythm section playing on their own*, with solos often taken by a guitarist and only one saxophone used. Rudi Pompilli aside, however, the Comets did not have the front-man for the job in Bill Haley – his voice did not even begin to suffice as 'foreground', and when more interesting rock-singers came along he could not compete.

Related to this failure was Haley's inability to inspire much identification among boys or romantic adulation among girls. Not only did his voice not command great attention, but the plump, energetic, affable, ageing Haley simply did not have the appeal of the conventional handsome young pop star, let alone the impact of Presley as I will describe it below. Perhaps for this reason, Haley and the Comets did not provide any great encouragement to amateurism, unlike skiffle, Presley, Buddy Holly and others. This perhaps is why their impact is played down in many rock histories. However, not only did they usher in a new phase in the development of *codal fusion* in general, especially in Britain, but they brought many particular elements of Afro-American practice, and one or two distinctive appropriations of it, into every young listener's store of known and possible sounds. Apart from the pulse-and-leads structure, other elements used by Haley were 'sax-riffing' ('See You Later Alligator') and 'call-and-response' between singer and sax ('Shake, Rattle and Roll'). The chief one, however, was the down grading of *melody* or *tunes* in the traditional, tonal-code sense. Of course, jazz improvisation had often laid greater emphasis on rhythmic and timbric intensionality than on melody, but almost all well-known jazz employed popular tunes, or imitations of them, as the basis for this improvisation. But some of Haley's songs were hardly 'tunes' at all. 'Melody' in tonal-code music is produced normally by its differentiations of *pitch* in relation to harmonic grounding, as explained in Chapter 3. But these vocal lines, as well as the lead guitar and sax lines, were defined at least as much by their rhythmic character – with, yet not totally 'on', the beats of the pulse – and their timbric roughness or smoothness, as by their melodic character in this sense. True, the vocal line of 'Rock Around the Clock' opens with a I–III–V figure, which Deryck Cooke has used as a standard example of a joyful melodic convention,[10] but the rest of the vocal, and the whole of, say, 'Shake, Rattle and Roll', does not fit Cooke's approach at all, and demonstrates instead the 'abandoning' of the tradition of melody, which had characterized earlier white light and popular musics in Europe and America. So softened have the tonal rules, or their remnant, become in Haley's singing, that almost any tone can be sung 'over' any chord in the twelve-bar structure, though those which 'clash' greatly with their grounding are passed through rather faster than others. The 'rules' of tonality have been relaxed and pushed into the background in such singing, though of course this is only actually possible because the simple harmonic sequence of twelve-bar blues is quietly insisted on and indeed rigidified by the instrumental accompanists. This is again very similar to the intensional practices found in most urban blues.

However, it is not true to say that Haley sings 'all on one or two notes', to quote a common complaint. To think this is clearly to experience the downgrading or absence of melody in the old tonal-European sense but not to notice the actual pitch range used or the rhythmicization and timbric variety of the vocal line which have largely replaced melody. In reality, Haley's vocal line in 'Rock Around the Clock' covers almost an octave, and contains some large intervals. But they are of very subordinate importance in the overall impact of the music. To miss this, and criticize Haley for it, is the response of someone for whom codal fusion has been arrested at an earlier stage, or for whom it does not apply at all – and indeed it was the 'older generation' who normally made such charges. None the less, with Haley the possibilities of the new kind of singing are not really developed. The main virtues of the Comets' music were in the energetic playing and singing, including some rhythmic and timbric intensionality, and in the collectivity which was clearly involved in the semi-improvised instrumental playing: Gillett calls it 'high-spirited feelings of togetherness',[11] and, as so often, his intuitive description/evaluation reveals a flash of insight.

Haley's influence in Britain was rapidly supplanted by a number of other rock 'n' roll artists, led by Elvis Presley. Here, however, I want to pursue the theme of *codal fusion* a little further by discussing Buddy Holly and the Crickets, and also mentioning the relationship between Haley's and Holly's music and the phenomenon of skiffle. Holly and his group played a more Country-influenced style of rock 'n' roll than the Comets, but such nuances of style were probably largely lost on their early British audiences of teenagers, whose knowledge of Country music was rather limited. What Holly did, which was *not* lost, was to develop the possibilities of the rock-*group*, for all to see, and to develop group-music in two major directions: bringing codal fusion into focus in *song-forms* themselves and, with the Crickets, introducing to young white British and American audiences a new kind of 'virtuosity' in singing and playing.

Holly led two overlapping collectives: a song-writing and producing group which comprised himself, his friend, manager and co-producer Norman Petty, his drummer Jerry Allison, and various others at different times, and also a playing and singing collective, the Crickets, who sometimes recorded under their name (with Holly on guitar and vocals) and sometimes as Holly's backing group. Towards the end of his brief career, Holly left the Crickets, and recorded with session-bands, including the well-known rhythm 'n' blues sax player, King Curtis. But the Holly-and-the-Crickets records which were successful in Britain all featured the group playing *as* a group – 'tight' backing for Holly's voice interspersed by breaks for the lead guitar, and exhibiting the work of the drummer, bass and rhythm guitar prominently throughout. The 'dance-band' sound which still lingers in Comets records (with the prominent saxophone) has been supplanted by a mixture of 'hard' rhythm 'n' blues and Country and Western 'small-group' sounds, in which no saxophone is used.[12]

Although certainly pre-planned, these records ('Peggy Sue', 'That'll be the day', 'Oh Boy', 'Not Fade Away', etc.) clearly declare their 'collectivity' and 'spontaneity' of production. The collectivity is evident, again as in Comets records, in the mutual dependence of the players, especially in the playing of off-the-beat rhythms which cannot easily be scored but which are 'picked up' from each other by the musicians. 'Oh Boy' and 'Not Fade Away' offer particularly good examples of this. The spontaneity of these records is evident in the 'breaks', where a sort of home-spun virtuosity flourishes. Holly's guitar (and the others' playing too) does not astound the listener, it does not sound inimitable or perfect; instead, it decorates the chords imaginatively, and in a way which could quite conceivably be changed next time, but which is far from skill-less for all that. The same is true of Allison's drumming, which he varies greatly from song to song without ever doing anything technically very difficult. This is musicality objectified not in the domineering, individualistic manner of composing a score but in a more ephemeral, yet also much more obviously exuberant, happy manner. It depends on only a little pre-planning, compared to an orchestral score, yet it manages to grow freely and without clash or breakdown into a genuinely collective performance. I think only such a description of these records can suffice to account for their extraordinary influence in subsequent rock and pop, both American and British, as evidenced by numerous re-recordings by other groups, and many tributes and inter-views.[13] These records showed what small-group rock, with limited instru-mental resources and even limited players, could none the less achieve. In this, they epitomized a quality present in most early rock. And they did this without ceasing to make good dance music like anything by Haley and the Comets. Furthermore, these records demystified song-writing. Holly, Petty, Allison and one or two others were the authors of almost every hit the Crickets made, and there was nothing about the records which suggested they had employed any complex specialist skills: merely they 'wrote' what they could play. This was particularly important in Britain where rock 'n' roll had, until Holly's success, seemed wholly 'American' even in its most popular forms, and therefore largely inimitable. Unlike the demi-god Presley, Holly did not come across as extraordinarily manly, sexy, powerful, etc.; his group did not sound perfect either – it was even more clearly a case of an ordinary kid showing everybody what he could do. Of course, all this can be said to be true of much small-group blues also. But Holly's impact on white teenagers was based on an identification they were not yet (*en masse*) ready to make with black bluesmen.

In fact, however, the simplicity of Holly's music is in one respect illusory. His song-forms break all the rules: twelve-bar verses will be followed by eight- or sixteen-bar breaks, or eight-bar forms will have twelve-bar instrumental breaks stuck in the middle, etc. 'That'll be the Day' consists of eight-bar segments (of which there are three in each vocal section) with a fully-fledged twelve-bar blues instrumental break in the centre. Furthermore, each verse begins, unusually, on the IV-chord, moving to the I-chord after two bars. 'Oh Boy' follows a pattern of twelve-twelve-eight-twelve, a twelve-bar break, then twelve-twelve-eight-twelve again, making the unlikely total of 100 bars in all. The eight-bar section in each 'verse' is an orthodox 'middle-eight' of the sort used in non-blues pop. None of these procedures is so rare or unlikely as to be at all revolutionary (indeed, many similar things were done in the rhythm 'n' blues field from time to time), but it is not Holly's 'greatness' I am trying to prove. It is the fact that these structures do not sound *avant-garde* or strange (so that it comes as a slight shock to count the bars and discover unusual combinations) which is significant: it tells us how far codal fusion, or the integration of Afro-American elements into the musicality of white people at a level deeper than self-conscious, superficial imitation – how far this development had proceeded, not only in Holly's musical imagination but among the listeners who welcomed these songs with open arms, on both sides of the Atlantic. (This penchant for somewhat unusual structures is found in the work of some other 'rockabilly' songwriters too – Carl Perkins being a well-known instance.) To put it another way, what is interesting here (and what comes to the fore again in the music of The Beatles and others) is that Holly was sufficiently at home with the style of music chosen to carry out successful experiments, increasingly leaving the twelve-bar form, if not at first the 'three-chord trick', behind. Furthermore, these developments were comprehended in some way, and enthusiastically accepted, by Holly's mainly white, mainly teenage audience, in both Britain and America.

Further evidence of the development of codal fusion is provided by skiffle, a phenomenon which occurred in Britain alone, though one or two skiffle records sold well elsewhere. Now skiffle was a school lunch-hour and church youth club kind of amateur music-making, taking as its models principally the recordings of Lonnie Donegan. It was not so different, musically speaking, from rock 'n' roll, as it is sometimes held to have been.[14] The use of home-made instruments and the absence of electrification gave it a different sound certainly, but in spreading the twelve-bar form, the rhythmic preoccupation, and the monopolizing of the foreground by a single singer for most or all of the time, it undoubtedly pushed the development of codal fusion in more or less the same overall direction as did the music of Haley or Holly. It is therefore unsurprising to discover that, whereas much rock 'n' roll sounds like a jazz or blues rhythm section plus singer much of the time, skiffle actually *was* exactly this, originating in the habit of The Ken Colyer Band (a jazz group) to provide a sort of break for the lead instrumentalists while the rhythm section played a simple, fast, highly danceable accompaniment for Colyer or Donegan (the group's banjo player) to sing a few American folksongs and blues.[15]

It came out of the 'Trad' jazz clubs courtesy of BBC Radio, who played several 'requests' for it, and also the popularizing efforts of The Chris Barber Band. It soon became a minor craze, and later an avalanche, when Donegan began to concentrate exclusively on it. BBC Radio then itself responded by running a specialized programme, 'Skiffle Club'. Much of the music of Donegan, The Vipers and so on was an unmistakable mixture of blues with white American folk song styles, together with a dash of music hall and George Formby. It was certainly an extremely important source of amateur teenage musicians, some of them to become successful professionals. Examples are The Beatles, The Shadows and also such highly influential, if less celebrated, early rock 'n' roll artists as Johnny Kidd, of Johnny Kidd and the Pirates. I should also mention that the skiffle movement, and the huge guitar-playing boom it catalysed, also fed into the British 'folk music' movement which enjoyed its own first 'boom' in the late 1950s.[16] This mainly middle-class movement then itself contributed notable musicians and song writers to British rock and pop later in the 1960s and 1970s: Donovan Leitch, Bert Jansch and others. Most of those who went on to become rock, folk or beat-group members lingered only briefly with the limited, rather antiquarian style of skiffle. Nevertheless, at the time this relationship between skiffle and rock 'n' roll was by no means clear to commentators; viz. the definition of rock 'n' roll in Gammond and Clayton's *A Guide to Popular Music*:

> Rock and Roll, Rock 'n' Roll, Rock. A more commercial form of skiffle generally using contrived themes instead of folk music, and with the emphasis on the rhythm or beat, which is magnified to frantic proportions. It does not employ the jazz inflection so completely as rhythm and blues and skiffle but rather a number of tricks and affectations which emphasise the crude rhythms. The effect is also generally emphasised by suggestive body movements. One of the most successful pioneers of the music was Bill Haley and his Comets, while its biggest individual star is undoubtedly Elvis Presley. It would seem to have the characteristics of a temporary craze rather than the more lasting folk element of skiffle.[17]

While Haley, Holly and Donegan were undoubtedly of very great importance, particularly Holly and Donegan in their encouragement of amateurism, there is no question that the survival of rock 'n' roll, the depth of its impact, and the reason why it proved a more important and lasting change than skiffle, must be attributed in large measure to the 'biggest individual star', Elvis Presley. Yet it was of him that Gammond and Clayton, speaking no doubt for many other listeners, were clearly thinking when they identified crude affectations and suggestive movements as central to the shallowness and commercialism of the style, prime reasons why it would prove to be just a passing fad. Presley as marketed, as a pop star, undoubtedly did represent a brash, vulgar hard-sell in popular music which separated him out from both skiffle and even Sinatra. But I want to suggest that his success was none the less originally and primarily based on a particular, musical dimension which he brought into white rock 'n' roll and which he represented *par excellence*: the prominence and dominance of the voice, and of a new (to most whites) type of singing, which has remained one of the central qualities of rock music ever since.

Elvis Presley

The impact of Presley in Britain began in the spring of 1956, when Haley had already had five or six hits, and Pat Boone two, within the broad category of rock 'n' roll. Presley did not have a 'Number One' until July 1957, with 'All Shook Up'. In this early period, then, Presley was certainly very famous, causing a media sensation with everything he did, but his actual popularity in Britain was confined to the hard core of the youth culture, and was roughly equal, in record sales, to that of Haley. Both had six hits from May 1956 to December 1956, with Haley having records in the Top Twenty for 76 weeks in all (including overlaps) and Presley achieving 72.[18] This youth culture audience, then, was not normally large enough or affluent enough to send its favoured records to the very top of the charts, though we can of course speculate about how often each record was listened to and how many people listened to one record. We might also find that charts of juke-box favourites would show rock 'n' roll records to have been more, and more repeatedly, sought after than some which outsold them on the undifferentiated record-store market, always assuming that the charts accurately reflected this, which is doubtful.

Even more so than some of the other artists, then, Presley at this time was very much the property of teenagers, and little more than a spectacle and a scandal to others. If they heard his music (and it was not heard much on radio or TV), they (parents, teachers, etc.) found it apparently to be either objectionable or, at best, unexceptional. Certainly in the USA there were numerous attacks made on Presley, notably that by the TV critic John Crosby who called him an 'unspeakably untalented and vulgar young entertainer', or *The New York Times*, which declared, 'He injected movements of the tongue and indulged in wordless singing that was singularly distasteful.' Another wrote 'He moved as if he was sneering with his legs.' As late as 1961, Edward Jablonski wrote that Presley 'seemed remarkably devoid of any singing talent'.[19] In Britain, the same sort of comments were being made too, with the added twist that many critics objected to everything American. I can myself recall very clearly what a shocking and bewildering effect Presley still had on older people in the early 1960s, a shock much greater than The Beatles, say, caused, and perhaps similar to that occasioned a little later by Jagger and the other Rolling Stones.

Presley was first and foremost a singer. He did not participate in a 'group', even though certain regular players and backing singers were used in the early years. He did not write songs, though he is credited with co-writing one or two. His repertoire was, from the beginning, a mixture of blues, Country songs, a few 'standards' and devotional songs. After 1957, there were few blues on his records, but specially written rock songs using blues-like elements were still included.

But if Presley was primarily a singer, this in no way belittles him. His singing made such an impact on the teenage listeners, that it cannot be said to have mattered that he was not in overall control, in the manner of Haley (or Holly) since, as far as his fans were concerned, he *took over* the recording and made it his vehicle. This prominence and dominance of Presley the singing voice was the most dramatic difference between Comets records and Presley records, and it was this big step forward, which rock 'n' roll took in the records of Presley, which quickly made him its most famous representative.

As I have already hinted in the account of urban blues above, Presley and other rock 'n' roll singers took their singing approach and particular vocal techniques from black blues singers. In Presley's case, the model we know he was particularly aware of, because he said so, was the hybrid Country-urban blues singer Arthur Crudup, known as 'Big Boy'. He probably also imitated an acquaintance at Sun Records, (Little) Junior Parker, and various black and white gospel singers. Presley's version of Crudup's 'That's All Right' actually comes from his very first proper session with a full backing group, and a comparison with Crudup's version can give us a clear idea of the initial similarities between the two singers. Gillett writes of Presley's singing on 'That's All Right':

> . . . he evolved a personal version of this . . . [blues] . . . style, singing high and clear, breathless and impatient, varying his rhythmic emphasis with a confidence and inventiveness that were exceptional for a white singer.[20]

This may be largely true, but it falls into the usual rock-book trap of mixing a description which purports to be objective, though based on no explicit terms of comparison, with a pre-formed and nowhere-defended evaluation. In fact, there *are* some descriptive and contrastive points which we can make about these recordings, and which are more susceptible to verification. First, Presley's voice is *not* as uniformly 'high and clear' as Crudup's, though it is less 'nasal'. In fact, Presley introduces audible 'swoops' into the lower register which is called for in the middle of each verse, while his singing of the lower-pitched phrases themselves ('That's all right, that's all right' and 'I need your lovin' in the last verse) contrasts (in timbre, or tone of voice) with the surrounding singing much more than Crudup's rendering of the same. Presley is clearly not copying slavishly, but using a more composite voice – 'full', 'open-throated' – which must derive from a wider listening-experience than just Crudup, as well as attesting to a strong and versatile voice.

Secondly, the instrumentation of the song has been altered. The 'rough' blues guitar of the Crudup version, playing in the same pitch-register as Crudup's voice, and coming in between his phrases with phrases of its own is replaced, on Presley's version, by a more lightly played, less intrusive 'strumming' and 'picking' on guitar, so that Presley's voice comprises more nearly the whole audible foreground than does Crudup's. This monopolizing requires Presley to sing with a greater 'fullness' than Crudup – hence the swooping, the sliding across tones ('ri-i-ght' and 'Mama' throughout) and the distinctness of the lower register as described above. The low-pitched, fairly homogeneous rhythmic introduction, and the low-pitched instrumental break in the Presley version 'set off' his voice by simple contrast, whereas Crudup is happy to engage in call-and-response patterns with a high-pitched guitar, and to use this guitar in the opening instrumental section. Again, the rhythm section work on the Presley version is relatively static, with the bass seesawing from one tone to another almost throughout, alongside an evenly strummed rhythm guitar, 'steady' and fast, a 'danceable beat', probably with influence from white Country music as well as black blues. On Crudup's recording, the bass player moves around incessantly, creating different patterns in different measures, while the lead guitar continues to improvise both melodically and rhythmically alongside the voice. The effect is to create a much more broken rhythm to which the word 'beat' is hardly applicable, though a steady pulse is of course maintained.

Thirdly, the song's form itself is an unusual one in both versions. Although Crudup's original (written by him) uses the three chords of the normal blues, it is a ten-bar rather than a twelve-bar structure and can be represented in the following form:

Chord	1	1	1	1	4	4	5	5	1	1
Measure (Bar)	1	2	3	4	5	6	7	8	9	10

(Bar eight might be rendered in two halves, with chords moving five-four, 'back towards' the one-chord.) This ten-bar form is itself perhaps a tribute to Crudup's songwriting skill, since the result does not sound lopsided or experimental in any way. However, Presley's version alters this form, cutting the tenth measure completely except at the end of the instrumental break. The effect is that no sooner has one full stanza of the lyrics ended than another begins. It may be that this gives the singing a quality of speed or urgency which accounts for Gillett's rather puzzling word 'breathless', since there is no audible breathlessness on the recording. Certainly, it increases the prominence and dominance of the singer in the performance, as he repeatedly usurps the foreground again following the very shortest of pauses.

To sum up, the differences between the two versions of 'That's All Right' tend to fall into two groups: first, the greater emphasis on rhythmic concertedness and simplicity in the Presley version, which gives the song a prominent 'beat' rather than just an underlying pulse and, secondly, the greater prominence of Presley the singer, who monopolizes the foreground much more completely than Crudup does. Thus with Presley, even as an untutored beginner in July 1954, the song becomes more danceable and more vocally memorable (and perhaps therefore more likely to be a pop-hit?) than Crudup's by no means incompetent version.

None the less, it was among the black listeners of Memphis that Presley achieved much of his early success with this and other recordings.[21] His manager-producer Sam Phillips (and later Colonel Parker and others) did however put a Country and Western song on the 'B-side' of most of his early records, and gradually both his repertoire and his appeal broadened. This was, in part at least, planned: Phillips later claimed he had consciously devised a way of mixing black and white (Country) elements in the music of many of his artists, in order to achieve a novel sound which would succeed with young whites,[22] and he fully intended to produce a big pop star rather than just another blues (or Country) singer, if possible.

Presley's first British hit, 'Heartbreak Hotel', his second, 'Blue Suede Shoes', and at least three of his others prior to his first British Number One, 'All Shook Up', preserved both the rhythmic emphasis and attack and the vocal dominance of 'That's All Right'. A comparison of Carl Perkins's original 'Blue Suede Shoes' with Presley's version reveals changes of the same sort which were employed in the transformation of the Crudup record: tighter, simpler rhythms, and a more prominent vocal. On 'Heartbreak Hotel', extravagant echo is used by the producer in order to further promote Presley's voice. Twenty months of schooling by Phillips and others are clearly to be thanked or blamed for Presley's development of a fuller, lower register than he had used at the beginning – and his use of it almost throughout these songs. He sings even the fastest numbers in this 'husky' voice, which was apparently considered very 'masculine'. This masculinity, combined with his 'lewd' stage act, formed the basis of his image of 'sexy', which his backers promoted in various photographs and press releases, and which also gained confirmation, no doubt, from attacks in the media on his obscenity and vulgarity. When, as in 'Hound Dog', Presley still sang in his upper vocal register, he now used a 'rougher', more shouted tone than earlier, no doubt to fit in with the more manly image he had acquired in the meantime.

In stating that Presley's 'husky' tone was 'masculine', I have begged a question I now wish to consider briefly: what is the nature of, what is the source of, these meanings in a singing voice, and what gives them their power? 'Heartbreak Hotel' as his first major international hit and a record which has attracted reams of commentary, mostly concerned with his singing, is the best example to consider. His echo-enhanced singing is so full of swoops, slides across tones, grunts and gasps that, in places, the lyrics become all but indistinguishable and the 'inarticulate' voice is all that can be heard. These elements do not come from light-white singing, but are found in the blues, and to a lesser extent the Country and Western, traditions. However, it is not necessarily a matter of particular tricks which Presley has pinched but a general *freedom* to use these resources, an approach, which is at stake here. The influence of these musics, and blues in particular, liberates for Presley a source of singing techniques which perhaps lies ultimately behind all song, but which is rather buried and forgotten in the formalized styles of tonal-code vocal music – namely, his own *speech*. The whoops, shouts, 'coarsenings' of tone, gasps and grunts in 'Heartbreak Hotel' and also in 'Hound Dog', 'Blue Suede Shoes', 'Jailhouse Rock', 'All Shook Up' and many others, express 'excitement', 'strong emotion', 'vitality', 'sexiness', etc., by virtue of the fact that they *already* express these things in the everyday speech of his cultural milieu and that of his listeners.

Of course, it is not in everyday speech as a use of the languages *system*, that such meanings reside, but in the ways in which people use the resources of vocalization, and of their faces and bodily movements too, to nuance their utterances in many ways. No two utterances of 'God, I feel awful' are the same, not only in terms of which word is emphasized but also in many less easily definable ways which can none the less alter the whole message. It is

possible to shout it out or whisper it, with a smile or a frown, in an un-
accustomed vocal register, perhaps, quickly or slowly, accelerating or slowing
down, while jumping in the air, waving the arms or stamping the foot.
Precisely this order of variability, and this type of resource, is brought by
Presley into his singing. Here is what Carl Belz says about Presley's voice:

> As an expressive vehicle it shifts from high to low notes, it groans, it slurs, and it
> produces breathless [!] changes of rhythm. To many listeners Presley's voice may
> have seemed crude, but its folk immediacy resided in this crudeness.[23]

Now the blues and Country and Western singing had both always been
close to the *enonciation*[24] of speech within the black/white rural American
milieux. But white crooning, and the semi-operatic style descended from
operetta, and still to be heard in 'Oklahoma' or 'My Fair Lady' in the
1950s, had been characterized by a quest for 'purity' of sound production,
rhythmicized breathing (which often respected the musical phrases rather
than the lyrics), and certain novel or fashionable tricks, like the 'whispering
baritone' of the 1920s or the 'vo-de-o-do' style in which all vowel sounds were
sung with exaggerated fullness. Of course, some crooners (notably Sinatra)
and jazz singers did use coarse tones and lyrically expressive phrasing, but
this was still widely regarded as a step or two down the ladder from 'proper'
singing. A good example of such traditions is Gershwin's 'Porgy and Bess', in
which the hedonistic black stereotype 'Sporting Life' is allowed to sing songs
(supposedly in a jazz style) which employ speech resources quite prominently
while the hero and heroine soar to Puccini-like operatic heights. The same
pattern occurs in other 'musicals' between the leading characters and the
comic characters.

The shouts, whoops, grunts and gasps of Presley all come from the youthful,
extrovert American male leisure style as it existed in the 1940s and 1950s, and
as it was reproduced and represented (to Britain, as well as America) through
the mass media. The shouting, chanting and screaming which accompany
baseball and American football games, the stock-scene of many a Western
film, in which the young bloods ride into town shooting off their guns,
whooping and yelling 'Yee-ha-a-agh', etc., the sullen, rebellious, sexually
threatening Brando and James Dean, apt to burst at any moment into a
shouting, punching frenzy, but for most of the time grunting and mumbling
semi-articulately – these were the sorts of representations of the *speech of
masculinity* which flourished at the time, which no doubt corresponded to 'real'
speech in some ways, and which formed, even in Britain, the familiar context
of comparability which enabled Presley's singing to be placed and understood.
Older people who found Presley brash and vulgar, crude and impolite, were
reacting to the same intelligible elements as his young fans: simply the young
fans felt like being brash and vulgar, crude and impolite, for whatever reasons.
It was a matter of identification – if you could and would identify with Presley
there was a delight in his crudeness and sullen, rebellious look, speech and
song; if you couldn't or wouldn't, there could be little pleasure in it. Of course,
this argument raises acutely the question of girls and women, and their

response to Presley and similar artists, and I will return to this in Chapter 6.

Presley took his vocal cue chiefly from the blues, but he also recorded Country and Western songs and straightforward ballads from the beginning, and had some of his biggest successes with them. As I have already remarked, the Country tradition had always been characterized by a degree of interchange with black music, and it is therefore not surprising that Presley's voice was able to be influenced by both sources without sounding like mimicry rather than his own vehicle. Despite Phillips's aim, of a white boy who could sing 'coloured', Presley was in fact received in the USA mainly as an 'integrated' singer rather than as black or mock-black. He might have been found a great deal less offensive in some (racist) quarters if he had been merely a novelty, a sort of updated 'coon-singer' or 'black-faced minstrel', rather than what he was, a white singer who was neither clowning nor apologetic when singing the blues. It is an interesting historical coincidence that this integrated singing burst out of its local and 'down-market' limitations at precisely the same time as the famous anti-discrimination campaign around the Montgomery, Alabama bus service began to escalate into an example and inspiration to urban and rural black communities throughout the USA (Spring and Summer 1956).

However, this integrated aspect of Presley's singing must be presumed to have had very much less impact in Britain, where the situation was so different historically, so that these connotations of Presley's singing voice would be less obvious and less important to the pop audience as a whole. The echoes of Country singing in his voice *would*, however, be somewhat familiar, especially to rather older listeners, since there had already been a Country-music 'boom' in Britain in the late 1940s and early 1950s, with Tex Williams, Gene Autry and Slim Whitman achieving success, while Frankie Laine, Guy Mitchell, Rosemary Clooney and Patti Page too had brought Country elements into their ballad singing, and Bill Haley had retained them in his rock vocal style. The basis for Presley's transformation into a 'mainstream' pop singer with appeal to all age groups, which took place in the 1960s, was laid in this stylistic ambiguity which was present from the beginning, in so far as Country and Western music was already well integrated into the field of universal (i.e. non-teenage) pop, and already included a large number of 'sentimental' ballads of a kind Presley later specialized in.

Another major difference between Britain and the USA as regards the character and intensity of Presley's impact, stems from the fact that he never toured Britain. His presence in Britain in the 1950s was comprised by the records, articles and pictures in magazines, and of course the early films 'Loving You' and 'Jailhouse Rock'. His early success among teenagers cannot even be said to have relied much on the films, since he achieved his first British Number One with 'All Shook Up' before either was seen in Britain, while the long string of Number Ones he achieved in 1960–1962 was made up mostly of songs with no blues or even Country basis ('It's Now or Never', 'Are You Lonesome Tonight', 'Wooden Heart') or of what might be called 'rock-pop' (see below) like 'Return to Sender', and signalled the success of his conversion into a pop singer with a much wider-than-youth-cultural appeal. If this aspect of Presley's early career seems to corroborate my claims about the centrality of his voice, it also offers strong evidence of the seriousness with which teenagers listened, the centrality music was achieving, regardless of 'packaging' and 'personality', in the emerging youth culture.

The aftermath of rock 'n' roll in Britain

I do not intend to go on simply discussing artists of the period in sequence. But before I finally leave the American artists of the early rock 'n' roll styles, I should mention three others who were of great importance in Britain; Little Richard, Chuck Berry and Eddie Cochran. Little Richard and Chuck Berry were among the most successful of the small number of black artists to achieve hits with the white rock 'n' roll audience in both the USA and Britain. Little Richard (a singer and pianist) is notable for his 'frantic' singing, full of shouts and whoops, and often using minimal or even apparently meaningless lyrics ('Tutti frutti, Hey rootie' or 'Awop bop a loo bop a lop bam boom'). Clearly this fits in with the tendency to downgrade and garble lyrics already noted in Haley and Presley, and perhaps confirms its connection with black sources. Chuck Berry (a singer and guitarist) had no big hit records in Britain in the early period of rock 'n' roll. For example, two of his best remembered and most imitated early songs, 'Maybellene' and 'Johnny B Goode', were never chart hits in Britain. But he was a very influential figure in the long term, almost on a par with Holly in his stimulus to amateurism, and continuing to sell rock 'n' roll records at a fair volume through the 1960s. His principal importance was that he toured frequently, reaching white audiences in both the USA and Britain, and also that he wrote a number of narrative lyrics of some style and wit. All in all he had a major impact on many young singers and songwriters: Gillett cites Dylan, The Beatles and The Rolling Stones, who are perhaps the three 'biggest names' in white songwriting in the 1960s.[25]

Eddie Cochran's importance is of a slightly different order: he had no great success in the USA but, taking advantage of Presley's failure to tour Britain, he did extremely well as a representative white rocker in the UK. A Country singer by background, he developed a rougher voice with a husky lower register and some coarse shouted tones, and set about singing rhythm 'n' blues-influenced rock songs from 1956 onwards. Some of them he co-wrote himself. His guitar playing too was developing in a blues direction at the time of his accidental death in 1960. Cochran combined these musical elements with 'teen-lyrics', all about weekend socializing, fighting parental discipline, coveting fashionable clothes, breaking up and making up with girls, and so on. Examples are 'Summertime Blues', 'C'mon Everybody', 'Somethin' Else', 'Pink Legged Slacks', 'Rock 'n' Roll Blues'. Like Presley, he also had success with 'cover versions' ('Hallelujah I Love Her So' by Ray Charles) and straight 'rock-pop' as I will call it, such as 'Three Steps to Heaven'. Cochran, along with his friend Gene Vincent, was a great favourite of the Teds, and his vocal influence can, I think, be heard again and again in early British rock and Beat, as in Wee Willie Harris, Johnny Kidd, Billy Fury, while his guitar style certainly influenced Joe Brown and others.

'Rock-pop' is a makeshift category of my own, of no real rigour; after all, some of the 'hardest' rock 'n' roll (whether by this is meant most prized by the youth culture or most rhythm 'n' blues-based) was also very popular indeed in terms of sales. What I mean by the term has two aspects:

1 There grew up a whole variety of music using some elements of rock 'n' roll, or rockabilly, alongside tried and trusted elements of older 'Tin-Pan-Alley' pop. The music of Pat Boone, Paul Anka, at times Presley himself, and others from America, offers many examples.

2 Also, some record producers and entrepreneurs signed up and launched various teenagers and young men (and a few women) who often could not play an instrument and had little background in blues or any other type of music, in an attempt to catch the boat of rock 'n' roll: this obliged them to write and arrange extremely simple songs using the most basic of harmonies and rhythms, with much straight repetition, and largely without the compensation of rhythm 'n' blues-derived elements of improvisation, spontaneity, rhythmic and timbric intensionality, etc. Hence the brief successes of Jerry Keller, Danny and the Juniors, Brian Hyland, Boddy Vinton, Johnny Tillotson, and others.

These two overlapping currents both had their British equivalents; indeed, this is how some very successful artists like Cliff Richard, Tommy Steele and Adam Faith began, as well as many now less well-known ones such as Terry Dene, Craig Douglas and Vince Eager. The manager and impresario Larry Parnes assembled a successful 'stable' of such singers, some with a background in other kinds of music, some just good-looking teenagers who could sing a bit. He also launched the careers of some important instrumentalists, who featured in the backing bands for his artists, both on tours and on television (the 'Oh Boy' show on ITV made a lot of use of his artists), as well as becoming small 'stars' in their own right. Perhaps the best-known were the keyboards player and singer Georgie Fame, later a member of the rhythm 'n' blues boom (and an early imitator of Jamaican music), and Joe Brown, one of the first white British lead guitarist/singers to develop a style close to American rock 'n' roll and blues.[26]

The rise of Beat music

However, just as the original American rock 'n' roll emerged out of small dance halls and small studios, played and sung by artists who had forged their style through some committed listening and hard practice (Holly, Presley, Berry, even Cochran), so there was now a groundswell of rock 'n' roll musicmaking in Britain, largely separate from this rock-pop, and influenced mainly by the American originals. This groundswell was in the first place amateur and involved mainly boys, a feature I will discuss again a little later. It was based on groups, rather than lone individuals, from the start, because it was especially necessary, in this virtually uncapitalized, spontaneous movement, to make the backing as well as deliver the vocal; and the influence of rock 'n' roll and skiffle settled the format of these groups as being guitar and drum based (usually bass and rhythm, and perhaps lead guitar, drums, and perhaps one or more other instrument – piano, organ, sax, harmonica). This movement survived the decline of the skiffle boom and the fall-away of rock 'n' roll records from America in the late 1950s, and came to provide an alternative, live style of music for many teenagers and young adults which they could hear at dance halls, youth clubs and pubs. Indeed, it was counterposed quite consciously by many makers and listeners to the 'sweet', 'bland' and 'boring' state of much chart-pop of the late 1950s and early 1960s. As Dave Harker recalls: 'If "they" wouldn't produce the music that "we" needed, "we" had to do it ourselves.'[27] Another factor may have been the failure by the big rock 'n' roll stars to tour Britain: Presley never came at all; others just played at one or two big venues. These were times when teenagers could not travel as freely or cheaply as they later did. Some artists who did tour (Cochran, Holly) were dead by 1960. Others had legal, financial or drug difficulties (Chuck Berry, Jerry Lee Lewis). Thus the romantic view, that the first blaze of rock 'n' roll consumed itself by about 1960, is not without some truth. Deprived of 'live' visitations from these star performers, the youth culture in Britain fell back on its own music-making resources.

It has also been suggested that the popular music establishment in Britain was rather monolithic, and largely uninterested in rock 'n' roll. There was no substantial fringe of radio stations, DJs, minor recording labels, etc., such as existed in America: just four major record companies and two radio networks (BBC and Luxemburg), 'one owned by the Government the other effectively controlled by the record companies'.[28] This structure was felt by youth culture members to be remote and unsympathetic, and they got on with their own music-making and live music-use without much early contact with it. This movement was then to culminate later in the rapid rise of British 'Beat music' on both sides of the Atlantic. As Gillett puts it:

> ...around 1962 Britain served the useful function of re-establishing popular music as a medium for personal expression rather than as the raw material for mass-produced entertainment which it had once again become.[29]

His terminology, as so often, is vague, the authenticity of Beat music ('personal expression') is asserted rather than shown, but it is fairly clear that Gillett is describing a real change. Cohn describes the same events as a re-emergence out of the 'Rue Morgue' of around 1960.[30]

Colin Fletcher describes the process by which Beat groups were formed, from his own first-hand experience:

> What mattered now was not how many boys a gang could muster for a Friday night fight, but how well their group could play on Saturday night... the Park Gang literally nursed its group. To enable the group to buy microphones and

speakers a system of 'shares' was set up which were to be repaid from the group's earnings . . . The trusted 'spiritual' boys became the director and manager respectively. An electrical apprentice acted as an on-the-spot repairer. . . . Girls too assumed a new role – they became the seamstresses.[31]

Again Hunter Davies' account of the early Beatles and Spencer Leigh's excellent survey of Merseybeat tell the same story.[32]

Out of the thousands of such groups which existed from the late 1950s onwards, and especially during the 'Beat-boom' of 1963–1965, a few hundred went on to semi-professional and professional status (George Tremlett claims there were 20,000 groups in Britain in 1963, 400 in Liverpool, 600 in Newcastle![33]). The majority of such groups flourished outside of the orbit of the big recording companies, and were largely ignored by TV and radio. They provided cheap, live, dance hall, pub and night club music, aimed at the 'affluent, free-spending' young people, particularly the working-class youth. Small, local studios and 'labels' did record them, and occasionally 'scouts' from larger companies would have demonstration tapes prepared. We do therefore have quite a number of good examples of the music of such groups available on record again now, such as various compilations on the Edsel and See-for-Miles labels.

From 1962 onwards, led by The Beatles, Gerry and the Pacemakers, The Dave Clark Five and a few others, many of these Beat groups (especially in the first few years the ones from Liverpool), achieved great success on the (singles) record market. The industry noticed, caught up with and, of course, inevitably transformed the existing Beat movement. As with the earlier rock 'n' roll boom, the larger record companies, who had been difficult to persuade to record such music at all before 1962, suddenly began signing up all manner of groups, and for a time Beat music literally swamped the British charts of top sellers. And for reasons which are really somewhat outside the scope of this book, these groups actually achieved unprecedented American success as well. The wave inevitably subsided, of course, but it has left an indelible mark on the patterns of music-making and music-listening in Britain. To this day, hundreds of Beat groups, often now wearing evening dress and calling themselves 'Cabaret', but Beat groups in musical terms none the less, provide cheap live dance music at parties, dance halls, Christmas 'dinner dances', British Legions, working-mens' clubs, etc., all over Britain, performing rock and Beat and soul-pop standards mixed perhaps with crooner-type ballads, Country songs and a smattering of whatever is in the pop charts this year. The 'plodding bass' and simple drumming are almost unchanged since 1963, but the organ, electric piano or simple synthesizer is often used to enlarge the range of sounds produced.

The 'heavy', 'progressive' and 'folk' variants of rock which flourished in the later 1960s were themselves very close to Beat music, in terms of the basic techniques used (drum styles, rhythm guitar, single string 'plodding' bass). The variety was largely a matter of superimposed recording tricks, or unusual instrumental decoration. This description holds for most of the early music made by bands as different as, say, Lindisfarne and Pink Floyd. Perhaps the most important single development in these later styles, which was not present to any great degree in Beat music, was the blues-influenced 'single-string' lead guitar style introduced into British pop by the white blues players Eric Clapton, Peter Green and others, and rapidly incorporated into the sound of The Beatles, The Rolling Stones, Pink Floyd and so on as the 1960s drew to an end. Otherwise, 'Beat music plus various distinguishing instrumental or electronic tricks' was the basic formula of most British pop until the early 1970s, and indeed is still to be heard now.

In *The Sound of Our Time*, Dave Laing puts forward the following brief musical description of early British Beat *c.* 1961:

> ... the chord playing of the rhythm guitar ... [compared to American rock 'n' roll] ... was broken up into a series of separate strokes, often one to the bar, with the regular plodding of the bass guitar and crisp drumming behind it. This gave a very different effect from the monolithic character of rock, in that the beat was given not by a duplication of one instrument in the rhythm section by another but by an interplay between all three. This flexibility also meant that beat music could cope with a greater range of time signatures and song shapes than rock and roll had been able to.[34]

Now this has the usefulness and also the untruth of most generalizations of its kind; the point about flexibility in particular is very important, as anyone who ever attended an early 1960s 'Beat-nite' or 'Beat-ball' can testify. The bands could cope with rock numbers, crude waltzes, pre-rock standards and new soul-pop importations with only slight variations in their format, or the 'texture' of their sound. Recorded evidence of this versatility is plentiful (though mostly from 1961 to 1962 onwards): The Beatles doing 'Red Sails in the Sunset', Gerry and the Pacemakers doing 'You'll Never Walk Alone', The Dave Clark Five pounding out simplified versions of old rock standards, etc. However, the precise description Laing gives of the Beat 'sound' is of limited application. Certainly, the fast strumming of the rhythm guitar had been more frequently found in early rock and 'rockabilly' music than it was among the Beat groups, and certainly a very simple steady 'plodding' style of drum and bass was widespread in Beat (Ringo Starr). But the Dave Clark thump was also common, and this could hardly be called 'interplay' in the rhythm section!

I would argue that Beat playing in general was a simplification of the sounds heard on, for example, Presley, Cochran, Lonnie Donegan and Crickets records, simplified in the first place because the musicianship of most young players in these early years was of a very rudimentary, start-from scratch character. It was ironic that this very simplicity enabled the Beat groups to tackle ballads, waltz-time numbers and so on. But Laing does not do full justice to the rapid technical strides made by some musicians or the great variety which soon developed.

The well-known 'Shakin' All Over' by Johnny Kidd and the Pirates, from 1960, is an excellent example of the technical progress made. There is a lot of recognizable Crickets influence in the playing, a shouted vocal which perhaps owes something to Cochran's 'Nervous Breakdown', and an intricate guitar solo in which the beginnings of a 'sound of their own' can perhaps be detected. This record was a hit, but dozens more of a similar kind were made in the 1957–1963 period which never achieved such sales.

One of the most striking things about 'Merseybeat' in particular, but true of bands in other areas to some extent too, was the great variety which was soon achieved. If King Size Taylor and the Dominoes were producing fairly good imitation rock 'n' roll from as early as 1957, others like Ian and the Zodiacs and Gerry and the Pacemakers were 'covering' rock-pop tunes from the USA and the British charts, and even experimenting with writing their own, Faron's Flamingos were working on soul-type sounds, and Sonny Webb and the Cascades were doing rockabilly and Country songs (and later evolved into the popular British Country and Western group The Hillsiders). The Swinging Blue Jeans, who had chart success in 1963 and 1964, began as a Trad jazz group in the late 1950s, and came to Beat via skiffle. Jazz and skiffle also gave birth to the extremely successful Shadows in Newcastle, while in the same town the embryonic Animals were mixing Beat with rhythm 'n' blues, and also imitating the Country/blues/gospel/jazz fusion music of Ray Charles. In the south-east the Stones, Zoot Money, The Zombies and others were making similar beginnings.[35]

Within all this variety, however, a fundamental musical trend is discoverable: the consolidation of a decisive advance in the century-long process of codal fusion among white British people. This is true in the first place at a simple technical level: British audiences, predominantly the working-class and middle-class young, became enthusiastic for the strong, loud beat, some 'intensional' foreground artistry, a strongly speech-derived singing style, etc., all of which originate mainly in the *blues*, as first appropriated by the American rockers Haley, Presley and Holly. The earlier successes of 'hot' jazz and of some of the more authentic Country music in Britain had been precursors to some extent, but these had really only achieved lasting popularity with minorities of listeners. In the second place (and this is perhaps the more important point), the take-up of rock in Britain established music-making, rather than just music-listening, as an important, respected, even central practice in the lives of huge numbers of (mainly male) youth culture members. Amateurism took root everywhere, among those hitherto most unlikely amateurs of all, working-class boys.

This development was truly extraordinary, and has persisted ever since. Now, as I have explained in Chapter 2, the true character of a 'code' is to be sought not only in its musical objects but also in its underlying assumptions about the nature of music and its relationship to the practices which surround it. It was at this deep level that young white British people embraced the Afro-American code during the 1950s, though of course without losing touch with the tonal-European one of which they already had limited experience. The elitist discourse of musicality as a rare gift, which is so prevalent in the writings and discussions which uphold and service the tonal-European code, was rejected by these young people, as, led by a few culture-heroes, mainly from America, they took up singing and playing, and discovered for themselves that they could derive great pleasure and generate important meanings out of *making* music as well as listening to it. It is fairly safe to speculate, I think, that the great majority of these boys would never have come to music-making through any knowledge they might have gained of either the 'light' or the 'serious' aspects of the tonal-European code. The failure of music education in the schools to really touch working-class youth in Britain since the 1920s has been documented,[36] while extra-scholastic pockets of working-class amateurism like brass bands and male voice choirs tended, then as now, to remain obstinately localized, minority pursuits. In any case, they were musically conformist and conservative in spirit, in a way which was unlikely to appeal to the youth culture.

Some of the music made under the banner of 'Beat' in Britain, especially later in the 1960s, and after the style had been made more universally popular (by The Beatles, The Kinks, The Small Faces, etc.), seems, when we hear it now, a long way from the sounds of the late 1950s and early 1960s. It is in listening to this later music that it is especially important to remember the *strength of the codal shift* which underlay its making. In the song-shapes of The Beatles, the clever chord progressions and snatches of other musical styles, as indeed in the jolly tonal melodies of Gerry and the Pacemakers, or the music hall echoes behind The Kinks, we can hear the very strong influence of light tonal music, of older folk music and even of the jazz-tinged pop of the 'swing era', etc., all clearly reasserting themselves.[37] There is really nothing to be surprised at here, but it is crucial to remember that, historically, this music would not have existed had it not been for the original impetus to amateurism given by skiffle and early rock 'n' roll.

This is why 'codal fusion' is the right description. It was not that British boys began singing and playing like Chicago bluesmen, though some tried very hard to do just that; the Afro-American influences which reached them (whether or not mediated solely through white American rockers like Presley and Holly) had an indelible effect, and an effect which went deeper than mere technical imitation, into the very basics of their approach to music-making and music-listening. Their existing familiarity with light and serious tonal music (and other earlier pop) was thus put into a new context, and when it surfaced again in their music-making, it emerged correspondingly trans-formed. Certainly, it was not lost.

There are two final areas I want to cover briefly in this chapter. The first is what I would call 'soul-pop', and is sometimes also known as 'crossover music'. Just as a kind of rock-tinged pop style grew up on both sides of the Atlantic in the late 1950s among mainly white artists (rock-pop), so there was also a movement within black American popular music away from the 'straight' blues, rhythm 'n' blues and gospel styles towards mixtures of these, and mixtures of all these with white popular elements. The overall term which came to attach itself to all these developments was 'soul' (though the word had much more specific original connotations in the jazz world, connotations it never entirely lost). As it developed into the 1960s, 'soul' became itself more and more divided between that which sold mainly to American blacks (occupying the market, now much expanded, which had previously been that of rhythm 'n' blues), and that which sold (or was aimed to sell) also or mainly to whites, and indeed outside the USA. The term 'crossover' was used by black artists and producers – such as Berry Gordy, the founder of Tamla Motown – to describe this latter type.[38] All in all, quite a lot of pop success on the wider, mainly white markets was achieved from the mid-1950s onwards, in several waves. This music, with its strong blues and gospel roots, its highly intensional vocal styles, and its use of vocal harmonies, a feature rare in early white rock 'n' roll, became hugely influential on young white amateur and semi-professional musicians in Britain, particularly after the decline in old rock 'n' roll in the late 1950s. In turn, this also led some British listeners and musicians to the 'blacker' sounds of James Brown, Etta James and so on. Ray Charles, with his extraordinary fusion (in both singing and piano style) of blues, jazz, gospel and Country music, was a hero to countless young imitators, such as The Animals' Eric Burdon.[39] Vocal groups like The Platters in the 1950s, and The Drifters and The Isley Brothers in the early and mid-1960s (as well as the white American Four Seasons who were themselves influenced by black models), inspired a lot of vocal-harmony arrangements by British Beat groups, perhaps the best known being those done by The Tremeloes in the mid-1960s. 'Do You Love Me' by the Tamla vocal group The Contours provided Brian Poole and the Tremeloes with their first big hit, as well as being in the repertoire of Merseybeat groups like Faron's Flamingos. The Rolling Stones recorded 'Can I Get a Witness' on their first album, a song by the prolific soul-writing team of Holland, Dozier and Holland. Many other examples could be given.

Finally, there was the 'British Rhythm 'n' Blues' (or 'R 'n' B') movement. There was a nationwide network of jazz clubs which had appeared in the first jazz 'boom' of the late 1940s and early 1950s, and expanded again in the late 1950s, Skiffle of course began in this milieu. Another aspect of this was a romantic 'folklorist' interest in Country blues. George Melly in *Owning Up* describes this very well.[40] Artists like Leadbelly and Big Bill Broonzy were widely regarded as the very essence of authenticity in folk music, and the latter made some successful tours of Europe on this basis in the 1950s, followed by numerous lesser known artists in the later 1950s and 1960s. Also, the ethnomusicologist Alan Lomax, a leading figure in a similar folklorist movement in the USA, and the famous folk singer Pete Seeger, spent part of the 1950s in Britain as victims of McCarthyism, and exerted considerable influence on the British folk and blues movements.

Most of these earlier blues (and jazz) purists had little time for contemporary, predominantly urban blues or rhythm 'n' blues, which was usually loud, electrified ensemble dance music. It seemed to them a compromise or devaluation of real blues under the pressures of the pop market, both black and white. But there was a smaller (white) group in Britain who did enjoy this music, and of course there was a growing population of West Indian immigrants who had often already been familiar with American rhythm 'n' blues in Jamaica, Barbados and Trinided. One or two American artists (such as Muddy Waters) bridged the gulf, enjoying the esteem of both the purists and the rhythm 'n' blues fans, who, in any case, increasingly overlapped by the early 1960s. It was out of this milieu that some of the more blues- (and even jazz-) based British bands of the late 1950s and early 1960s sprang, such as Alexis Korner's groups, or those of Cyril Davies or John Mayall. Later, there developed numerous groups who were willing to play 'commercial' rock, Beat and soul-pop as well as rhythm 'n' blues, and yet who always played their more popular numbers with a lot of rhythm 'n' blues (and sometimes jazz) influence in the singing and guitar playing. This description holds good for The Rolling Stones, The Animals, The Zombies, Georgie Fame and the Blue Flames (said to have been particular favourites of black British listeners) and Chris Farlowe and the Thunderbirds. This set of groups had a lot of pop success in the mid-1960s, paving the way for other blues-based music such as Fleetwood Mac (and also experimental blues–jazz–rock mixtures such as Cream) to achieve some pop success in the 'year of the blues', 1968,[41] and after. The long-term effect of all this was to set higher standards of playing (especially of guitar) in British pop than had previously been accepted, and to make the particular 'single-string' lead-guitar style (adopted from black models like B.B. King, but with added special effects) of Clapton and a few others an almost universal element in 'rock' performance – and, to a lesser extent, on records – for a time in the late 1960s and 1970s; it is still widely to be heard on pop records today. Of course, this was not due solely to the British rhythm 'n' blues artists. A parallel movement existed in the USA associated with such people as Mike Bloomfield, Ry Cooder, Captain Beefheart and Canned Heat.

The rhythm 'n' blues-based groups of the early 1960s tended to have a more middle-class and 'intellectual' audience and background than the ordinary Beat groups, and were especially popular in the universities, art colleges and sixth forms. The case of Mick Jagger, whose father was a lecturer and who studied briefly at the LSE, would be more normal in rhythm 'n' blues, and quite rare in, say, Merseybeat. However, this difference should not be over-stated, lest it blind us to similarities: after all, the Beat group singer John Lennon had art school connections too, while Eric Burdon came (via art school) from a 'solidly' working-class background straight into the rhythm 'n' blues movement. An examination of the repertoires of, say, the early Stones and early Merseybeat shows a lot of overlap: the Stones performed Rufus Thomas's 'Walking the Dog', but so did the Liverpool group the Dennisons. The Stones and Animals alike performed many 'commercial' soul-pop songs from black American models, while Merseybeat groups like Derry Wilkie and the Pressmen and The Big Three were quite at home with rhythm 'n' blues songs by Ray Charles and others, such as 'Hallelujah I Love Her So' and 'What'd I Say'. Again the Stones had only their second substantial chart hit with 'I Wanna Be Your Man', written by Lennon and MacCartney.

A picture emerges of rhythm 'n' blues influence on all the young pop music-makers of the period, but of the more purist, romantic version of that influence remaining largely, though certainly not exclusively, a middle-class phenomenon. But a process of advancing and consolidating codal fusion (even, it seemed for some musicians, of the supplanting of the European code by an almost total immersion in blues) was clearly proceeding very widely among young music-makers and music-listeners, and proceeding *across* the class boundaries. Certainly one cannot pair off class 'backgrounds' with musical preferences in any simple way. One finds many anecdotes of unlikely, yet apparently fairly straightforward, musical progressions such as The Swinging Blue Jeans starting in Trad jazz and finishing as an archetypal Merseybeat group; Sonny Webb and the Cascades, accepted as a Merseybeat group of the early 1960s but performing largely 'Country' songs; or Wee Willie Harris, an exhibitionistic early rock 'n' roll singer/pianist who dyed his hair pink or green and often sang self-mocking lyrics in a style influenced by Cochran and Little Richard, but was also 'Fingers Harris', the small-time jazz pianist of Wimbledon Jazz Club.[42]

In this mainly narrative chapter, I have tried to introduce, or offer a snapshot of, the main currents, and some of the main artists of the period in British pop music-use begun by Haley and Presley and ending with the triumph of The Beatles and others like them in 1963 and 1964. Of course, this account does not follow sales figures for singles and LPs – no doubt Doris Day 'shifted more plastic' than 90 per cent of the names I have mentioned! I have concentrated on new tendencies, patterns of new music-*use* rather than just sales (notably the rise of amateurism and the growing black American influence) and I have dealt with the music-use of young people, teenagers and very young adults, in particular. I have advanced the idea of ongoing (accelerating) *codal fusion* as a way of describing these developments, a unifying thread running through them. However, to describe rock 'n' roll and Beat music as instances of codal fusion is only a beginning. My central question remains that of meanings and functions, and it is, therefore, not enough to simply say young people adopted Afro-American meanings and functions. The attraction of rock 'n' roll and blues for young British whites must be accounted for in terms of *their* position, their needs and concerns. This is what the next chapters will attempt.

5 *British Society and Culture in the 1950s and Early 1960s*

The general economic context of rock 'n' roll

The decade with which I am most concerned (1955–1964) falls wholly within that period of British economic history which is known as the 'long boom'. An excellent account of this is contained in Hobsbawm's *Industry and Empire*,[1] and I have relied heavily on it for this section. The social and cultural character of the period is also surveyed there as well as in another famous 1960s book, Raymond Williams's *The Long Revolution*,[2] and I have made a lot of use of these accounts. The book *Policing the Crisis*[3] from 1977 offers a useful later view of the same matters, written in the 'cultural studies' tradition.

After the Depression of the 1930s and the upheaval of the Second World War, the late 1940s, 1950s and 1960s saw Britain settle into a state of steady economic development, punctuated by nothing more serious than occasional currency crises and credit squeezes. Old industries declined, new ones such as electronics and petrochemicals grew, and the state took on a larger role than ever before in the economy. As far as the working population was concerned, unemployment became negligible (unless you lived in a 'declining area'), real wages grew (slowly at first but later more rapidly), and consumption grew even more as a result of the expansion of consumer credit (overdrafts and hire purchase). Of course the break-up of the Empire, the slowness of the rate of investment in new productive plant and in infrastructures, as compared with some other countries, and the relative 'overmanning' of certain industries, were all major features of the period, and were all storing up economic and political problems for the British Government and for private and public enterprises which became acute later in the 1960s and thereafter. Finally, during these years the 'safety net' of the Welfare State was elaborated to something approaching its highest level of development.[4]

This, then, was the overall economic context for my musical decade. If we examine the condition of the working population more closely, we find a certain recomposition of the working class as traditionally defined. Hobsbawm cites the relative decline of manufacturing industry and the relative growth of 'tertiary' occupations in distribution, transport and various public and private 'services'. He also notes the decline of manual and growth of 'clean-handed' work within each industry.[5] In the so-called 'middle classes' taken as a whole, the self-employed and small employers were now relatively less numerous than earlier in the century, while the 'salaried' – who considered themselves middle class, but were none the less employees of some sort – were becoming relatively more numerous.

The last point I wish to make here concerns the political and cultural climate that was encouraged by this economic situation. After the post-war Labour government's partial reconstruction of the economy, the Conservative Party held office for 13 years. The later years (from 1957 onwards) were those of 'never had it so good' politics, when a complacent mood was fostered throughout society. The rise of consumption and the factors of full employment and developing welfarism promoted a belief, orchestrated by the mass media, that the old class conflicts were now becoming irrelevant, and that the future held more and more leisure time, more and more affluence and better consumer goods for everyone.[6] It was a naive and insular view, but none the less probably a majority one for some years. Fears about 'the bomb' and 'moral panics' about Teddy Boys and Communist shop stewards were strong, certainly, but only as a counterpoint to the general mood. This, then, was the atmosphere in which rock 'n' roll (and skiffle, rock-pop, Beat music and early British rhythm 'n' blues) developed, and had their life. I will, however, be looking more closely at these matters later in this chapter, and suggesting that there was a widespread vague disorientation and uncertainty underlying this mood among working-class and middle-class people, especially the young. This undercurrent found expression in youth culture and its music-use, as we shall see.

The popular music industry

The first thing I wish to signal here is the *age* of the commercial music business in Britain. Certainly music, in one form or another, has been sold as a commodity for many centuries. We know that Handel, for example, and a little later Haydn, made their livings (with mixed success) by presenting concerts of their own music to paying London audiences. There were also considerable numbers of professional and/or semi-professional players and singers in existence. Thus almost all the 'standards' of the modern 'serious' concert repertoire were composed during the period of music-for-profit, though individual musicians did often rely on private patronage to some degree too. The charge of 'commercialism' against modern popular music is therefore largely a misunderstanding. The main differences from an economic point of view, between the earlier music business and the moden industry, are of *scale*, *market* and *technique*. The commodity form and the profit principle were already virtually ubiquitous by the nineteenth century.

The *scale* of the modern industry in Britain is vast, having grown virtually non-stop from 1945 to the mid-1970s. More capital is involved than ever before, and the techniques, attitudes and priorities of 'big business' may naturally be expected to accompany this growth. This development has been accomplished by the successful penetration of a *new market*, beginning in earlier centuries with sheet music and music hall concerts, but developing into the largest sector of the music market only in this century, via records and radio; namely, the (broadly defined) *working class*.[7] At this same time, *internationalization* of the industry and of the market has proceeded rapidly, chiefly in the form of an overall growth of American interests and products in the British market and, to a lesser extent, vice versa.[8]

The chief musical 'commodities' of the music industry today, by far, are records and cassettes (and now compact discs), the chief 'media' stereo-sets and radios. Film, TV and video also occupy a place. 'Live' music is still important, of course, but sheet music sales are now very much less significant than in the last century or the early part of this. A veritable revolution of techniques, and of the forms of artefacts which sell, has thus taken place. This revolution can be placed in time; despite earlier successes, the recording industry was reduced to a tiny shadow of its old self during the Depression and the Second World War, and the modern industry took shape in the late 1940s and 1950s, when new materials (vinyl) and techniques ('hi-fi', tape and later stereo) were developed. Radio has been established since the 1920s but was transformed in the late 1950s and early 1960s by the arrival of the portable or transistor radio.[9] Transistorization represented a further development in sound quality too. And TV became established in the 1950s. We can thus see clearly that the period of rock 'n' roll was also a period of great change and accelerating development for the techniques of the music industry and their social dissemination; one of the decisive periods of the century so far. A music industry employing new media of sound to sell a new type of product (singles, LPs and small radios), and to sell these goods to a market comprising mainly the working people and their families within the producing nations, on a scale never previously approached – this is the musical *infrastructure* of the 1950s, the economic framework for the studies which I shall go on to attempt.

Now the capitalist process of music production is somewhat exceptional as a type of capitalism. The production function is subject to a division of labour, in which certain functions (pressing the records, packing, etc.) are fulfilled via factory production, using 'proletarian' labour power, but a lot of others are left in a much less rationalized form – the 'creative artist', the loose definition of roles in recording studios, the 'big-name' performers who are their 'own bosses' and contract themselves out, etc. 'Artisanic' production relations, of a sort normally considered pre-capitalist, thus survive in the music industry, as they do in some other areas of mental or intellectual work; perhaps nowhere else do they survive so strongly. Related to this is the continued existence (and even growth, in the 1970s and 1980s) of a fringe of small, shoestring record labels, studios and distribution networks, which, while only occasionally achieving significant growth, manage obstinately to avoid the 'tendency towards monopoly' – they are *not* swallowed up, or, alternatively, those which are swallowed up by larger concerns are rapidly replaced, like the Hydra's heads, by new ones. This survival of older relations of production is to be attributed, I believe, *not* to the calculated maintenance of an illusion by the industry, as Adorno implies,[10] but to a certain *unrationalizability* and resistance to quantification, characteristic of music as of visual art, creative writing, etc.

However, the effects of production for profit, and payment for labour power (i.e. of the 'commodity-form' itself) on musical practices are by no means wholly negated by this unrationalizable character, though they are inhibited. From about 1600 onwards, musical specialization increasingly removed musicians from the milieux which provided their audiences, through institutionalized training and ever wider travel. As a result, the professional–amateur division became harder and harder to cross, so that much musical production – music-making among non-professional people – was cut off from professional musicianship. Amateurs eventually became, with few exceptions, people who bought already-written scores from a 'music-shop' and took them home to play or sing from. Amateur composition dwindled, and more and more people became listeners only, with no knowledge of music-making, except for singing in the bath.

These developments constitute an undoubted threat to the very existence of music as we know it. Musical activity always meets two needs: the need of the music-maker to make music and the need of the listener. The success of the relationship requires that together the two parties realize meanings. Now music has probably never occupied a parallel position to spoken language, i.e. where *everyone* is both speaker and listener for much of the time. Music-making has, more or less always, like visual art, been somewhat marginalized by language. Nevertheless, the development of a situation in which the majority of people partake only of the listening experience, and in which any music-making faculty, drive or need is largely thwarted by their socio-economic situation, threatens to destroy musical meaningfulness itself, by leaving listeners with no grasp or handle on the codes used by music-makers, or progressively reducing the range of codal elements understood by listeners, and the depth of that understanding.

In this century, however, the new media have transformed music-making as well as music-listening: the *studio*, with its team of experts collaborating to produce the recording; the *tape* with its alterability; a vast range of ways of altering ('distorting') sounds as they are produced and the possibility of composing without scores now that a different method of storage has been invented (the record or tape), all of these developments tend to undercut, at least in their potential, the composer–performer division. It is now possible for people without a full technical training of the older sort (score-reading, theory of harmony, etc.) to make music (in the studio, usually with the help of the studio team), which may be the result none the less of a high degree of honing, perfecting and judgement. The period of the domination of the score thus meets a serious challenge, and perhaps the beginning of its end.

In potential, then, though not necessarily in realization, the threat posed by widespread listening without music-making can now be averted by a new sort of music-making which need be bound by neither the training norms nor the elitist justifying discourses of the older sort. A contradiction is thus set up. It must, however, be placed in the concreteness of the society and the times, if we are to see how real contests and developments have worked it out and pushed it from phase to phase.

The cultural context of rock 'n' roll

In this section, I discuss some of the discourses, ideas and values which surrounded the reception of rock 'n' roll in Britain, and influenced its development. Later, I will delve a little deeper into some of the areas which are represented or constructed in these discourses, bringing some hindsight and some 'social science' to bear on them.[11]

Teenagers

The term 'teenager' was an invention of the late 1940s or early 1950s, spreading rapidly from the USA to Britain.[12] It fitted together with the discourses of affluence, classlessness, juvenile delinquency, promiscuity, the 'generation gap' and others in the common sense of the time, at least as mediated and directed by newspapers, radio and TV, and educationalists, clerics, etc. Behind many of these hovered more 'serious' and 'academic' debates about class, about the long-term effects of universal education, about 'mass culture' and so on. These discourses were the means by which people represented the social changes around them to themselves and each other, and they were consequently effective in the actual actions, reforms and efforts to direct or prevent change which characterized the period, notably the policies of the mass media and educational institutions.

'Growing up' or 'being young' had apparently changed and become strange in some ways to older people, and the new term 'teenager' (and to a lesser extent 'youth') came to signify all that seemed different about it. However, the term did not merely connote the differentness of the young but also delivered it up as explained, contained, bracketed off, as something separate from everyday, normal life and, to some extent, neutralized and solved. In other words, 'teenager' became a label, though not such a damning one as some others. Whenever the word 'teenager' was used, the expressions 'just a phase' and 'they'll grow out of it' were never far away.

The definition of teenagers was a matter of *style*. Unlike the term itself, which was foisted on the young, the clothes, haircuts, slang and musical preferences were the chosen means of self-expression and group differentiation adopted by the kids themselves. Of course – and this was part of the intention – they were also the obvious and spectacular signs by which teenagers could be identified from outside. Specifically teenage was a style of *leisure*, not of work, and teenagers often rigidly demarcated their leisure time from their school or working time.[13] This leisure style was created through the appropriation of consumption goods – clothes, haircuts, records, etc. The unavoidability of this definition-by-consumption (rather than work) led some authors to believe that class in the older sense (defined mainly by type of work) was dying out, and that either a vast new class or true classlessness was coming into existence. Thus in 1959, Mark Abrams,[14] argued that an affluent, teenage group had come to dominate the market for certain commodities in Britain, including music. Although his own findings indicated that the category 'teenager' comprised mostly, or most typically, 15- to 25-year-old boys and men, employed and unmarried, he felt that the consumption style associated *with* teenage was actually a phenomenon which embraced most other young people too. He wrote:

> ... under conditions of general prosperity the social study of society in class terms is less and less illuminating. And its place is taken by differences related to age.[15]

This expressed in sociological terms a view which was then becoming the 'common sense' of the time, and which reigned supreme for a period during the 1960s.

This 'prosperity' should not be overstated however. Harker, for example, recalls the years 1959–1962 thus:

> Musically it was a *bloody desert* [his emphasis]. Older brothers and sisters could perhaps go to a local jazz club. But outside the major urban areas this meant having access to transport. Going by bus usually meant leaving early: railway lines were being cut; and the ownership of private transport (even a motor bike) amongst most working-class families was rare indeed. So much had 'affluence' contributed to the material culture of the post-war working-class generation![16]

Another who was well-acquainted with working-class realities was Richard Hoggart. He did believe, however, in 1957, that a major change in class structure was taking place, of which 'the young' were primary evidence. He was, of course, much less favourable to it than Abrams:

> I have in mind ... the kind of milk-bar – there is one in almost every Northern town with more than say, fifteen thousand inhabitants – which has become the regular evening rendezvous of some of the young men. Girls go to some, but most of the customers are boys between fifteen and twenty, with drape suits, picture ties and an American slouch. Most of them cannot afford a succession of milk-shakes, and make cups of tea serve for an hour or two, whilst – and this is their main reason for coming – they put copper after copper into the mechanical record-player.... Compared with even the pub around the corner this is all a peculiarly thin and pallid form of dissipation.... Many of the customers – their clothes, their hairstyles, their facial expressions all indicate – are living to a large extent in a myth-world compounded of a few simple elements which they take to be those of American life.... They are ground between the millstones of technocracy and democracy: society gives them an almost limitless freedom of the sensations but makes few demands on them – the use of their hands and a fraction of their brains for forty hours a week. For the rest they are open to the entertainers and their efficient mass equipment. The youth clubs, the young people's institutes, the sports clubs cannot attract them as they attract many in their generation ... they are in one dreadful sense the new workers.... It is true,

as I have said, that they are not typical. But these are the figures some important contemporary forces are tending to create, the directionless and tamed helots of a machine-minding class.[17]

In the context of studies of youth culture which have since been made, Hoggart's comprehension of the Teddy Boy (for it is more or less he) seems very weak. But he was one of the more serious and open-minded students of cultural change at that time, and any charges we find in his book were certainly repeated far less fairly and more stridently by many another writer, broadcaster, vicar and teacher, and accepted by many a parent of the period.

Delinquency

Another aspect of the teenager was still more threatening; namely, the juvenile delinquent, and (to many the same person) the Teddy Boy or Ted. To many parents, teachers and others the term 'Teddy Boy', from referring initially to the 'Edwardian' clothes these boys and men wore, came to connote nothing so much as violence on the streets (flick-knives and bicycle chains), the destruction of phone booths and bus shelters, and the writing of graffiti in public places.[18] Fighting and street-roaming became forever associated with rock 'n' roll in Britain by the so-called riots at cinemas – and afterwards in the streets – at showings of the film 'Rock Around the Clock', and by those 'rumbles' at dance halls which had long been part of Saturday night in Britain.

The generation gap

The 'generation gap' was another 1950s invention, this time coined and promoted chiefly by social scientists such as Margaret Mead.[19] It referred to the supposed acceleration of social and cultural change in every way (from changes in fashions and lifestyles to the growth of government), which had been proceeding since the Second World War. This process was creating such new and different conditions for the socializing of the young that they came to seem largely incomprehensible even to their own parents and teachers. The impact of this theory probably owed a lot to its evolutionistic, apparently objective spirit: the development was made to seem inevitable, irreversible, and therefore to be accepted, and it even seemed to contain the hint that young people might be better survivors than their elders; that is, that out of some apparent regression, progress might yet proceed. I will be arguing later that there was truth in the general view that the processes of socialization of the young had radically changed.

Girls as 'teenagers'

The category 'teenager' was, in the 1950s especially, a male one. Of course, there are teenage girls, but, in the 1950s, these added little or nothing of their own to the style as perceived from outside, and nothing much to the connotations of the label. There were girls who saw themselves as Teddy Girls, but they did not really enter the popular imagination as such at all. Girls were either the conjuncts and consorts of boys, or merely the daughters of their parents, the girls of the school. They were not the *subjects* of the teenage culture(s), whether as they saw themselves or as others saw them. They did of course have their own secretive, much less spectacular but very strongly established 'bedroom culture',[20] but this went largely unremarked at the time.

The teenage culture was seen by most parents, teachers and other grown-ups primarily as a threat to girls rather than an attribute of them, a threat identified almost wholly with 'sex before marriage' and, worse still, 'promiscuity'. In 1959, several authorities on this subject collaborated in producing a pamphlet entitled *Teenage Morals*, in which we can examine quite a range of popular intellectual reactions to this 'problem'. Most of the articles are patronizing in tone, condemning while offering to understand, but one or two are a little more liberal and even 'permissive' (as it would later be called), notably that by the anthropologist Geoffrey Gorer.[21] His article is guilty of the now-famous double standard, identifying sexual activity by 'girls only' as the problem, as though that of boys were entirely acceptable, not to mention separable. None the less, he does put forward most of the elements, and some of the assumptions, of the debate as it then existed, as a result of his claim to be objective and scientific, and to take the longer view. 'Declining parental supervision' and 'earlier physical maturation' are the chief elements of his approach. At one stage, he presents quite an interesting theoretical characterization of the process by which teenagers have come into existence: the 'social childhood', defined by the upper age-limit of schooling, has lengthened since the 1940s, while the physiological childhood has remained the same or even shortened. A gap has opened, during which teenagers are physically adult but excluded from the routines and responsibilities, and from the leisure pursuits, of adulthood.

A further version or image of girls and young women, largely that of Hollywood and American pop, in which girls were the pleasure-objects of brave, handsome young men, was, of course, available via the cinema, radio, records (later TV) and magazines, and there was undoubtedly a process of balancing these models and discourses against more traditional and parentally endorsed ones, and of moving from one to another, going on among girls and young women of the 1950s. I shall discuss this aspect of the period again below. What was almost totally lacking in the popular discourses of the time was any sort of *feminist* view of teenage girls; it was not until the early 1960s in America, and later in Britain, that Betty Friedan and others began to offer their critique of, among other things, growing up feminine in the 1950s.[22]

America

Since the Second World War, there has been a tendency for American cultural artefacts to acquire a value in Britain simply by virtue of their Americanness. The size and profitability of the American entertainment industries enabled them to colonize the British working-class market; in this they were assisted by a deep traditionalism in the equivalent British bodies (the BBC, many of the newspapers, etc.), so that to many 'ordinary people' in Britain, 'American' became almost synonymous with excitingly new. An image of the USA was thus created which was to be greatly intensified by the contrast between the 'austerity' of post-Second World War Britain and the boom in America. The car and the television set in particular became the symbols of that affluence which, in the late 1940s and 1950s, it seemed everyone in America and very few in Britain enjoyed. But perhaps the most successful of all the American products marketed in Britain was music. Not only did American records sell well in Britain, often reaching the 'top of the charts' (after their inception in 1952), but, as a result of decades of influence, much British popular music was itself written and performed in an 'Americanized' style.

For the protagonists of 'mass-culture-criticism', following Eliot, Leavis and other pre-war sages, there was a negative value in all things American just as strong as the positive one which attracted 'the masses'. Such a view flourished in the education system, the older newspapers, the professional middle classes and, of course, the BBC, and was found particularly in reactions to music. Hoggart once again provides a good example of it:

> ... almost all [the records on the juke box] are American; almost all are vocals, and the styles of singing much advanced beyond what is normally heard on the Light Programme of the B.B.C.. Some of the tunes are catchy; all have been doctored for presentation so that they have the kind of beat which is currently popular.... The young men ... [still those of the 'American slouch' described above] ... waggle one shoulder or stare, as desperately as Humphrey Bogart, across the tubular chairs.[23]

One might ask which practices of arrangement, performance or recording come under the heading 'doctoring for presentation' and which do not, though it is not really fair to ask Hoggart to dabble in musicology. It is clear, however, that he is not saying anything very damning at all about American pop; he even comments elsewhere on its 'precision' and 'competence'.[24] The condemnation arises solely from the fact that it *is* American. The integrity of British culture has been breached; a debilitating foreign body has been injected into the bloodstream of the national way of life.

Hoggart was certainly not alone in this sort of opinion, as we might indeed infer from the fact that he felt free to use the unqualified word 'American' as an insult or derogation. In the BBC itself, the main provider of radio music, there was a policy of playing a lot of live serious and light music, and only a little modern pop, and, over and above this, a tendency among programme makers to counterpose British to American and to hold up 'folk music' as the true popular tradition. Very little Elvis made its way through this set of filters![25]

Black America

An element of the mid-1950s appropriation of America which I have not touched on yet, but which was of very great importance, was the discovery or rediscovery of that 'other America' which owed its distinctness to the black communities. Of course jazz, blues and rock 'n' roll, which all enjoyed the attention of overlapping audiences in Britain during the period, were musics originating in the black communities. The early rock 'n' roll audience of teenagers and young adults exhibited, on the whole, little interest in 'authentic' urban blues as such, though they enthusiastically accepted Little Richard, Chuck Berry and others into the pantheon of rock stars. Indeed, Presley-loving Teddy Boys were apparently blissfully unaware of the contradiction (if there was one) when they involved themselves in the Notting Hill street-fights of the late 1950s, and the harassing of newly arrived blacks. On the other hand, and in the first place *through* artists like Berry and Little Richard, individual teenage listeners, and small groups of like-minded enthusiasts within the broader rock 'n' roll audience, embarked on that exploratory listening-and-buying process which would lead them to blues, jazz, soul and so on, and which was to bear fruit in the directions subsequently taken by British amateurism and the semi-professional and professional music-making of the 1960s. Here is Eric Clapton's account of his early musical influences:

> At first I played exactly like Chuck Berry for 6 or 7 months. . . . Then I got into older Bluesmen. Because he was so readily available I dug Big Bill Broonzy; then I heard a lot of cats I had never heard of before, like Robert Johnson. Later I turned on to B.B. King and it's been that way ever since.[26]

The enthusiastic listeners who emerged out of the rock audience as 'collectors' and often also as amateur musicians themselves, swelled the ranks, and altered the hitherto rather exclusive, normally middle-class, normally 'anti-commercial' character of the existing constituencies for the products of American black culture, especially music, in Britain. The enthusiasm of these musicians and listeners was intimately related to the strength of the attraction which black America as a whole exerted for them, an attraction expressed for many not only in music but in the reading of cult books from the 'Beat' and 'hipster' sub-cultures, in slang, drug-use, and even in the deeper elements of self-conception. Some of the strength and zeal of this embrace is no doubt to be explained as a counter-reaction to the racism which many people – older people especially – openly expressed in their comments on rock 'n' roll and rhythm 'n' blues. Horrified reactions to 'jungle' drums, 'primitive' rhythms and sax and guitar-playing, 'African' dance styles, etc., were in good supply in Britain, even if not quite so strong as in parts of the USA where white racists savagely attacked concerts both in the Press and physically, and where Cold War propagandists added a further twist to the reactions, holding the music to be 'communistic' as well as primitive.[27]

Reactions to rock 'n' roll

This point brings me nicely to a brief consideration of discourses about rock 'n' roll itself, which were significant at the time of its first impact in Britain, and which have, in some cases, persisted ever since. The first point to be made here is that favourable discussion of the music, in the media, the schools and other institutions, was very thin on the ground in these early years. The young fans themselves tended to use only a very limited, evaluative vocabulary, of no great descriptive or analytical potential: it's 'great', it's 'fabulous', it's 'got a good beat', 'I'll give it five out of ten'. Musicians had, of course, their own terms, often derived from the slang already in use in jazz and older popular music. There was almost no favourable discussion of rock 'n' roll or Beat (until around 1962 or 1963) in the Press or on television. Only three significant music papers were in existence, *Melody Maker*, *New Musical Express* and *Record Mirror*. *Melody Maker* was mainly a paper for musicians and jazz fans, though it began to change in the early 1960s. And *New Musical Express*, though it concentrated mainly on 'chart-pop', gave almost no attention to criticism, analysis or history writing, being content mainly to praise what was popular and review what was new in a trivial vein; *Record Mirror* was not much different.[28]

However, there was quite an abundance of unfavourable discussion of rock 'n' roll and early Beat music, led by various self-appointed pundits of TV and radio, the newspapers, the churches and the teaching profession.[29] Now this discourse was in part rooted in honest reactions to the music, and the new young stars it brought to prominence, and should not be lightly dismissed by an investigator who is searching for musical meanings and functions. I will mention here some of the main *charges* laid against rock and Beat at the time, and they will turn up again later at various points. I refer to my own memories of the early 1960s, as well as to various writers, for this list.

1 Rock and Beat were widely found to be 'too loud', something I will discuss under the heading of 'sound-sense' in Chapter 6.
2 'You can't make out the words'. While this charge could be made against some light and classical vocal music too, it was certainly very widely repeated with reference to early rock 'n' roll and Beat music. It represented a reaction to the 'new' kind of singing employed by such artists as Presley, and also to the down grading of lyrics and upgrading of overall sound and 'beat' in some of the music.
3 Many people found rock 'n' roll 'crude', 'brash' and 'vulgar'.[30] In comparison to the slick, smart, well-dressed artists of British pop in the late 1940s and early 1950s, artists as different as, for example, Elvis Presley and Tommy Steele seemed briefly to represent a common trend of crudity and vulgarity. The very qualities in their singing and stage acts which occasioned this widespread response were, of course, among the qualities most appreciated and imitated by the young fans, and this worried the anti-rock commentators greatly.
4 As I have already noted, there were many writers and broadcasters who noted a resemblance between rock 'n' roll and 'jungle music', though it is doubtful what knowledge of the musical cultures of the world's jungles they had. This was a repetition of a response to jazz which had been widespread in the 1920s and 1930s.[31] Undoubtedly, this response was in part just a

racist dislike of the presence of major black artists within the music. But it was also a misconceived reaction to a real change in the nature of the music itself, a large step forward in the century-old development of *codal fusion* between the European and Afro-American codes. The importance of both prominent rhythmic 'monotony' (the beat) and rhythmic variety (improvised singing and playing 'against' the beat) in the music was recognized as an element foreign to the tonal-European tradition. The audience responses of 'uncontrolled' dancing, swaying, clapping, etc., were recognized as something different, too. The tags of 'tribal dancing', 'jungle drums', 'primitive voodoo rituals' and so on were seized on to describe and, generally, to condemn, and even to ban, the new music and dancing, by listeners who were not prepared to make the identification and the effort made by the young fans. George Melly recalls 'No Jiving, No Rock and Roll' signs in dance halls of the mid- and late 1950s.[32]

5 Another viewpoint which was canvassed in the period can be summarized as follows: the new popular music is so limited in form, so stereotyped in content, so undemanding on the listener, that it promulgates bad listening habits. These include the tendency to treat music as a mere background to the performance of other tasks, and also a 'deconcentrated' mode of listening which only really wakes up and takes notice of startling sounds and unexpected twists. Thus the composers and recorders of the music pack it with novelties (twangy bass guitars, echo-machine vocals, etc.) and these novelties are more highly valued by the fans than any 'deeper' or 'more serious' qualities of structure, or expressive meaning. We have already encountered this argument in Adorno, of course, but it is repeated in, for example, Francis Routh's *Contemporary British Music* from 1964, once again in Hoggart's *The Uses of Literacy*, and also in 'Francis Newton's' (Eric Hobsbawm's) 1959 book *The Jazz Scene*.[33]

I am now going to look behind, as it were, this discursive context of rock 'n' roll, to certain major social trends (and the sociological categories and theories required to study and explain them), which I will be claiming as relevant to my account of the meanings and functions of the music.

Class in Britain 1955–1964

The British popular music industry is basically a capitalist industry, with its group of entrepreneurs, owners, shareholders and directors at the top of each company or corporation. Indeed, it is more capitalist than most in this sense, having little state involvement. But I am concerned in this book with popular music-use, and the music used, and this means essentially the buying, listening and music-making behaviour of the working- and middle-class people who make up almost the whole popular music audience. I will not spend any time at all, therefore, on the economics of the industry or the lifestyles of the owners, producers and star artists who are its major figures. Other books cover that area well.[34]

The great change in music-use among young British people in the 1950s took place in both the working class and the middle class. Both groups listened to and bought more musical goods, absolutely, than ever before, and both groups exhibit quite clearly the processes of advancing codal fusion and the rise of amateurism. These facts were no doubt among those which led Mark Abrams to cite music-use as prime evidence for the class-convergence and even class-disappearance theory which he and many others put forward at that time.[35] I myself think there was some truth in the idea of convergence, certainly at a cultural level, though class disappearance turned out to be an illusion (I have elaborated on these conclusions in my thesis). But beyond this, I believe the virtual *universality* of the new music-use among young people is evidence that it provided them all with some sort of response to conditions of social life in the post-war period which seem to apply, albeit differentially, to both working-class *and* middle-class young people. More of this in due course.

As I see it, the middle class of post-war Britain consisted of first, the small businessmen, farmers and autonomous professionals who had been around for hundreds of years (those whom Marx called the 'petit-bourgeoisie') and, secondly, the 'salaried', the 'managerial', the 'professional' but not necessarily 'self-employed', the better-off white-collared workers and their families, whose numbers have grown steadily since the Victorian era, and grew quite fast in the post-war period, with its expansion of education, the Health Service and Welfare State, and the employment of specialist managers in industry. The latter group probably now outnumbered the former. This composite middle class is not the 'capitalist class' of Marxist economics, though some of its members are small capitalists. It is not *a priori* impossible for it to converge with the working class, economically or culturally, and I believe it did so, culturally at any rate, in the 1950s and 1960s.

Many factors can be cited in this context: the greater numbers of working-class children staying on at schools and colleges and obtaining white-collar jobs afterwards; the 'slum clearances' followed by dispersal of working-class families to outer-city estates (which on the one hand led people to *believe* they had moved up a notch on the class scale and on the other hand did actually help destroy a number of old working-class communities which had traditions of class-consciousness and class independence – this happened in the East End of London, Birmingham, Glasgow, etc.); the rise of radio and TV, especially the latter, which increased the amount of *common* cultural fare experienced by both classes, and especially the young; the political climate after 1952 in which 'class politics' and 'class rhetoric' were deeply unfashionable, even for many in the Labour Party, while the rise in living standards which was gathering pace by then led people to believe in a future of plenty for everyone, in which class differences would cease to matter.[36]

Certainly, rock and Beat music-use seem to fit this pattern. Rock 'n' roll became popular in the mid-1950s *across* the class divide, though at first more so among working-class boys and girls. Rhythm 'n' blues and Beat music and various in-between styles then became very popular with grammar school boys and college students of the late 1950s and 1960s, and a lot of middle-class musicians featured in the explosion of these styles into the pop charts in 1964 and after. There were 'Beat Balls' held at Oxford and Cambridge Universities where much the same songs were played in much the same way as in the Cavern in Liverpool at a lunch-time 'Rave'. For a few years from the mid-1960s to the early 1970s, the generation-consciousness of teenagers and young adults, boys and girls, was so strong – and it centred around music – that they seemed, both to themselves and many observers, to have more in common with each other, across class boundaries and even across the ocean, than with their often bewildered parents and elders. This spirit I can recall clearly from my own youth in the late 1960s. Certainly, consciousness of 'class' was at least partially dissolved by this heady cocktail of cultural changes. Eric Burdon, the working-class tough from Tyneside, was transformed effortlessly into the San Francisco hippy guru. John Lennon and others can be seen in the same terms.[37]

On the other hand, we can clearly see the reproduction of class differences in music-use and music-making. The Teds were a resolutely working-class sub-culture, in their dislike of other non-Ted youths, their territoriality, their racist attacks on immigrants, and the 'I know what I like', inarticulate certainty of their musical tastes. They rapidly diverged from the skiffle crowd, seeing them, broadly speaking, as conformist 'cissies', and they re-emphasized in this rejection the traditional 'tough = masculine = working class' identification characteristic of unskilled workers over the previous two centuries.[38]

When the rhythm 'n' blues boom came in the late 1950s and 1960s, it often centred around the existing jazz clubs, with their overwhelmingly middle-class atmosphere. Along with the taste for listening to and imitating blues records, there often went a certain Bohemianism, romantic anti-racism and a tendency to *discuss* music and musicians at length, to read music reviews, etc. All of these characteristics mark this milieu out as a middle-class one *par excellence*.[39] None the less, rhythm 'n' blues was widely listened to outside this milieu, while some modern soul-pop from America was accepted into it. We must not overstate the pairing off of styles of music-use with class backgrounds, since it is constantly subverted by the facts.

All in all I do not think that a search for the fundamental meanings and functions of rock and Beat music will find much to satisfy it in the investigation of class differences and class reproduction among listeners. What I do believe is that deeper underlying aspects of what modern industrial capitalism is like to live with, for both working- and middle-class people (though obviously with great variations), *are* involved in the task of explaining the meanings and functions of the new musical styles, and these are what I will now go on to examine.

Mass culture and mass society

Many of the social changes I have just listed, in the context of the limited class convergence which occurred in the 1950s and 1960s, are frequently cited in support of another theory, namely what is known as 'mass society' and 'mass culture criticism'. The argument runs as follows: the heterogeneous class society we associate with Britain in the eighteenth and nineteenth centuries has been replaced gradually by a more homogeneous one, in which the mass of people are organized and manipulated in big patterns of sameness and slow change, both in their working lives and in their leisure. Large private interests and the state cooperate in this rationalization of the masses. The 'mass culture critics' use this description to underpin their critique of the uniformity, banality and mediocrity (at best) of the new cultural commodities – film, radio and TV programmes, popular music, advertisements, etc. Other commentators are more interested in its political and economic dimensions.[40]

This set of ideas has become rather less fashionable since the 1970s, with other Marxist and pluralist views challenging the over-generality and elitism of mass culture theory in particular. But I believe that 'the baby must not be thrown out with the bath-water'. The basic argument about the homogenization of the majority into a *mass* with a lot of experiences in common ('massification') and the related argument that older, more cohesive forms of community (village life, extended family, class solidarity) have dwindled away ('atomization'), so that people find themselves *alone within the mass*, solitary even in their sameness, part of a 'lonely crowd'[41] – these two principal propositions of mass society theory seem to me to have a lot of truth, and a lot of potential explanatory power in their application to various modern cultural forms and practices.

People live in increasingly small family units, and more and more people live alone. Young people move away from home for education and/or work. Old people go into state-run homes. 'Estates' spring up on which people hardly know their neighbours, since they work in different places and travel to work in separate cars. Yet they lead very similar lives, as clients of the same agencies, payers of the same taxes and rates, consumers of the same goods, viewers of the same TV programmes. All this description can be pushed too far, of course, and we must be aware of all the exceptions and counter-tendencies which exist. But if there is any truth in it, then it must certainly be true that the period from 1945 to the mid-1960s was a period in which all these tendencies developed and grew.

The term 'series' (serial, seriality) which I have borrowed from Sartre,[42] is a good way of pinpointing a central aspect of these changes. A series is a set of people who share the same, basically *passive* relationship to some other person, object or institution but have no necessary or significant contact with each other. The 'mass' society is characterized by more and more seriality, in terms of consumption in general, cultural goods in particular and also the statuses of citizen, taxpayer, client of various public agencies, etc. And the mass culture, as conceived by many critics and commentators of the 1950s and after, is essentially and increasingly a serial culture, with films, radio, TV and records, as well as the older forms of books and magazines all promoting to varying extents a passive and individualized mode of reception, whose ultimate examples are such things as the personal stereo, the transistor or TV in the teenager's bedroom, and the cinema show in deep darkness with all eyes on the one screen and virtually no social contact among the viewers.

A characteristic of many cultural forms in this serial context is their invocation of 'togetherness', 'community', 'friendliness' and so on, even though their very structure contradicts these. Hoggart calls it 'centralised palliness'.[43] So we see the pop DJ chatting in familiar, pally tones to millions, the innumerable advertisements identifying various commodities (scents, sweets, Coca-Cola) with an idealized vision of friendliness, healthy young people laughing together in the sun, etc., and the 'Hit Parade' or pop chart which serves to boost record sales by enabling fans to identify themselves with the 'in-crowd' as defined by last week's aggregated musical preferences.[44] This invocation of (often illusory) togetherness, whose power stems from its function of compensating people for their actual loneliness and atomization, will turn out to be a significant element in my account of musical meanings in the next few chapters.

Of course, the true 'mass culture critics' take this argument and others very much further than I do. Authors like Adorno, F.R. Leavis and Denys Thomson, and the rather different Richard Hoggart and Hall and Whannel (significantly mostly active in the 1950s and 1960s), combine their critique of 'mass society' and the decline of older communities with a view of most popular culture as crass, unoriginal, vulgar and corrupted by commerce.[45] They accept that there is a *consolation* function in popular mass culture, that it provides a compensation for loneliness, but they do not see anything positive here, condemning it as 'conformism' and 'mass manipulation'. What I hope to do is to present a view of the same cultural practices, and even the same aspects of them to some extent, which is less pessimistic, and which explains the genuine pleasures and even 'resistant' feelings which are to be found there, particularly in the youth cultures and subcultures which have developed in Britain since 1955. The youth culture, then, is the subject to which I will now turn. This does not mean that I disagree totally about the depressing side of popular music-use to which those authors point: I do not. But there have been many such contributions, and their ideas even filter into rock journalism and history writing themselves, in the form of the 'commercial trash' category which many authors use. I am more interested in exploring other aspects.

Youth culture

In the early 1950s, the Teddy Boys began to appear in London and later in the 'provinces'. Such close-knit and rather spectacular groups were not new, but over the next 20 years or so they, and others like them, were to grow in numbers, in influence and in the intensity of participation they inspired, until a very widespread 'youth culture' could be said to exist throughout society, complete with spectacular sub-cultures within it. These developments were widely studied by sociologists and others of the 1970s and 1980s, producing one of the main strands of what is called 'cultural studies'.[46] I make free use here of arguments taken from all those authors as well as my own memories of youth and youth culture in the 1960s.

A feature remarked on by many authors is the 'resistance' or rebelliousness of youth culture and sub-cultures. The members of youth cultural groups were almost always up against aspects of the parent culture, both immediately, in terms of their own parents, teachers, police, etc., and in a wider sense, of disaffection from a lot of the values and priorities preached at them by schools, parents, the media, politicians and so on. One of the best known studies of youth culture is actually entitled *Resistance through Rituals*.[47] And yet these writings are often tantalizingly vague about exactly *what* is resisted by youth cultural practices and styles. The more detail they provide about clothes, language and music-use the more the bigger questions get lost – *why* does this happen, what *function* does youth culture fulfil, if any, for its participants? And what function if any for society at large, or for the 'system'? Of course, the works of Hebdige, Willis, Hall and Jefferson, etc., are not entirely lacking in suggestive hints on these matters, many couched in terms of a loose sort of Marxism. But they remain, for the most part, just hints. Hebdige explicitly rejects several possible overviews of 'the function of sub-cultures', ending up with a view that they merely 'express' the tensions of social power and subordination in different ways.[48]

I believe that youth culture involves a resistance to atomization and massification, and to the boredom, the loneliness, the fear and the experiential vicariousness they produce. The unique position of post-war teenagers, physically almost adult yet excluded from adult roles and responsibilities, with considerable disposable cash, and familiar from early childhood with the products of the modern mass media, healthy, well-fed and energetic, yet involved in less hard physical work than many of their ancestors – this privileged, new position seemed merely to throw into sharp relief for them the limitations, frustrations and oppressiveness of their existence in other respects, and to give them the opportunity to respond in new ways to these conditions. Music-use became one of the main chosen instruments of their response.

Let me be more specific. Youth cultural resistances (by which I mean all manner of tensions, frictions, refusals and defiance, not just those which can be readily seen as radical or political in some way) can be described under several broad headings:

Family, school and mass media

If it is accepted that these three agencies play the largest roles in the socialization of the young, then it will readily be granted that tensions among them will have discernible consequences. Average school careers lengthened in the 1950s and 1960s, creating a larger and stronger 'peer-group' reference to set against the influence of parents. And film, radio and especially TV came to occupy an unprecedentedly large place in the lives of children and young adults. The whole world was represented in the living room, and a vast new range of stars and fictional characters became available as objects of identification and desire. The role of *parental imitation* as the chief channel of 'maturation' was thus increasingly challenged and supplanted, as alternative role models aplenty, including singers and musicians, became important.

Thus the embrace of some elements of mass culture was itself a resistance in relation to parental roles, values and aspirations for their offspring. It was an older culture, a traditional pattern, which was resisted here, rather than the new mass society or culture themselves. But what the 1950s teenagers did about their disaffection, their rejection of certain traditional expectations, was *not predictable* in the terms of mass culture criticism as argued by Eliot or even Hoggart. They were not content to become couch potatoes fantasizing about Elvis or Marilyn Monroe, but developed a range of communal practices which ran counter to the atomizing tendency and the vicariousness which might seem to be built into the film, radio and TV experience. They selected from the range of mass-cultural commodities those which could be altered by use, whose meanings could be inflected and even expropriated, to give expression to their concerns. Music was the chief of these.

Boredom

If one were to ask a youth-cultural member, almost any time in the last 35 years, what he or she was trying to rebel against, avoid or get away from, then the word 'boring' would very rapidly crop up. Woe betide the investigator of youth culture who ignores such a ubiquitous claim! And yet no generation of young British people before the 1950s had enjoyed the cultural provision or the relative affluence that were now enjoyed by most working- and middle-class young people, albeit with exceptions and pockets of poverty. This contradiction is to be explained by considering the vicariousness and passivity which are central characteristics of film, radio and TV reception. Even the most exotic ingredients, while they certainly eclipsed for many teenagers the school curriculum and the attractions of the local library, were made commonplace by their casual repetition and by the fact that any excitement experienced by the TV watcher, say, is rapidly short-circuited by the comfort, domesticity, smallness and familiarity of the living room. The restless young were bored by the cosy and jolly sit-coms, 'variety entertainments' and children's shows, and craved more exciting stuff, only to find that this too often cheated them in the same way. So it was that, sated from an early age with the main courses of cultural fare on offer, they sought out within the range of the commodities on offer those whose excitement did *not* quickly pall, those which seemed capable of holding and retaining a worthwhile meaning. Clothes, haircuts, bikes and cars were used as gestures of youth cultural identity, and rebellion. But above all, *music* was chosen, because it could be used in ways which gave real and repeatable pleasures, not vicarious and not passively domesticated. Just why and how this was possible I will examine in the next chapter. Music-*making* then followed, something no-one really expected from gangs of working-class boys, something serious, active and communal which mass culture criticism could and did not really predict or explain. This was not mere 'mass culture' in a 'mass society', but an autonomous development of a new cultural practice as a *response to* mass society, specifically a *refusal* of the boring, largely vicarious, cultural fare it offered.

Private and public worlds

Youth culture was brash, loud and exhibitionistic, and its participants took pleasure in shocking people, with their noisy music, loud behaviour, sex-play in public and so on. Now the *boundary* between acceptable public and private behaviour is always a shifting one, but these young people shifted it quite a long way, with their abandoning of 'manners' and formality of address to a large extent ('Who called the English teacher Daddy-O?' asked The Coasters), their preening exhibitionism of dress and hairstyle (especially the Teds), and their contempt for the 'older generation's' values of 'domestic bliss', gentility and thrift.

To a great degree, they were probably shouting loud to convince themselves. For in a wider sense, too, the discourses of public and private were in a state of confusing change. All sorts of state activity were expanding, a 'public' sector had appeared in the economy, yet there was no sense in which an ordinary member of the public could really feel that he or she owned or controlled this. The apparent collective entities of citizenship, even of Britishness, of being a consumer, being a member of the public *for* certain media messages, etc., were very *abstract* collectives, involving little or no commitment or activity, and to which it was hard to feel much allegiance. The more rationalized and planned the nation and the whole world became, the more mysterious, remote and 'out of control' it also seemed to be. The world was threatened by nuclear war, leaving people feeling very small and helpless, and certainly not feeling that something as small and boring as their vote, or their views as given to an opinion poll, could have much effect on anything. Undoubtedly, this set of feelings and fears generated – and still does generate – *a retreat*, especially among older 'mature' people with their responsibilities and personal effects hemming them in, into a private, domesticated, small-scale, apolitical existence, with great emphasis on family life, made bearable by the acceptance of cosy, soothing 'family entertainment' transmitted directly to the home. Young people, educated and energetic, not yet prepared for this retreat, found in youth culture – in a period when radical politics were highly marginalized for various reasons – the excitement and the (unfocused) rebelliousness which were squeezed out of 'normal' family life. They found a way to join in the big world as a *spectacle* – since this was how it reached them on film and TV – by 'making a spectacle of themselves'. They *were* Teds, or Mods, or bikers, not just (to recall a redolent 1950s and 1960s phrase) 'faceless masses'.

Groups

All these exciting and rebellious practices were done by *groups*: the gang, the in-crowd, the secret sub-cultural gathering, were essential to all the styles of youth culture, and especially to the intense styles of music-use which grew up within it. These groups might crystallize out of classroom friendships, neighbourhood peer groups, or around an institution such as a youth club. But they acquired an autonomy, creating and sustaining themselves, relying on their own closed ranks for survival, non-institutionalized, informal, unendorsed and even sometimes repressed by the parent culture, in the form of the police and the Courts. Music-use – which involved the making of secret meanings, and a lot of activity, from record-collecting and dancing up to the serious, collective and on-going project of actually learning to play together – became the most central of the groups' inner resources for resisting or evading 'normality', 'growing up' and 'settling down'. Music-use and music-making were the *social cement* which held youth culture together.

In more theoretical terms, these strong and sometimes quite lasting groups were the *defences* of young people against the threat of atomization, the pervasive seriality, of the mass society. Faced with having to make a largely solitary way in a complex and somewhat hostile world, they sought some support other than just the 'retreatist' solution of normal family life. At the same time, the same groups functioned as channels for identification responses which challenged and partially replaced identification with 'parents and elders'. The participants identified with each other and also with the group's heroes – such as pop stars – and supported each other's choices. This may have served to socialize these young adults into the fast-changing world of modern work and leisure, so that, by an often-observed irony, their 'resistances' turned out in fact to be adaptations to the conditions of their present and future lives.

In all these ways, then, teenagers and young adults engaged in 'resistant' and rebellious cultural practices, which defined them as youth or sub-cultural members. And music-use, including music-making, was tied up with the process from the beginning. In the next chapters, I will explore what the music meant to them in much more detail. But first there is another important area I wish to cover.

Gender, sexuality and the youth culture

It was widely perceived by the media, authors and educationalists of the 1950s and early 1960s that teenagers were heavily preoccupied with sexuality. We can accept, I think, Gorer's general description, to which I have already referred; namely, that the 'social' childhood, chiefly delimited by the school or college leaving age, was expanding during the 1950s, while the 'physiological' childhood was constant or shortening. The interlude of teenage which opened up was thus in part actually *produced* by the fact of sexual maturation in the new social context.

The period between 1945 and the early 1960s was a period of particularly intense oppression of women in general, expressed in their exclusion from many sections of the national workforce (after being employed in almost all capacities during the war), and in the 'baby boom', as well as in the dominant discourses of the time. Women as 'sex objects' and women as housewives and mothers were the two most generalized representations, everywhere encouraged by the newspapers and magazines, radio, TV and films, and in the schools and churches, to a much greater extent than had been true of the war years or even the immediate pre-war. The famous 'childcare experts', Bowlby and Spock,[49] were in the van of an orchestrated exhortation to women, to return to their 'natural' and 'most fulfilling' place, the home and copious motherhood. The theory of 'maternal deprivation' was invented to berate nurseries and 'child-minding', and extol the virtues of turning motherhood into a full-time commitment to child-rearing.

In the standard fare of the mass media, the processes of gender specification and reproduction were polarized in the extreme. American post-war films were perhaps the best examples, full of he-men who fought, drank and swaggered through plots designed to flatter their masculinity in every scene, picking up and discarding, often with astounding sadism, the extravagantly beautified women who multiplied at the time in Hollywood, and who did nothing much in many films except be picked up and discarded. Humphrey Bogart, John Wayne, Audie Murphy, Burt Lancaster, etc., were the men, Rita Hayworth, Jayne Mansfield, Marilyn Monroe and Jane Russell, etc., the 'girls'. Products, too, of the 1950s were the James Bond books, whose extravagant sexism was even more fantastic and insulting, with the addendum that, since at this time he inhabited print not celluloid, Bond could actually fornicate merrily, whereas the screen heroes normally – on screen – stopped just short. Alternatively, there were the romantic films, and the in-between ones like sentimental westerns (such as 'High Noon'); here love and sentiment triumphed over vicissitudes which enabled the man to prove his qualities of courage and spunk as well as those of honesty and integrity, while the woman was able to exhibit a clinging and dependable loyalty, sometimes despite temptations or misunderstandings, and to dispense tender loving care in generous helpings. The 'modern' films of James Dean and Brando, if anything, exaggerated these characteristics.

In the cultural climate which gave rise to such strong stereotyping, in films, TV, books and magazines, it is perhaps unsurprising that girls and women continued to be largely excluded from music-making except in the traditional role of singing. With the exception of a middle-class career opportunity for a few in symphony orchestras, there was virtually no role for women in professional music-making other than as singer. And when rock 'n' roll, skiffle and Beat developed in Britain, girls played perhaps even less part in them than in the musical life of the 'parent culture'. Fletcher[50] recalls how the music group grew from within an existing gang of boys, becoming its focus or centre, and how the girls who were involved in the gang (already and always in a subordinate role) naturally became the 'seamstresses', making and decorating the boys' elaborate stage clothes. In Britain as in America, some women singers flourished briefly on the rock-pop fringes of the rock 'n' roll movement (Brenda Lee, Helen Shapiro), but it was not until the mid-1960s that more than a trickle of women artists became active in rock and Beat music. One or two notable exceptions existed of course, as always: Jackie de Shannon and Carole King the American singer-songwriters, Sharon Sheeley who co-wrote songs with Eddie Cochran, and so on. They only serve to point up how absent women as a whole were. A rough measure of this is to examine the lists of British 'Number Ones' from, say, 1955 to 1960: out of some 90 titles, 11 were by female artists, of whom only one – Winifred Atwell – was anything other than a singer. Of the remaining ten singers, only three were British (Alma Cogan, Anne Shelton and Shirley Bassey) and none of these was really associated with rock 'n' roll, skiffle or Beat music.[51]

If rock 'n' roll was masculine in its conception and execution, however, it none the less set out to elicit a feminine as well as a masculine response. I have not counted but I would be prepared to assert with confidence that some 90 per cent or more of rock 'n' roll (and 'Beat') lyrics sung by males are wholly or partly concerned with boy–girl relationships, whether they take the form of boasts ('I gotta girl, ... long blonde hair, eyes of blue, ... you should see her dance ... she's mine ... etc.'), of warnings (The Coasters' 'Poison Ivy', Dion's 'Runaround Sue'), or of direct pleas, exhortations or orders addressed from male singer to girl. Many songs which are initially or centrally concerned with something else (e.g. 'blue suede shoes', 'pink legged slacks', the weekend, parental strictness) repeatedly return to the girlfriend or female object of desire in each verse or chorus. Of course this preoccupation is nothing new; it simply continues the preoccupation with sexual relationships and 'romance' which characterizes most popular songs, including most blues, of the whole twentieth century. There are, however, some differences, which directly shed light on the teenage phenomenon, on teenage gender construction and sexual practices, and on the importance of these in any theory of the relationship of rock 'n' roll to its social surroundings.

A large body of rock 'n' roll and rock-pop lyrics, particularly from the USA between about 1957 and the early 1960s, can be categorized as 'teen-lyrics'; viz. the songs of Eddie Cochran, The Coasters, most of The Everly Brothers' hits, and famous singles such as 'Teenager in Love', 'Runaround Sue' and 'At the Hop'. Teen-lyrics normally projected quite overwhelmingly the stereotypes of American teenage sexual behaviour, namely 'dating' and 'going steady', with questions like what clothes to wear so as not to be 'square', and the rules of sexual conduct (first kiss, boy getting girl home at an acceptable hour, etc.) very much to the fore. In his 1969 account, Dave Laing calls this the 'High School Courting Code'.[52] Although Laing does not point this out, the rules of the code were discriminatory through and through: girls are chased, they do not do the chasing; boys chase as many girls as they like, but girls get a bad name if they 'run around' too much; boys are entitled to try it on, girls are supposed to resist. Courtship has sites as well as rules: the weekend, the car, the drive-in movie; outside these times and places nothing much happens. The important thing which these lyrics demonstrate (and no doubt at the time helped to reproduce and to generalize), is that these sexual practices were seen as the symbolic *centre* of teenage life, its climax and purpose.

But such 'teenage' and 'high school' songs were not by any means the whole of rock 'n' roll, and they were also mainly American. In Britain, the American artists who seem to have made the greatest impact on the youth culture were, with the exception of Eddie Cochran, *not* the teen-idols who sang of little else other than the 'courting code' (Dion, Fabian, etc.), but Haley, Presley, Buddy Holly, Little Richard, Chuck Berry and perhaps Pat Boone. And these singers, by and large, *avoided* teen-lyrics, except on rare occasions, though Chuck Berry wrote and sang some humorous songs about teenage courtship which might be included as exceptions within the category. Native British rock 'n' roll and Beat songs attempted to imitate mainly these other lyrics; viz. The Beatles, Gerry and the Pacemakers and others of the early to mid-1960s. There were few British 'teen-lyrics' of any note.

Most of the songs of Buddy Holly, Little Richard, Jerry Lee Lewis, Presley and the black 'rockers' (Fats Domino, Lloyd Price, Larry Williams and others who enjoyed some success in Britain) were concerned, certainly, with sexual relationships, but not those which were confined within the high school code. The love and sexuality *they* sang about were more generalized, and normally more adult in language, reference and style of singing and presentation. The very adult model of the urban blues is clearly present behind such songs as 'Hound Dog', 'All Shook Up', 'Great Balls of Fire', 'Whole Lotta Shakin' Goin' On' and (appropriated a little more distinctively) Buddy Holly's 'Oh Boy', 'Peggy Sue' and 'Not Fade Away'; several of the black rockers were actually already moderately successful urban blues artists (Fats Domino, Lloyd Price). This tradition of adult and even 'explicit' lyrics, about sexual relationships undoubtedly of the 'full' sort, worried many moralists in both America and Britain now that it was reaching the white youth.

In terms of the representation of femininity, the standard type of address or reference to girls and women in the lyrics of these songs was one which stressed beauty, sexual willingness and a kind of energetic, care-free style, the capacity to provoke and favour the man/boyfriend up to and beyond the point of 'surrendering' to him. 'I gotta girl, name of Sue/ She knows just what to do/ she knows how to love me, yes indeed/ boy, you should see what she do to me', sang Little Richard in 'Tutti Frutti', one of the archetypal songs of this sort, while Presley insulted his girl most crudely in 'Hound Dog', and confessed his arousal in similar earthy terms in 'All Shook Up'; he even turned the apparently innocent lyrics of the non-rock song 'Its Now or Never' into such an urgent message that romantic ardour seemed to give way to the threat of rape. Presley's output in these years was exceptional, however, containing fewer songs which praised women than almost any other rock artist. Songs which were perhaps almost teen-lyrical but 'raunchier' and less sentimental, like Buddy Knox's 'Party Doll', The Diamonds's 'Little Darlin', The Big Bopper's 'Chantilly Lace', Johnny Tillotson's 'Poetry in Motion', Johnny Kidd's 'Linda Lu' and many more give perhaps the best indication of the way in which femininity was being frankly reconstructed as 'sexiness' in these songs, as in other aspects of teenage culture of the time.

A less virginal, less 'protected', more sexually willing representation was thus being promoted. It was, however, no less *passive* than other conceptions of the female sex role, and should not be confused with any sort of liberation of women. The nature of the change which was taking place can be grasped a little better if we examine other developments of the period. Peter Lewis, arguing that 'the current of liberation really began to flow in 1953' (!),[53] cites three important events of that year – the Kinsey Report and the debuts of *Playboy* and James Bond.[54] Clearly, any potential for women's 'liberation' contained in the pages of Kinsey (which was briefly a bestseller in Britain and America) was hardly likely to be reinforced by the overwhelming 'sex-object' approach to women in the two new literary ventures. Lewis's pre-feminist category of 'moral freedom' obstructs his understanding of this, but he does make some good points; for example, that the older type of magazine picture, of women as creatures of high style, such as Barbara Goalen and Suzy Parker, was being challenged by the new 'sexier' type, and not only in the pages of *Playboy*, e.g. Marilyn Monroe and Jayne Mansfield. The same process in films saw Vivian Leigh and others 'outpaced in the beauty stakes' by the same Monroe and by Brigitte Bardot. Britain came up with Diana Dors. Of course, it had all happened before in the 1920s and 1930s, but this time it was to go further and last longer. Similarly, the promiscuous Bond can be contrasted with Bulldog Drummond or the heroes of John Buchan novels. Whether or not we go as far as Lewis and say that 'the Puritan ethic was being replaced by the Hedonist ethic'[55] it cannot be denied that a change in what was openly permitted to men, and of necessity *some* 'girls', was underway, and it tends to fit broadly with the tendency I have already noted in rock 'n' roll lyrics. Its enemies discovered a name for it a few years later – the 'permissive society'.

We should be cautious in generalizing from America to Britain. Lewis himself claims to be writing chiefly about Britain, but in the chapter on 'A Woman's Place' it is noticeable how much of his discussion actually concerns America in the first place. His only apparent source of feminist-critical ideas is American too, i.e. Betty Friedan. The fact is that we have a work of primary-source research and oral history to perform before more confident generalizations can be made. Secondly, we should beware of supposing that a development of 'permissiveness' in discourse corresponded simply and proportionally to any real increase in extramarital sexual activity among adults, or among teenagers. Lewis notes: 'It was the fact that people believed sexual liberation was going on – somewhere else – that was influential, even if it was not really happening.'[56] However, there are figures and studies which, no matter how cautiously interpreted, do point to a considerable rise in *pre*-marital sexual activity at this time.[57]

If some such change was indeed occurring during the 1950s, then we must surely accept also the truth-content in the commonsense view of the time that rock 'n' roll was in the van of this movement. The 'open', 'frank', 'explicit' expression of 'sexuality' (i.e. of aggressive male sexuality) was indeed involved in the impact of Presley, Jerry Lee Lewis, The Big Bopper, and even the less risque Eddie Cochran and Buddy Holly, and I think these artists had a very considerable effect in transforming the representation of acceptable masculinity. The same social scientists and psychologists who had promoted fecund motherhood as the ideal role for all women had also popularized, especially in the late 1940s and early 1950s, an image of the pram-pushing father, and the serious, restrained, responsible young man who would become such a father. It was a time of very considerable social and moral conformity for both working-class and, particularly, middle-class men, both in America and 'austerity' Britain: the sort of 'normality' which is so hated and ridiculed in influential novels and plays of a little later, like *The Catcher in the Rye* or *Absolute Beginners*, *Lucky Jim* or *Look Back in Anger*. True, the he-men films offered a conflicting image, but it was rock 'n' roll which really *celebrated* it brashly, openly and wildly. The impact of Presley's 'lewd' movements, or of the defiant lyrics of 'Blue Suede Shoes' and 'All Shook Up', can only really be explained in terms of the dull conformity which had genuinely preceded rock, both in media discourses and in austere reality. In the absence once again of feminist critique, the reaction to the dull, conformist sexist who kept his wife chained to oven and sink, was the wild and extravagant sexist who helped himself to other mens' wives and girlfriends, and held domesticity in contempt (Brando, Bond).

If 'earth mother' and 'sex object' were the contradictory burdens of the two sermons most frequently read to women by the male-dominated media, then an equivalent duality developed in their exhortations to boys and men also. The ancient double standard was revived to permit the sowing of wild oats, while at the same time responsibility and hard work were the virtues for husbands to cultivate. But whereas women and girls were in no position to successfully play both of their roles for long, the situation was, in theory, simplicity itself for men and boys, providing only that they knew how to 'take advantage'. Of course, in the way of these things, the bizarre revenge of shyness, perplexity, inability to 'make a move', total gauche-ness, was visited on boys and young men, as their licensed obsession raced ahead of their actual attractions and opportunities, while girls and women employed their only weapon and put a price or conditions on their sexual willingness. A large part of the pattern of teenage sexual behaviour, for the next two or three decades, was thus set, even though 'the Pill' had not yet become available.

The world of popular music-making, and especially the jazz scene in Britain in the late 1940s and early 1950s, was, among its other distinctions, a haven of a kind of Bohemian sexual freedom (again mainly for men) in the midst of the puritanical climate. In *Owning Up*, George Melly takes a rather unpleasant delight in recalling the life of 'knee-trembles' and one-night stands which he and other musicians enjoyed while touring the provinces during those years. The women involved, of course, are depicted as 'scrubbers'.[58] On the other hand – and as part of a long, anti-puritanical tradition in the world of musicians – male homosexuality was not particularly frowned upon in this milieu. Taken as a whole, this 'artistic', 'Bohemian' fringe, thriving in these years as a reaction against the wider conformist climate, fed into the rhythm 'n' blues (and to a lesser extent the Beat music) culture which came along later in the 1950s and in the 1960s, giving it a sexually promiscuous atmosphere along with its traditions of dope-smoking and romantic anti-racism.

To return, finally, to the level of generalization about youth culture as a whole, it is clear that one of its central characteristics was a great preoccupation among its male members with sex, and with the expression of a brash, aggressive masculinity. This type of sexist behaviour and self-conception entered rock 'n' roll from the ghetto culture of urban blues and, in finding an echo among white teenage boys eager to assert their masculine personalities, it formed a sort of bridge between the two cultures, enabling an appropriation of not only the music but also dress, slang and a certain approach to 'style' in general. Furthermore, a similar relationship of envy may also have underlain the relationship of middle-class to working-class boys, with the latter often seeming to 'get girls' and enjoy an uninhibited life which the former could only long for. Sexism of a particularly intense sort thus became a common denominator for boys and young men, and it came to constitute a discursive and practical site for the transcendence of the frustrations of teenage life, as penned in by class, income, mobility and other restrictions on the parents and the boys themselves. Through the oppression, real and imagined, of girls and women, the boys asserted their own desire for control or power over their lives. Several rock 'n' roll songs (e.g. Eddie Cochran's 'Weekend' and 'Rock 'n' Roll Blues') actually express this relationship more or less explicitly in their lyrics, and it is implicit in many more ('Oh Boy', 'Bye, Bye Love', 'Party Doll', 'At The Hop', etc.); these and other songs also aptly capture the sort of humiliation of women out of which many teenage boys fashioned their fantasies:

Every morning when the sun comes up   [hints of living together]
She brings me coffee in an old tin cup   [a sort of Bohemianism]
Thats why I . . . Hallelujah I love her so
(Ray Charles, Eddie Cochran, The Animals and others)

Oh why can't there be
Two loves for old me   [meaning young me]
One on the dance floor   [date]
And one hanging round the door   [wife, or 'steady']
(Eddie Cochran again)

You say you're gonna leave
You know it's a lie
'Cause that'll be the day when I die.
When Cupid shot his dart
He shot it at your heart
So if we ever part
Then I'll leave you.
(Buddy Holly)

This pattern of boasting, of idealized self-transformation-through-sexism, was not perhaps so desperate and deep-rooted among white teenage boys as in the black ghettos. None the less, it is true that this element was central to the teenage appropriations of rock 'n' roll and to youth culture generally. A consequence of realizing this is that we must accept also, however, that the conditions and experiences of the teenagers, which called for such transcendence or symbolic transformation, must have been felt to be oppressive and frustrating in some way. Thus we see that the *embrace* of ghetto music by white male British youth, while 'facilitated' by the shared sexism of the two cultures, must also be related to the wider oppressiveness, loneliness, fear and boredom which characterized the life of the white male youths themselves. In the next three chapters, I will examine meanings and functions of rock and Beat music-use which can help account for this embrace.

6   *Resistance Through Rituals*

Introduction

In this chapter, I propose to show that rock 'n' roll (and some, at any rate, of the related styles) *included*, as a meaning encoded by makers and available to listeners, a capacity to function as a central part of *rituals of resistance*. This consisted, as I have already suggested, chiefly of resistance to 'atomization' and 'seriality', and to the resulting fears and the boredom which were newly intensified in post-war life. The manner of resisting was, in its very heart, communal, a reaching-out to a community that was elsewhere denied to the listeners. The people involved in these rituals were, first and foremost, the *youth*, the participants in youth culture and its component sub-cultures. Indeed, it is my belief that this music-use, far from being merely congenial or 'homological' to the youth culture, actually acted as the most central and important 'styling' practice of all.[1] And this resistant element was also involved in music-use *beyond* the youth culture, among non-participants, and among ex-participants as the years went by, with the youth culture acting as a cultural example for others to follow in their musical lives.

World-sense in rock 'n' roll

Time-sense

In the section on urban blues above, I explored the way in which a perform-ance can become an image, even a 'quasi-symbol', of the collective mastering of external, alienating time. The music does not merely fill or pass through its duration, but does something very specific and potentially meaningful with it. This effect stems from the collective character of the music-making, which consists of the transcendence of the composer–performer split through inten-sional variation and improvisation, and the mutual reliance of rhythm section and leads, and is expressed also in the way the whole structure becomes 'negotiable': repeats can be played or omitted, 'breaks' may go on for one verse or several (or less than one), there can be any number of breaks, etc. These qualities of prominent intensionality, mutual reliance among performers and overall negotiability, were carried over into British (and white American) rock playing, as well as jazz, rhythm 'n' blues and Beat music, from the very beginning. Thus, even when the early groups played nothing 'of their own', they were in no way slaves to someone else's conception, they were free to make changes of all sorts, and frequently did, both within and between performances. They inherited from jazz and urban blues – even if they did not know it – the control over the virtual duration (and actual duration) of their music-making and the downgrading/rejection of the instructions in the score. Often, they used no score at all, or just a chart of chord sequences. This meant that the potential meanings I have indicated in urban blues and jazz, of communality and of the collective victory over alienation, are present, again *potentially* (requiring sympathetic listening by people sharing the time-sense of the musicians), in rock 'n' roll from the start.

This collectivized control over the virtual duration of the music rests on, and is most obviously demonstrated by, 'the beat' itself. For even in the simplified procedures of Country-influenced white American rock 'n' roll (The Crickets, etc.) or early British rock imitations and 'Beat music', the creation of the beat is normally done by a cooperative process of performance, in which the drummer, the bass and rhythm guitar players will often depart from an exact ('marching') beat into a slightly lilting one which varies from one group to another. Here too, then, the subordination of the scored indications (if a score is used at all) to the value of 'doing it' afresh in performance, which is central to the Afro-American origins of the music, is clearly in evidence. I will deal at more length with the 'beat' a little later.

The pleasure or value derived by musicians from *making* this sort of music – each time slightly remaking it – is the first of several reasons we shall discover why 'live' music (or at any rate a certain kind of live music) is the central practice of youth cultural music-use, and the one in which the most intense meanings are realized.

In the same section on urban blues above, I also pointed out the way in which 'foreground artists' (singers, guitarists, sax-players) become symbolic to some extent of an individual struggle against the alienating externality of time, and thereby against the alienating social and physical environment as a whole. In rock 'n' roll and early Beat music, this particular type of articulation survived mainly in singing, at least in the early years.

Rock singers in general have employed a type of singing which makes use of rhythmic intensionality to detach the voice from the 'backing', and thus to realize an individualized *persona* or *presence* for the singer, him or herself, as opposed to the composer of the song. They do not only derive this directly from blues, of course. Of all Afro-American elements to be adopted in white American popular music, this one had already become the most fully absorbed, even before rock 'n' roll came along. The influence of Louis Armstrong's extraordinary singing, of other jazz singers after him, and then of white crooners like Sinatra who distinguished themselves from their contemporaries by using some of the tricks of jazz instrumental phrasing, had already become pervasive in American popular singing, and well-known in Britain too, by the late 1940s and early 1950s. From the beginning, rock singers detached their voices from the backing through such phrasing, often doing it less extravagantly but more spontaneously than the careful technique of a Sinatra. This even occurs in the orchestrally backed ballads of Presley (and others, from Pat Boone to Billy Fury), but is more obvious in their 'rockier' numbers.

This 'privileging' of the voice, and the individualizing of the singer as a musical persona which results, lays the basis for listeners to concentrate or 'fix' on the singer singing.[2] But of course there is nothing natural or inevitable about such fixing. A large part of the meaningfulness of jazz, blues and rock can exist without the detachment of the voice, and does so in instrumental music. However, it would be true to say that most rock music is vocal music and I will discuss singing again at length in Chapter 7.

But if (temporal) foreground artistry of the jazz/blues type was limited mainly to the singing voice in earlier rock 'n' roll and Beat music, it later burst back into white pop music in spectacular fashion, in both the USA and Britain, in the form of lead guitar-playing. All the pulse-subverting tricks of T-Bone Walker, B.B. King and others were copied slavishly, and later brilliantly, and even rapidly excelled in some ways, by the young British rhythm 'n' blues guitarists Eric Clapton, Alvin Lee, Peter Green, and so on, and their American equivalents Jimi Hendrix, Mike Bloomfield and Ry Cooder. And (in terms of *timbric* variety especially) these young guitarists were soon to leave the original models far behind. A 'rock guitar' sound was gradually produced which became universal in the pop music of the late 1960s and early 1970s, and is still widely to be heard today.

Sound-sense articulations

Now much urban blues and also other dance music of the late 1940s and early 1950s (certain white Country styles included) was, by previous standards, very loud music. This was not just a matter of the total volume of a performance but also the amplification technology by means of which a small group could fill a great hall with as much ease as a big 'swing' orchestra. A single guitar twang could be made to virtually deafen the listener who ventured too close to the loudspeaker. This technology played a role in the movement away from large bands towards smaller ones, even in Britain, in the late 1940s and after.[3] It also influenced the development of new instruments (electric bass, electric organ, as well as electric guitar) and new ways of playing them. These features were all basic to rock 'n' roll and Beat music from the beginning.

In *The Sound of Our Time*, Dave Laing suggests a connection between the development of this 'electrification' of pop music and a new kind of dancing. He writes:

...there was a new intensity in the dancing of young people to rock 'n' roll. Its loudness gave it a physical presence not possessed by the earlier music...with jazz and skiffle dancing attention was concentrated on the steps, and on dancing with the partner. The enveloping loudness of amplified music cuts out all other sound and encourages the tendency for the dancer to empathise with the music. From rock 'n' roll onwards the partner has become decreasingly important, until today it is no longer obligatory for a dancer at a progressive concert to have a partner at all.[4]

This 'enveloping loudness' of the music is a quality which has increased steadily in rock music from Bill Haley through Presley, through instrumentals like those of Duane Eddy, through Beat music in Britain, and culminating in the 'heavy' rock of the 1970s and 1980s. I will deal here first with meanings involved in sound production as such, and then with the 'beat' (a combination of sound and time articulations) in the next section.

Just as the rhythmic intensionality of urban blues and rock 'n' roll becomes, in certain circumstances, the image of a communal (and individual) victory over alienating time, so the use of volume in (especially) rock and Beat music can become an image, or even a quasi-symbolic acting out, of a victory over alienating sound. Let me try to explain exactly what I mean by this. The disproportionality between the human sound-producing faculties – speech, singing, shouting, clapping, striking objects, etc. – and the sonic environment or 'soundscape' which is the necessary accompaniment to modern urban life, full of great blocks and rhythms of mechanical and industrial noise, is more or less evident to everyone. It is evident by virtue of (a) the contrast which the 'silent' countryside and the 'silent' night can still afford, (b) the discourses of the 'natural' and the past, which condition our response to the countryside and the night etc., (c) the actual pain of noises beyond a certain level, which is surpassed more often than in the past, though still fairly rarely, and (d) the irony that, as we have seen, almost all mechanical sounds are the *incidental* by-products of production and transportation techniques; that is, rather than being utilized, or being essential, they are the uncontrolled but unavoidable side-effects (or avoidable only by a 'pointless' technical effort) of the process.

As we have seen R.M. Schafer[5] draws up speculative schemes of the sound-scape at different times and places in world history, moving from those dominated by natural and human sounds to those of cities in which people cannot hear themselves speak on the streets, due to the predominance of mechanical sounds. Even in cities and towns where this extremity is only occasionally reached, we can say with confidence that music-use in urban environments almost always masks incessant non-musical sound, and that this is a major distinguishing characteristic. My radio does not actually 'drown' the hum from the roads around my house, and certainly not the sound of passing cars on my own street, but in so far as it creates a composite listening-time around its own messages, these other sounds sink into the unnoticed background, unless something very loud should happen. I can, up to a point, ignore extraneous sounds, i.e. they are *masked* by music.

Now the title of Gillett's book, *The Sound of the City*, and its opening paragraphs, can be seen as an attempt to relate contemporary popular music to this urban soundscape:

> ... the city's sounds are brutal and oppressive, imposing themselves on anyone who comes into its streets. Many of its residents, committed by their jobs to live in the city, measure their freedom by the frequency and accessibility of departures from it.
>
> But during the mid-50's, in virtually every urban civilization in the world, adolescents staked out their freedom in the cities, inspired and reassured by the rock and roll beat. Rock and roll was perhaps the first form of popular culture to celebrate without reservation characteristics of city life that had been among the most criticised. In rock and roll the strident, repetitive sounds of city life were, in effect, reproduced as melody and rhythm.[6]

But this account is puzzling to say the least. Why should adolescents hit themselves over the head with extra amounts of the 'brutal and oppressive' sounds which were already all around them? In fact, of course, only a tiny fraction of the sounds of the city can be described as physically painful. Indeed, to grow up among city sounds may raise the threshold of familiarity, so that sounds too loud to be enjoyable to parents can give their children 'a buzz'. The truth of Gillett's claim that city sounds are oppressive, resides actually in a sociological rather than a physiological insight: that these sounds are oppressive by virtue of being uncontrolled, even pointless, and intrusive; they are themselves part of, and become readily symbolic of, the alienation from control over, or direction of, the social process as a whole, which working-class and middle-class people 'live'. Therefore, to be able to produce and control loud sounds by one's own efforts – to fill every corner of a dance hall with a twang of one guitar string – is a reversal of the social odds between the individual (or group) and the environment. It becomes readily (quasi-) symbolic of resistance, of an impulse to escape from alienation.

In the context of the male domination of rock and Beat music, the sexist example of the urban blues, and the emphasis on 'getting girls', etc., this loudness also comes to symbolize and reinforce masculinity, the masculine power and success of the singer or player. This occurs particularly when the voice dominates the backing to a striking degree, but another form of it is found in electric guitar-playing. An early example was Duane Eddy, a bass guitar player whose extremely loud (for the time), but quite restrained, unshowy way of playing brought a wave of imitators, in Britain especially. On the record 'Rebel Rouser', the 'cool controlled' power of Eddy, as rock writers might call it, is pointed up by the 'frantic honking' of a saxophone. Strictly speaking, this sort of thing only articulates masculinity when a discourse of interpretation says it does. Indeed, the same might even be true of calling it 'powerful' in any sense. But such discourse was of course readily supplied by Eddy's promoters, by reviews, disc jockeys and so on. A superficially very different case of exactly the same process was the loud, arrestingly different, lead guitar style of Jimi Hendrix in the mid- to late 1960s, again supported by commentary and some crude visual symbolism, and also by lyrics in his case, as an expression of extraordinary masculine potency.

The 'beat'

One of the most striking characteristics of rock 'n' roll and Beat music, both for people who disliked them and for the fans, was 'beat'. The very names 'Beat music', 'Big Beat' and 'Merseybeat' illustrate this fact. The beat is not just a steady pulse such as we find in almost all tonal-European music, but a prominent, loud rhythmic pattern which refuses to be ignored. It is, as such, a use of both time and sound and thus works on the listener's time-sense and sound-sense to realize its functions and meanings.

In the tonal-European music of the eighteenth and nineteenth centuries, very precise and predictable rhythmic patterns (on the small scale) had become almost universal: two–four, three–four, four–four, etc. This relative simplicity in the use of rhythm is related to the harmonic/melodic priorities of the music. Often the harmonic sequences and melodic phrases might be said to *produce* the rhythmic parameter, without any need – in normal circumstances – for extra instruments (e.g. drums) or particular stresses of volume, to mark out the measures or bars. As Collier argues:

> ...the beat is abstracted from the melody itself. Even without training, we are able to tap a foot to a Christmas carol or a symphony. We can do this because the music is written in such a way as to give prominence to certain notes at regular intervals, suggesting an underlying pulse.[7]

A simple example is the well-known 'Blue Danube' waltz by Johann Strauss, in which the second and fifth tones of the principal theme require only a small extra stress by the players to establish the 'waltz-time' or 'three–four time' of the music, since the accompanying chord patterns themselves outline it (especially when the opening nine-note phrase is repeated with a slight chord change) without any use of drums or other rhythm-section device. The role of rhythm in this music is (a) to hold together the players in exact simultaneity and (b) to enable the construction of small and large symmetries and asymmetries, such as pairs of bars, pairs of pairs, sixteen-bar sequences and larger structures. And, of course, the simplicity of the rhythm within each bar in this case, and its clearly defined repetitions, are helpful to the dancers who must execute set *steps* repeatedly, and need to be able to refer easily, almost unconsciously, to the groups of three beats which guide their feet.

There is no such thing as a 'rhythm section' in this music. Orchestras do have 'percussion', but the instruments thereof are rarely if ever used (with the exception of some military march music) to underpin whole passages with a 'beat'. Rather they are most often used for *structural* purposes (to articulate phrases) or for iconic effects; for example, the snare drum and timpani are used for 'martial' or 'heroic' effects, the cowbells are a 'pastoral' icon, the cymbal is 'Oriental' and so on. But in jazz and urban blues, on the other hand, a duality of rhythm section and leads soon became ubiquitous. And in the latter music, the rhythm section very often provided a loud, heavily accented, unremitting beat which directly anticipated what rock 'n' roll and Beat musicians later developed.

A particular type of beat is central to rock 'n' roll and Beat music. Laing calls it 'syncopation', though I suspect many jazz and Latin musicians would wish to reserve that term for subtler shifts and delays. It consists of accentuating the second and fourth beats of the usual four-beat pattern (the 'off beat' or 'back beat'), either through the drumming itself or a combination of drum and other rhythm section instruments. Laing goes on:

> Syncopated rhythms of this kind . . . draw the listener into the music to 'supply' the 'missing' first and third beats either mentally or physically, through hand-clapping, nodding or dancing. The presence of a recognisable syncopation in the music is a precondition for all dancing in the rock-based popular music sphere.[8]

Although Laing does not say so, this 'syncopation' of course depends on the continued four-beat harmonic and melodic pattern of the music, known as 'four beats to the bar'. In other words, something – in the chord changes or the melody or the singing – must continue to realize the first beat of four *as first*, so that listeners do not merely slide into hearing the accented second (or fourth) beat as the beginning of each bar. This produces a more or less permanent tension in the music which is only rarely or intermittently heard in, for example, marches or polkas. Think of 'Rock Around the Clock', where the opening lines are sung by Haley with only a minimal accompaniment, which stresses (using drum and bass and perhaps rhythm guitar) the first beat of the first bar and of the third. When the twelve-bar blues structure proper begins (at 'Glad rags'), this pattern immediately changes: the singing-stresses and chord changes continue to fall into line with the first beat of each bar, but the drummer and/or rhythm guitarist heavily accent the second and fourth beats, *against* the lyrical and harmonic pattern. This continues through the verses and is especially clear in the instrumental breaks. At times, the saxophone plays a little variation (hitting beats two and three, then one and three of the bar, though with a slight syncopation), reminiscent of the horn riffs from 'big band' and 'dance-blues' music of the 1940s. Again, during the last break, a strong 'surface' rhythm obscures the pattern for a time, but it is still there and soon reasserts itself. In the table below, the central, most indispensable element, and the one found in most other rock 'n' roll is the middle line, the drum stress on beats two and four.

Such effects are found throughout the faster rock 'n' roll records, in most Beat music and in most soul and soul-pop. The drumming of Benny Benjamin on countless Tamla Motown dance records of the early and mid-1960s was perhaps the most striking case; so strong was his 'back beat' that John Lennon is reported to have asked if he used a tree![9]

(Put Your)	Glad	Rags	On,	Join	the	Hunt(?)	We'll	Have	Some	Fun	when	the	Clock	strikes	One
Bar beats	1	2	3	4 1	2	3	4	1	2	3	4			1	2	3
Drum stresses	W	S	W	S W	S	W	S	W	S	W	S			W	S	W
Sax riff		↑	↑	↑		↑			↑	↑			↑			↑

W, weak; S, strong.

Dancing to the beat

The key to understanding the beat is *dancing*. Even when not danced to, rock 'n' roll and Beat music are recognized as dance-music or danceable, and often tend to produce some movement in the listeners, such as swaying, clapping, finger-clicking, toe-tapping. But the dance-response is the crucial one, and these others can be seen as lesser forms of it. In all dancing, the synchrony of the responses of different listeners is *externalized* in a physical movement which is also a visible sign. And the more the act of dancing is concentrated on the effort to fit, complement and even extend the spirit of the music heard (rather than on, say, sexual play with the partner or the execution of set steps), the more this element of synchrony is brought to the fore of the experience and the more it shapes or constitutes the experience, both of the music and of the surrounding people, for the dancer at that time. I believe that, paradoxically, the decline of dancing styles which involve frequent or constant contact between partners, and exact, pre-determined patterns of movement, and the rise of 'free' styles with little formal patterning, signify not an individualization of dancing but a collectivization. Each dancer enjoys a direct relation – through the synchronization of his or her movements to the beat – with the music, and is thus part of a collective (comprising the musicians, the dancer and the other dancers present), whose visible sign is the diverse but unified crowd on the floor. No group of dancers looks more disorganized than the typical rock or Beat dance-floor crowd, yet truly none is more together, in a sense not available to the formalized executors of 'steps' in the 'ballroom' styles. Almost invariably the singer, and sometimes the other musicians of the Beat group, engage in some dancing themselves, while many clubs, dance halls and discotheques (as well as TV shows such as 'American Bandstand', 'Oh Boy', 'Top of the Pops', etc.) have been known to employ dancers (sometimes girls only, sometimes of both sexes) not only to add to the spectacle but also to get the audience started. Again, later in the development of rock, the climax of many live performances was (is) marked by dancers from the floor leaping on to the stage itself, further emphasizing the inclusive musician–audience collective which such music and dancing temporarily bring into being.

But in what *sense*, exactly, is the group on the floor more collective, more communally together than the ballroom floor of old, or the concert audience hearing a classical symphony? What is it that is shared, what is the content of this shared experience? To answer these questions requires that I begin to develop an argument about the very structure of subjectivity itself, which I intend mainly for the next two chapters. Suffice it to say here that, whereas other styles of dancing are very closely controlled, pre-determined and decorous, this 'free' dancing (which increasingly accompanied rock and Beat music) is relatively uncontrolled, only very vaguely pre-determined, and quite brashly 'physical' in its execution: the dancers throw themselves into it like a strenuous exercise routine, stretching and twisting, perspiring without concern and happy to keep going until they are breathless. A 'dancer's high' comes into existence, which commentators of the period were quick to compare with 'primitive rituals', 'voodoo trances' and so on.[10] Now such dancing had probably always existed to some extent in British and white American culture, but it had been frowned on, frequently suppressed, and had certainly always been unrespectable. The relatively sedate 'cakewalk', for example, was considered scandalous at the beginning of the century (along with ragtime, the music to which it was danced), while in the 1920s and again in the 1940s certain rather wild dancing styles associated with first jazz and later swing music were able to shock the easily shocked.[11] The jiving and other styles which accompanied rock 'n' roll and Beat music were a further development of this tradition, and an intensification of the 'free', unplanned element within it. And they were adopted more widely, including among the 'respectable' and the middle-class youth.

If we accept the description of this dancing as relatively uncontrolled, hardly pre-determined and brashly physical, then the key word for my argument is certainly *uncontrolled*. Of course, the movements are not mere reflexive knee jerks. What seems to be at stake is degrees and/or types of control exerted by the brain over the rest of the body. It is possible for listeners to sit still to such music if they wish. Clearly, however, these movements are not the same sorts of controlled, precise, instrumental movements as, for example, wielding a knife and fork to eat one's dinner. It is not consciousness which is at stake here – after all, one does not have to 'think about' the knife and fork in a conscious sort of way. But some difference between the different types of movement certainly exists. Now I suspect that a familiarity with both experimental psychology and physiology would be needed in order to define precisely and explain this difference, and this is something which I do not possess. However, I want to make a few tentative points here, which at least suggest how this problem might relate to my more general argument. The sense of one's own body, of the permitted and forbidden, the normal, and so on, in terms of bodily acts, movements and processes appropriate to social situations, is an aspect of world-sense. It is another dimension of the deep-down ideology which includes time-sense and sound-sense. It is an area in which both British people and white Americans have, in the capitalist epoch, been subject to a strong combination of what might be termed puritanism and instrumentalism; *puritanism* in terms of the forbidding of bodily pleasures beyond certain levels or in certain public contexts, and *instrumentalism* in the sense of disciplining the body, keeping it in check in order to conserve its energies for work, or subduing it so that more mental work can proceed undisturbed. Repressiveness in relation to sexuality, rules of social etiquette, the bodily 'drill' of getting up at the same time each working day, working to the clock, etc., and the moral strictures against laziness, and indolence, even in leisure time, are all ingrained characteristics both among people who subscribe to ideas of working-class 'decency' or 'respectability' and those who believe in the 'bourgeois' notions of self-help, social duty, and 'I didn't get where I am today by...'. Is it by and large such people, perhaps, who are capable of watching a black man dance and believing he has a 'natural rhythm' which is not natural to them?

In this social and historical context, the discovery by young white people of a type of dance, to a type of music, which goes against this puritanism and instrumentalism has a potential for 'resistance' – resistance to the repressiveness and limitations of the traditional body-sense. Like the resistant responses to time- and sound-senses which I have outlined, this takes place in an extra-discursive, extra-linguistic way, which certainly is not conscious in our everyday sense of the word, and may even be denied by those experiencing it. And it is learnt, or passed on, by being *shared*: young dancers learn by doing it, alongside their older models. It consists of relaxing a control, or inhibition, about movement, but retaining some negative control: some movements are *not* appropriate, and there is a general style of loose-limbed movement which is specific enough to function as a secret: the uninitiated stick out on a dance floor like sore thumbs. On the one hand, such dance is in some way deliberate or willed, but on the other it is 'taken-over' and directed by the music, by a kind of pied-piper effect.

The key point I wish to make on this subject here is that such uninhibited dancing is inevitably not just a resistance in relation to the sense of one's own body, but also in relation to norms of how to behave in the company of others. The flouting of an inhibition about public movement, among a crowd of people all doing the same, inevitably draws the crowd closer together than people normally come in everyday social contact. Not only are they united in their identical relationship to the music, and the group making the music, but they are also communalized by this shared, somewhat deviant and secret experience of dancing itself.

Of course, it must also be said that alongside the 'free' styles of dancing there still flourished, especially in the 1950s, styles of 'jiving' and 'rock 'n' rolling' that were very far from uncontrolled, involving careful, practised and well co-ordinated movements, most often with a partner. Such dances were also descended from earlier popular dancing (the Cakewalk, the Foxtrot, the Charleston, the Jive of the 1940s) and, indeed, there were still a few attempts in the 1960s to promote new dances in this tradition, usually associated with particular records. The best known was the Twist – others had very limited success. Though these dances were not 'uncontrolled' in any real sense, they were still highly strenuous and physical. (The Twist was almost a 'free' style in fact, being a repetition of one brief movement, more or less, over and over again.) When performed by competent dancers, they could produce a 'dancer's high' not dissimilar from the uninhibitedness and communality described above, so long as the dancers were good enough to be able to forget, as it were, the moves they were making, so accustomed to them had they become.

I will conclude this argument here by presenting two interesting quotations which describe the behaviour of live, dancing audiences, and outline two very different responses to them. Here is what Peter Townshend of The Who had to say:

> We all share the simultaneous experience of forgetting who we are at a rock concert, losing ourselves completely. When the music gets so good, and the audience are so relaxed and free and happy, the music isn't just good music it's

also *dance* [his emphasis] music – it makes you want to dance. Everybody for a second forgets completely who they are and where they are, and they don't care. They just know that they are happy, and that now is now and life is great. And what does it matter if you're a big star – you just know that you are one of a crowd of people. If you have experienced that enough times, it starts to become something that you strive for, because it is so sweet.[12]

I think this quotation sums up nicely the very experience I have been trying to analyse, and confirms first-hand that the musicians feel, and are aware of, the same joyful communality they produce in the audience at live concerts, even if they know little of its precise causes and effects. Certainly, this description contrasts sharply with the following, which is Wilfrid Mellers' attempt to describe the same (?) phenomenon:

In a very literal sense the rows of nubile young females who faint away at a Beatles performance have found the nirvana that Tristan was seeking, and the ecstasy of being 'sent' becomes a communal and collective activity which is also a sundering of identity. The fact that young people dance *alone* [his emphasis], not with partners, to beat music is interesting in itself. They evade the togetherness of relationship with another person ... in order to enter into a collective unconsciousness. There's no coming together of individuals; their lonesomeness merges into a corporate act, and belonging to the group asserts ones livingness, such as it is.[13]

This vague passage ('corporate'? 'livingness'?), which is undoubtedly also sexist, seems to imply that the listener/dancer experiences something very powerful but rather depressing: it is almost just a mechanical compulsion to 'be there' and 'be sent', alongside others but not in any real contact with them. In Sartre's terms, this would be a very peculiar kind of 'series'. But what Mellers misses is the joy, the fun of what is happening, which comes over clearly in Townshend's account. This pleasure derives in the first place from the togetherness brought about by the musical performance, from the inhibition-flouting involved in such dance, and of course from the sub- or semi-consciously grasped articulations of resistance to the socio-physical environment of time and sound enjoyed by listeners. It is because these decodings are present that even the hostile Mellers cannot help but notice some of the same communality as the favourable Townshend. Mellers misses the pleasure of this, however, probably because he cannot identify closely with the young people (girls) involved, and perhaps also because of his commitment to a European, 'art-music' model of what musical value ought to consist of.

This element of fun or pleasure will play a part in the further development of my argument. Therefore, I will introduce some ideas about it here. The pleasure of being 'lost', 'sent', 'transported', 'taken out of the self' by a musical performance such as The Who, or other Beat and rhythm 'n' blues groups could provide, is an instance of *jouissance*. *Jouissance* is the term used by Lacan, Barthes, Kristeva[14] and others, following Freud, for the thrills, the shivering climactic bursts of pleasure which we sometimes experience. Perhaps sexual climax is its most intense or characteristic form. It is to be contrasted to *plaisir*, which is the pleasure of being constituted or reaffirmed in one's ego-structure, a 'cultured', everyday kind of pleasure.

Rock listeners experience – and know and recognize – *jouissant* pleasure in listening. It is mainly this which brings them back for more. They do not, in all probability, know it stems from ego-loss, deconstruction, the thrill of a radical negation of, or resistance to, aspects of the dominant world-sense. But the pleasure does stem from this, is dependent on it, and also reproduces and strengthens it. In the case of music which apparently has little or no iconic content, the thrill of *jouissant* pleasure might seem to be the only definite meaning or function involved in listening. Such music will seem to the unsympathetic listener who favours the serious or light tonal code, and does not feel any *jouissance*, empty of meaning, and words like 'vacuity', 'hypnosis', 'passivity' etc., inevitably crop up when such a listener tries to criticize or analyse it. But once we grasp some of the significance of the *jouissant* pleasure enjoyed by the sympathetic listeners, this sort of analysis becomes irrelevant and wrong-headed. There is, of course, also a lot of rock and Beat listening in which both *jouissance* and *plaisir* are realized and the former enhances, or gives an edge to, the latter, making the experience more memorable than *plaisir* alone would normally be. More of these terms in due course.

Resistance through rituals

In the previous chapter, I set out certain aspects of the way youth culture can be seen as 'resistance', under the broad headings of 'family, school and media', 'boredom', 'private and public' worlds and 'groups', I anticipated there the ways in which popular music-use and music-making of the 1950s and 1960s could be shown to relate to these resistances. Now I wish to go into more detail, with more attention to the musical practices themselves.

I think I have already established various arguments which contribute to an overall description of rock music as a collective, collectivizing, communal phenomenon. Not only is music historically among the most collective of the 'arts' or signifying practices, in both its making and listening aspects, but rock 'n' roll, Beat music and related styles undoubtedly brought the resurgence of this collective character, in contrast to say light music or symphonic styles, with their single composers and individualized, even cerebral modes of listening. The collective control over the virtual and actual duration of the music, found in urban blues, is carried over into rock, and group composition is common, while the dancing which accompanies the music is highly communal, as we have seen. And, finally, there is the spread of group amateurism itself.

But, of course, as the above quotes from Mellers and Townshend make clear, communality of musical response might mean many different things. Adorno sees it as mass manipulation serving the interests of an oppressive social system. Others such as myself, Christopher Small and John Street see an articulation of freedom in the music and its use, even a moment of

Utopianism.[15] In fact, I think contradictions run right through rock 'n' roll and the other styles, so that both views have some truth in them.

However, communality is not the only underlying common element in all this music-use. There is also *resistance*. Leaving aside for the moment the wide definition of youth cultural resistance I suggested in the previous chapter – all the social frictions, tensions, etc., which shape and are involved in the youth culture – let me merely gather into a list the resistances we have discovered in rock music-use itself: the image of the 'foreground-artist' struggling with a hostile sonic and temporal environment, the counterposing of the group's *control* over time to the lived experience of time as alienatingly external, the flouting of inhibitions in dance, the forming of groups (of dancers, but even more importantly of music-makers) out of the given seriality of musical consumption, and the simple rejection of earlier and concurrent 'boring' styles of music in favour of rock 'n' roll and Beat.

Now I do not think that we have to look at this stage for a politics of resistance or a political-economy overview of the whole society, in order to relate this view of rock music-use with the view I set out above of youth culture as resistance. In so far as an overview does inform my approach, it is that the conditions broadly known as 'mass society' are what is being resisted by and large, though not exclusively. If an investigator is tempted to go further than this and, for example, pin down 'capitalist exploitation', the 'labour-process', the 'oppression of women', as 'things resisted' (as some writers, marxist and otherwise, have tried to do, in relation to cultural and sub-cultural forms in the 1960s, 1970s and 1980s), then I would merely wish to warn such a person against too great an attachment to dogmas. We must be wary of all *a priori* models of what music is, where youth culture fits in and where it is going, and how 'politics' and 'culture' relate. I distance myself from such writings, not only for the general reason that *a priorism* is always wrong, but for the particular added reason that *musical* meaning is so difficult and intractable that they are in grave danger of wringing the neck of the live pigeon in order to stuff it into their pigeon-hole. What in fact tends to happen to such studies is that they make lots of good points about the politics of lyrics, about artists' views, commitments, careers, and of course about the exploitation and cynicism that are rife in the music industry, and yet they say little about the music itself, except perhaps to re-hash the descriptive-evaluative, essentially subjective mode I have earlier described.[16] My approach is to find out as much as possible about musical meanings and functions, using – but not being blinkered by – some concepts and generalizations which seem to help, and to arrive at politics later rather than sooner, without too many preconceptions of what I will find there.

It is my central argument here that rock music and youth culture went together because rock music was the most central constituent of youth culture and force for intensifying and spreading it. It is no longer a matter of 'homology' – an apparent 'fit' or 'appropriateness' between a cultural practice and a social group[17] – but of the 'production' and 'reproduction' of the group, and of the individual subjects who make it up, by music-listening and music-making. It is true that the youth culture preceded rock 'n' roll to some extent; in the case of Teddy Boys, by a few years. But it so rapidly became central *to* youth culture, and did so much to intensify and spread it, and has remained so totally intertwined with it ever since, that my argument must surely stand. The embrace by a youth culture formed in resistance to atomization, seriality and boredom, of a music which *actually encoded such resistances in a communal practice* must form, I believe, the heart of any overall explanation of rock music. Around this can then be ranged its attractions as a fad from America, the identification responses of boys and girls with its stars, the shared sexism of ghetto and youth culture and so on, in order to approach a more comprehensive account. But the basic hypothesis is that of 'resistant communality'.

It is important that we understand that youth-cultural listeners – and indeed others too – did not primarily relate to rock music as an kind of 'art'. Music as an 'art' had always carried with it the problematical requirement of *performance*: even the most learned student cannot gain a complete musical experience from reading a score! And performances – whether by one artist or many – had always contained elements closer to 'ritual' than to a 'pure' concept of art, as a self-contained object of contemplation (the picture, the book, the poem). This ritual element is reinstated as central in rock 'n' roll and Beat music-use. The music is used, by makers and listeners, to relate, in a resistant and communal way, to the socio-physical environment: the sound and time environment, the seriality and atomization of 'mass society', and the inhibitions brought to the occasion by the participants to be flouted or shed there. This is ritual in the true sense, recognizable to anthropologists, who see rituals in terms of their communality and their function of mediating with a hostile environment.

The central rituals of rock 'n' roll and related styles are 'live' concerts and dances. The group on stage and the dancing crowd share in a build-up of a communal atmosphere to a level of great intensity, which also transfuses all the other pleasures and meanings which are involved there. But we must not imagine that the ritual element does not figure in other listening also, even in solitary listening to records and radio. The single listener can decode the resistant meanings and the communal feeling in the performance, particularly by reference to remembered occasions of more collective and involved listening experiences. It is a question of *orientation*, a sympathetic approach by the listener. Thus when rock fans and musicians wear badges proclaiming 'keep music live', and others lament the distracted and casual way in which domestic, especially radio listening is done, they are expressing their valid experience that live music is the central ritual of rock music, but they may be doing some slight injustice to the pleasures of solitary listening to records and to radio programmes, which *can* still be considerable.

I turn now to the particular broad headings of resistance I have already signalled in Chapter 5.

Family, school and media

The first type of resistance encompasses conflicts within the family and between the family, the school and especially the media. It is the nature of the
developing codal fusion over the years that young people should be more
familiar with, and less puzzled or affronted by, the Afro-American elements in
popular music than their parents and elders. This fact gave rock 'n' roll,
rhythm 'n' blues, soul and Beat their shock value and their capacity to act as a
'secret' for the young.

This shock value of rock 'n' roll and related styles was undoubtedly enhanced
by certain non-musical aspects which came as part of the package: the brash,
sexy artists, sporting outrageous clothes and haircuts, the 'dirty' lyrics in some
cases, and the fairly novel idea of encouraging teenagers to identify themselves
as such – as in Eddie Cochran's and The Coasters' songs and lyrics, the early
rock movies such as 'Jailhouse Rock' and 'The Girl Can't Help It', and such
British imitations as Cliff Richard's 'Expresso Bongo' and 'Summer Holiday'.
Furthermore, in Britain the dreaded early rock 'n' roll was not heard much on
radio and a rather sanitized version only was seen on TV. This changed only
gradually (ITV launched 'Oh Boy'), and by the later 1950s, the initial supply
of 'raw' and 'hard' white rock 'n' roll from America ground to a halt somewhat anyway. So the seeking out of rock records, rock juke-boxes in seedy
cafes, and so on, by the young listeners, was itself a communally resistant
thing to do. It was a rejection – in groups of friends – of the tastes of parents
and elders, by and large, and of the standard offerings of the main musical
media. This aspect, which of course declined later in the 1960s, as Beat
and soul music gradually conquered the musical media, and Radio 1 was
eventually launched in 1967, was very important in those early years and
should not be underestimated.

I have mentioned already the shift in certain *values* which took place among
the young people of both the working and middle classes in the 1950s. I went
on to argue that a certain reconstruction of gender and sex roles was itself
promoted by rock 'n' roll songs (the lyrics, the type of dancing that was
increasingly favoured). Clearly, rock 'n' roll and Beat music-use embodied
and promoted other aspects too: the belief in leisure as the purpose of work, a
certain decline in deferential and formal social behaviour, the beginning of
'permissiveness' – all of these *claimed* rock 'n' roll and were themselves claimed
by it. Think of the lyrics of countless 'exhortative' rock songs – 'Lets Get
Together', 'C'mon Everybody' – their frank use of slang and other familiar
language, their endless emphasis on sex and courtship as the *centre* of teenage
life.

Thus we see a pattern of music-use which simultaneously *relies on* the new
media, and yet turns the 'freedom' of the record market against the staid
narrow-mindedness of much radio and TV programming. And in relation to
the family, the new music-use is similarly ambiguous: it is produced by, and is
a part of, a growing challenge posed by the new media to the family and
'home life' (and also school), as the main agencies of socialization of the

young; yet it does not represent a mere *acceptance* of the most widely available products of the new media but involves the 'resistant', group-based search for marginal and deviant musical products, and the counterposing of these to mainstream' offerings, represented in 1950s music by the cross-generational music of dance bands, 'crooners' and Country and Western. The producers of music (both localized small-scale artists, studios, entrepreneurs, etc., and, later, the large recording and radio companies) then reacted to this with more products of more or less the type the young listeners wanted. By the mid-1960s, say, these musical tastes were extremely well catered for by the music industry as a whole, in both Britain and the USA, and the element of deviance in being a rock fan (in general) had largely disappeared. It was, however, replaced by deviant listening *within* rock, as youth-culture members sought out obscure rhythm 'n' blues and soul, Jamaican music, 'underground', 'progressive' and 'heavy' music, which was not to be heard much on radio or TV and could again function as a secret. This process has continued ever since (Northern soul, punk-rock, reggae, hip-hop, acid-house).

Through every phase of this ongoing process, the most resistant musical styles (those using the Afro-American codal elements most, the most intensionally constructed, the ones producing a strong potential 'takeover effect'), are generally the ones most associated with the youth culture, and especially its spectacular sub-cultures. Thus Teddy Boys were keen on 'hard' rock 'n' roll, Mods followed American soul and some Jamaican music (including much which had not been originally intended as 'crossover'), and later on the hippies, followed 'progressive' styles featuring a lot of improvisation and unusual sound production. Again, in the late 1950s and early 1960s, some teenagers and young adults followed Trad jazz, others modern jazz, and others again rhythm 'n' blues. All of these sub-cultural groups were fairly contemptuous of most 'chart pop'. Furthermore, almost all these youth-cultural styles involved music-making as well as just listening. Although this invariably began as an imitation of favourite records and artists, these young musicians inevitably began to produce something different from the originals. Such differences then gelled into new styles: the musicians quite literally learned to 'express themselves' in music.

For example, I can, by and large, tell British rhythm 'n' blues from black American rhythm 'n' blues of the 1940s and 1950s, though not infallibly. Certainly a lot of listeners of my age and older can distinguish early 1960s British Beat from almost any other black or white style. These divergences all began, no doubt, by making a virtue of necessity, in that the musicians had limited vocal and instrumental skills, but, since they did not take place in a vacuum, they themselves came to articulate the particular world-sense, the particular resistant feelings, the particular longings for togetherness and excitement and so on of the British youth culture, rather than just a borrowed, generalized or *ersatz* version of these. This takes place, strangely enough, less at the obvious level of lyrics – where there is much that can be considered *ersatz* – than in certain musical ways, which can be summed up as the banishment of everything 'laid back'. There is a certain universal franticness in British Beat, and in the more youthful rhythm 'n' blues of The Stones, Chris Farlowe, The Zombies, etc., which no doubt stems from the youth of the makers and listeners, and the defiance of parents and other authority figures which lurks close to the surface of the whole musical project. The melancholy, the batteredness or 'blueness' of earlier black American blues, is largely missing in both the Beat and the white rhythm 'n' blues of the early 1960s: this presumably reflects the greater poverty and oppression and the deeper self-questioning which characterize the black experiences of the ghetto, as opposed to the relatively secure or comfortable, but rather frustrating lives of the young British amateurs and semi-professionals. Again there is the ubiquity of young voices, relatively high in pitch and undamaged by smoking and working, in the British music, as against the usually more adult tones of the black American blues. The attempt to sing in American accents, found widely in British Beat and especially rhythm 'n' blues at this time, produces a strangled tone, not quite managing the American twang. This can be clearly heard on, for example, early Beatles and 'Silver Beatles' recordings, and many Rolling Stones tracks. The drummers of the British styles tend to favour simple loud patterns, as opposed to both the subtler effects of rhythm 'n' blues and the generally 'light' drumming of most early white American rock 'n' roll (e.g. The Crickets). This relates to the promotion of the loud 'beat' itself to even greater importance (in Beat music especially, which was almost wholly developed as live dancing music) and also, no doubt, to the limited competence of many of these 'first-generation' British rock drummers. Similarly loud, simple bass guitar patterns, leaving little space for the nuance or improvised detail, also became common.

A more problematical development in British Beat music was the emergence of a lot of 'modal' melodies and unusual harmonic sequences, which did not really come from blues or rock 'n' roll, or from the recent light tonal tradition (nor even from white American Country music). Several authors have pointed to instances of this in studies of The Beatles.[18] It can be heard to a lesser extent in the work of The Searchers, Gerry and the Pacemakers, The Hollies, The Rolling Stones and others too, and indeed also in American music by The Byrds, The Lovin' Spoonful, etc., from a little later in the 1960s. At a technical level, what I believe is involved here is not some welling up of the race-memory, as it were, producing medieval, 'romantic', 'primitive' and folk patterns in the song-writing of Lennon and McCartney, but a combination of factors: one is the way melodic invention can wander from the light-tonal pattern once the harmonic priority of light-tonal music is partly abandoned (and can then be intuitively harmonized afterwards); another is the rise of the guitar, which encourages unusual chord patterns simply because moving the fingers in parallel or one at a time along the fretboard from existing conventional chords produces some novel sounds, in comparison with those commonly arising from similar experiments on the keyboard. Bypassing the sophisticated chromatic evolution of tonal-European harmony (and indeed 'big band' music), the young Beat musicians arrived at what Edward Lee calls 'freshness without complexity'.[19]

However, it is not a mere coincidence that these new elements appear in British (and white American) rock and Beat at this time, rather than in, say, earlier black blues. These steps could probably only be taken by people whose 'givens' included the modes and unusual harmonies involved, or something very close to them. White British and American people inevitably had a certain knowledge of both old traditional songs ('Greensleeves', 'Danny Boy'), pre-rock 'standards' and 'advanced' music (from film and TV scores, for example), even when they were largely unaware of it. It was due to such priming, as it were, that people produced the fusions of blues influence, light-tonal influence and these other less expected influences and departures, so rapidly and un-self-consciously. (Some black Americans, from Duke Ellington to Charles Mingus, had themselves produced such fusions and experiments.) This, then, is another way the music came more and more to express who its makers were, their backgrounds and education, etc., and to diverge from blues and early rock 'n' roll.

Finally, it was not only because of their 'givens' that these Beat musicians took the steps they did, but also because a climate of experimentation had been ushered in by rock 'n' roll; the slightly strange sequences contained in 'She Loves You', 'Help', 'Yesterday', 'Michelle' etc., were in this sense the continuation of the formal experiments of Buddy Holly and the Crickets, Duane Eddy's bass sound, the use of echo-boxes and the discovery of new ways of making, tuning and playing instruments (e.g. the bass guitar, lead guitar, electric organ), which had begun in the 1950s and even earlier. Rock 'n' roll and Beat musicians were 'modernists' from the start; it never occurred to them to be anything else.

Before I leave this area, I should point out again that in music-making of these kinds young people were also resisting the respectable discourse of 'musicality' as a rare gift, and one which only a certain kind of formal training could develop. This discourse, widely believed in by parents, educators, broadcasters, etc., was even found, in a deviant form, among some jazz and blues musicians and listeners. But other teenagers and young adults would have none of it: mostly they did not argue on its own terms but simply ignored it and got on with their own honestly vulgar, cheerfully homespun music-making efforts.

So it was that the 'fit' between the youth culture(s) and the resistant musical styles developed and grew ever closer, as those youth-cultural leaders, the musicians, actually made the music their own in every sense of the words. What had begun as a loose 'homology' – a potential correspondence between elements in the music and concerns of the youth culture – ends up, in rapid time, with the youth-cultural musicians actually making, changing and reproducing the music, and (largely unconsciously, of course) bringing their concerns into the music, at the same time as they brought the music to more and more youth-cultural members, and eventually on to the wider record market. In the process, they reproduced and transformed themselves, their social relationships and their futures.

'Boredom'

The second item in my list of aspects of youth-cultural resistance is *boredom*. I have already commented that rock 'n' roll and the related styles were like an oasis of real affordable pleasures and accessible meanings, within the general blankness or blandness of mass-cultural offerings. Music did not seem to 'cheat' like much light entertainment, fashions for clothes, hair-cuts, certain film stars, etc., were felt to cheat. The reason music did not cheat is, of course, that it actually articulated in its interiority, and via the new patterns of listening it brought with it, resistant meanings related intimately to the concerns of youth culture: the alienating socio-physical environment and the threat of atomization. Whereas clothes and haircuts were all ephemeral *gesture*, some music yielded more meaning the more it was used.

If listening did offer this excitement, then music-*making* offered it ten-fold. And, as the amateurs developed their skills, and also as the demand for live music outstripped the handful of American touring artists, such as Cochran and Gene Vincent, the excitement of making music also became the excitement of a possible way of life – of making a living – for many music-making groups and individuals. It was a type of work which hardly looked or felt like work at all. The idea of an unalienated, exciting, fast-paced life in rock 'n' roll, enjoying the adulation of thousands and the sexual magnetism of stardom, appealed not only to the few hundred groups who took this path, some of whom achieved real fame, but also to the countless thousands who merely dreamt of it, and perhaps made humble 'garage' beginnings but got no further. The dream of the rock 'n' roll life became a central myth and aspiration of teenage boys (and girls to some extent), even if they neither sang nor played an instrument. And, of course, it is worth adding that in believing in rock 'n' roll as a way of making a living, and setting out to do so, teenagers were also resisting certain widespread discourses about what was possible and permissible. They were refusing to erect a barrier between leisure and work, they were refusing the 'boring' jobs/careers placed before them by parents and schools, and they were traversing the deep division between amateur and professional which existed in the world of music-making, simply by getting on and doing it in a small, localized way; and eventually the record companies and big money offers came to them, as happened on Merseyside in 1962, 1963 and 1964.

Private and public worlds

I have tried to explain that youth culture is to be seen as, in part, a response to a situation in which the relationship between the individual and the 'big world' has become deeply problematical. The teenagers, 'shouting loud to convince themselves', still sought a place in the big world, while fearing and trying to avoid the seriality and other threats it involved. On the other hand, many (older, but not only older) people 'retreated' into an apathetic, private, domesticated existence, eschewing any world-changing role, and avoiding the full blast of atomizing social forces mainly through immersing themselves in immediate family relationships, while yet accepting from the mass media (radio and TV) a type of entertainment that stressed cosy, narrow and apparently non-political values, and thus encouraged such passivity: light music of various kinds, bland situation comedies, trivial magazines, game shows. This pattern was true across the divide between the traditional working class and the middle class, though it was perhaps especially true of the former.

We do not have to look very far to see how rock 'n' roll shook up this pattern of retreat and cultural conservatism. It involved loudness, showing off, getting together in crowds to do uninhibited things: it even had the glamour of being widely banned by clubs and dance halls until around 1960.[20] Even if there seemed no point to the shouting, no political, religious or moral message, it certainly shouted loud, resisting in this respect both the parents' attitudes (or those widely ascribed to parents) and the mainstream of mass-cultural offerings and commodities. The new music-use expressed frustration and protest – admittedly of an unfocused sort – by the very virtue of its *not* taking place mainly in the living room, *not* being 'bland' and *not* embodying a clear endorsement of 'cosy' values.

In addition, the teenagers who frequented dance halls and juke-box cafes were grabbing for themselves a free and unchaperoned space for courtship practices. And they had the defiant, perhaps slightly exhibitionistic, pleasure of doing this in places which were public, i.e. open to older people too, but which they made theirs by their frequent presence, and the kissing, teasing and leering which went on there. Nothing very terrible happened much of the time, but the visibility and unashamedness of the 'goings-on' shocked many people none the less.

In the dance styles of the new music-use, we can clearly see these elements. Energetic, sweaty, often sexually provocative dancing served to advertise the person's bodily presence, in a public, crude, unabashed way, as youth-cultural member, and as potential sexual partner. Many people experienced some difficulty in 'letting themselves go' enough to do this dancing passably well, so that it functioned as a defiant secret for those who could. Through such display, a 'nobody' in the world of work, or the parent culture, could be a somebody on the dance floor. This area of meaning (display, self-advertisement, 'making a spectacle of oneself'), then, is to be added to two others already mentioned, in order to get close to an understanding of the rock 'n' roll and Beat dance styles: first, the resistance to controlled, everyday functional movements and, secondly, the obvious, but easily overlooked point that young, healthy energetic people, mostly strangers to really exhausting, back-breaking work, used the dancing as a way of 'letting off steam' (literally, if Spencer Leigh's account of the steam rising out of Liverpool's Cavern Club is at all typical[21]), a relief from the boredom and relative physical ease of most everyday life.

Groups as resistance to atomization and seriality

Beyond the points I have just made, the resistance to the norms of privacy and 'modesty' involved in the music-use becomes inseparable from the rise of self-generating and self-sustaining groups, the 'gangs' and 'in-crowds' of youth culture. I have already given this some attention in the section on youth culture in Chapter 5. Now in the urban black ghettos of the USA, the solidarity of the 'brothers and sisters', getting together and sticking together in a hostile environment, were elementary defences against oppression (police harassment, racial violence). They served also as an opportunity to develop leisure practices that were independent and capable of expressing a black identity, in relation to the white-dominated culture which surrounded everyone. The *oppression* of young British whites in the 1950s was a great deal less intense, direct and obvious. But the undeniable conclusion which emerges from a study of youth culture, and of the rise of rock, Beat, rhythm 'n' blues and soul as the musical styles of that youth culture, is that something similar to ghetto togetherness, and ghetto music-use, definitely develops – quite quickly and unexpectedly – among some of the working-class and middle-class white boys and girls, and young men and young women, of Britain.

The young Teddy Boys, and others, consciously and determinedly socialized their leisure outside the main sanctioned collectives of the parent culture, preferring the largely self-generated group existence of the gang or a few musical co-thinkers. A case in point is the reaction among hard-core Teds against skiffle, which quickly became the acceptable, even slightly 'cissy', face of youth, patronized by teachers, vicars and youth club leaders. The audience at a live Lonnie Donegan concert in 1960, say, would be very different indeed from the audience for Johnny Kidd and the Pirates, and the latter band would never dare, or wish to, sing a patronizing apologia for the less deviant youth such as Donegan's 'Putting on the Style' from 1957.

It may be part of the explanation of the overwhelming maleness of rock, Beat and rhythm 'n' blues in Britain, that they were nourished in these self-generating groups of Teds and other rebels. The freedom granted to girls and young women by their parents, and by the dominant discourses of femininity, was very limited in comparison with that granted to/taken by boys. Also, the average disposable income of the girls and young women was normally a lot lower. Thus the move towards independent group styles (based on the use of commodities like records, clothes, bikes, scooters, etc.) took place mainly among boys and young men, with girls and young women normally either absent or as a minority 'tagging along'. This would necessarily also apply to the amateur music-making generated within the groups. Add to this the male domination and sexism of the music business, which still saw women as playing the role of vocalists only, and the maleness of both British Beat and rhythm 'n' blues as they reached the record and concert markets of the early

1960s, can be seen to follow. Thus *patriarchy*, and the 'sex roles' characteristic of the 'parent culture', were most certainly *not* among the things normally resisted through the rituals of the new music-use, but were reproduced there in only marginally altered forms.

The music-making group, and in particular the group which achieves some success, locally or nationally, and even internationally, does not only function as a self-generated collective in its own right, with the exciting ritual and resistant elements – for its own members – contained in that function, but also becomes a symbol of togetherness or communality for the youth culture to imitate, and an apotheosis of it for the youth culture to idealize. In the very earliest period of white rock 'n' roll, there was perhaps no particular symbolic charge attached to musical groups as opposed to individual artists. Several vocal groups (white and black) had big successes without producing great waves of hero-worship or imitation – at any rate in Britain – while the solo artist Presley did inspire these things. However, the gradual rise of groups like The Crickets, who made the *whole* of their music together, became, in the Beat music movement, an irresistible tide. And from the beginning in Britain, amateur skiffle and jazz flourished as group enterprises rather than individual ones. As British 'rock-pop' and Beat music grew up, it became noticeable that whereas the former – very entrepreneurially-led, market-conscious music in most cases – featured numerous individual 'stars' and 'starlets' (Vince Eager, Dickie Pride, Cuddly Dudley, etc.), however limited their actual contribution to the records issued in their (usually false) names, the latter was a group phenomenon from the start. Most early Beat groups had collective names (The Shadows, The Merseybeats, The Beatles) or leader-and-group names (Gerry and the Pacemakers, The Dave Clark Five). Where they *wrote* songs, they generally *co-wrote* them. The members of many groups stayed together for some years, often for several years even before achieving any record success, and for several years thereafter, and many members who left would join/form other groups. This pattern was also true of the British rhythm 'n' blues movement of the early and mid-1960s (The Animals, John Mayall's numerous groups, The Rolling Stones).

To make my argument more precise, let me suggest here that these groups were symbolic (to their youth-cultural followers) not just of 'togetherness' or 'communality', which, as I have already remarked, can mean very different things in different cases. What they symbolized, in fact, was 'fusion' – the fused group, the true, ideal opposite of the series.[22] The fused group is a collective formed (and not usually maintained!) by the free action of its members, without coercion, shaming, scandal or institutionalization, or any of the other features which betray the unfree character of most collectives. In the fused group, the projects of the members coincide, and continue to coincide even as they change by conditioning each other, and by response to other factors. Just as a totally unalloyed series never, or almost never, exists, so history offers few if any examples of pure fusion, and certainly none which last very long. Sartre cites the crowd which stormed the Bastille. Many of the events of the next few years (and even days) in revolutionary France are then to be grasped in terms of the factors which creep in as fusion gives way to coercion, codification, corruption and so on.[23]

Now, in their roots Beat groups were very fragile and marginal. The youth culture consisted of economically and politically fairly powerless groups, in any event. And its music-use was confined at first, of course, to its leisure time only. But on the basis of their disposable income and the available media of records, transistor radios, juke-boxes, and guitars, drums and amplifiers, and fuelled by an urgent impulse to escape or transcend an atomized, lonely and boring existence, groups developed, and in particular music-making groups developed, which were closer to fusion than almost anything else in the society at the time. These groups were not sanctioned (except negatively by a degree of tolerance), nor were they directed from outside; they were as near as any group can be to being entirely voluntary, and they had a central, serious, *ritual* project, in the case of music-making groups, which was itself communal – the making of Beat music, or skiffle, or jazz, or rhythm 'n' blues. And, further- more, they could offer to listeners (and dancers) a symbol ('quasi-symbol') of fusion which, for the brief duration of the musical performance, was so strong as to be almost the real thing. Not just a symbol, in other words, but a 'magical invocation of communality'.[24]

In a social context of widespread loneliness, and perhaps some 'centralized palliness'[25] of a superficial sort, rock 'n' roll and Beat music offered listeners a glimpse of a possible togetherness which was real, intense, enjoyable and free. Truly, as Small argues (for both rock music and some *avant-garde* styles), a sighting of a better world, a world of better friendships, better inter-subjective relationships of all kinds. This is the Utopianism at the heart of rock music and, I believe, the root of its enormous and lasting appeal.

However, the recognition of this strong Utopian articulation was certainly not the be-all-and-end-all of the communal listening of young people in the period, and not even always the dominant feature. It is to be seen as one extreme of a continuum of collective listener-responses to music, at the other extreme of which would be a quite 'deconcentrated', almost indifferent, barely attentive mode. This latter mode might be more common in individual listen- ing situations, of course, such as the sleepless teenager, the bored housewife, the swotting student. But it can invade and constitute listening in group situations too. Being in a group does not guarantee the experience of 'symbolic fusion'; being alone does not preclude it.

But we can state, in general, that group listening to live music by youth- cultural members making the basic effort of orientation, is likely to be the site of the strongest collective experiencing of the articulation of resistant com- munality, up to the level of 'symbolic fusion' and its 'magical' or ritual character. The only stronger experience would be collective music-making itself. I do not think an oral historian would have much difficulty in obtaining confirmation of this hypothesis from people who participated in the youth culture and sub-cultures of the rock 'n' roll and Beat years. There is also abundant evidence of an anecdotal kind in rock 'n' roll books, articles and interviews, such as the Townshend comments already quoted, Eric Burdon's account of seeing Ray Charles live for the first time – 'The most memorable night of my life'[26] – or George Melly's account of sharing a bill with Tommy Steele and witnessing the overwhelming audience reaction.[27] Certain recordings, too, can give us an idea of the atmosphere at live youth-cultural musical events. The Big Three's 'At the Cavern' recordings and 'The Animals with Sonny Boy Williamson', both from 1963, are excellent examples.

Having made a case for the superiority of the 'live', however, I would go on to qualify it as follows. Accounts by Alan Freed and Gillett suggest that the groundwork for rock 'n' roll listening among American teenagers of the early 1950s was laid by the availability of 'dance-blues' and other styles on jukeboxes and radio shows. And in the early 1960s in Britain, the early 'Mods' prized their American and Jamaican import disks very highly, and attended 'all-niter' record sessions in London clubs, despite having little access to live performances in their favourite styles at that time.[28] Furthermore, fast, dance-designed, loud music is very limited in terms of the types of lyrics which can be sung with, or within, it. Simple exhortative phrases, lines of nonsense, or brief conventional love lyrics which require and demand little attention, are the most common lyric types found in early rock 'n' roll and, especially, in Beat. As a matter of fact, some narrative verses, and some witty descriptions, are found in the work of Eddie Cochran, Chuck Berry, The Coasters, etc. These all but disappear in British Beat in its early years. This is probably partly because a degree of skill – especially rhythmic sophistication – in the singing of such lyrics, was found difficult to imitate within the volume and at the pace that were typical of Beat music. The demands of 'liveness' here, then, actually contributed to a certain loss of potential, a certain narrowing of style, in Beat music. The homogeneous, rather formulaic sounds (especially rhythms) of a lot of early British rhythm 'n' blues occupy a somewhat similar relationship to their black models.

When Beat music began to develop in new ways, from say 1962 to 1963 onwards, one of the first currents to emerge was a greater 'seriousness' and imaginativeness in lyrics, whether freshly written, as most of The Beatles' songs were, or borrowed, such as some of The Animals' and Rolling Stones' early hits. And with this went a recouping within British Beat of the singing styles of rock-pop (e.g. 'intimate' vocalists of the 1950s like Rick Nelson), soul (Ray Charles and others) and both British and American 'folk' singing, especially Dylan. Although the basic format of the three-, four- or five-strong Beat group was very flexible and versatile, as we have seen, these developments, along with the commercial pressure for 'novelty', put more and more strain on it. Individual artists came to the fore, and groups had recognizable leaders. Session musicians, arrangers and clever studio effects also began to be introduced more and more. The *record*, as Laing has pointed out,[29] allows for a quite artificial balance between individual vocalist and 'backing', a balance which is more or less retained whether the record-player is set at very low, medium or even top volume. This balance, which at the time of rock 'n' roll and Beat music was extremely difficult if not impossible to reproduce live (except perhaps in small-scale rooms with small, 'folk club'-sized audiences and relatively low volume), made possible the 'intimate' vocals of rock-pop and soul-pop, and also the rather different sort of lyrical impact of, say, the young Bob Dylan. To the extent that in both these styles the (different) audiences attended very much more to lyrics and qualities of singing than to the backing or the overall group sound, these styles cannot be said to be 'better live' in the full sense. Something would certainly be gained in a live situation, but a good deal might be lost.

Conclusion

I wish to conclude here by making clear the following points, which are central to my overall argument. If we are asking 'What are the most important meanings and functions of rock music?', then we must go to real listening practices to find the answer. In doing so, however, we must not be gullible in accepting too quickly what seems to be the obvious. To ask a teenage boy of 1957 why he worshipped Elvis Presley might be to get a reply such as 'He's just a great singer', or 'He's so wild', or 'That's how I'd like to be', and so on. Any of these replies could have referred a few years earlier to Frank Sinatra or Eddie Fisher. Yet Sinatra and Fisher did not inspire a huge (or even a small?) wave of amateur imitations in Britain, nor did they inspire (and benefit from) a great and sustained boom of record sales and radio listening among young and very young British people. This change requires a view of the needs and desires which fuelled it, such as cannot be altogether deduced from such replies. This is what I have tried to provide in this chapter.

It is my belief that, if we adopt the overall view of youth culture and music-use I have suggested here, the unavoidable conclusion we are led to is that the overall communalizing function of the music (as used in live and other situations) is a very central meaning indeed. In a world of seriality, atomization and the consequent feelings of loneliness and boredom, the music involves its listeners, if they are sympathetic, in a ritual of togetherness which by its very nature is Utopian in its implications, because the meanings discovered and shared in the ritual are in tension with, are resistant to, basic qualities of the present socio-physical environment (namely socialized senses of time and sound, and of the human body), and because the togetherness itself offers relief from a serial, atomized existence. Thus what I have called 'resistant communality' is the most central meaning and function of rock music-use.

This is perhaps one of my two or three most important claims for rock music and music-use. Along with my view of codes and 'codal fusion' and the argument I shall put forward about subjectivity and 'ego-loss' in the next two chapters, I believe it to be a hypothesis which, if correct, must inform everything else we can say or discover about rock 'n' roll, Beat music and the related styles. These hypotheses, or something very like them, will I believe prove to be the *sine qua non* of progress in writing and thinking about rock music. Without them I think rock writing would be condemned more or less for ever to the level I criticized in Chapter 1.

7 Singing Styles, Identifications, Icons and Pleasures

Resistant communality is not, of course, the be-all-and-end-all of the meanings and functions of rock music. I now wish to complement that argument with a view of what I believe to be the main *other* meanings and functions to be found there. I shall discuss (a) singing and responses to singing, (b) identification responses in general and in the particular forms they take among rock listeners, and (c) iconic meanings in the music; and I shall consider all these in terms of the *pleasures* involved in them.

Singing

Singing is both speech and music. Its character in both respects is worthy of careful analysis. The first point to be made is that the 'sense' of words as speech is not lost when they are sung. There can be 'nonsense-lyrics', of course, and rock 'n' roll contains quite a few, but these apart, songs-as-listened-to will always have a 'literal' meaning, and this will almost always play a part in what the listener decodes.

Furthermore, singing is always related, closely or distantly, to the speaking voice of the singer. The singer of a 'lied' or operatic aria usually adopts a vocal sound that has been systematically distanced from his or her everyday speech, by training in breathing, sound production, purity of tone, conventions of interpretation, and so on. Often the song will not be in his or her native tongue anyway. The conventions of expressiveness in such singing can probably be traced back to patterns of 'heightened speech' and 'rhetoric', which existed several centuries ago. There have been one or two waves of expressive naturalism since then, and, of course, operatic 'recitative' is often allowed to be closer to the rhythms and resources of (the composer's) contemporary speech than is the aria. But the basic situation is of an 'artificial' approach to singing, far removed from the singer's own speech. On the other hand, the various styles of folk song, both European and North American, and indeed some styles of white popular song from the nineteenth and early twentieth centuries, uninfluenced by blues and jazz, do allow the singer to use the resources of his or her own speech directly, to articulate and enliven the song. Shouts, whispers, 'coarse' tones and *portamentos* are to be heard in music-hall song, Celtic folk song and white American sacred and secular song. But, as with instrumental music, nowhere do these and other non-tonal-European elements occur so widely as to be universal, and nowhere do they *define* the styles, standing on their own as central qualities, as they do in Afro-American song.

The speech that is employed in Afro-American singing is, of course, chiefly heightened speech; it is the cry, groan, gasp, whoop and scream, rather than the merely conversational tone. But the singer also uses the rhythms of speech, even of ordinary conversation, cutting across the musical metres in infinitely varied ways. These two elements have been bequeathed to modern popular singing, of virtually all styles, by the influences of blues and jazz. Furthermore, when instrumentalists in blues, jazz, rock, soul and Beat music seek to phrase their playing 'against' the beat, as I have already explained, it is often to speech rhythms that they turn, both consciously and unconsciously. So it is that saxes, trumpets and guitars are sometimes said to be 'lyrical' or even to 'talk'.

In more theoretical terms, we can say that there are two 'realms' of language: the symbolic and the semiotic.[1] The *semiotic* realm has been defined as 'sound, rhythm and movement anterior to sense, and linked closely to the impulses', whereas the *symbolic* is the 'semantico-syntactic function of language necessary to all rational communication about the world'.[2] These definitions are not really rigorous but I think their general sense is clear. In ordinary speech, the symbolic realm is usually in charge and binds the semiotic resources into syntax, but in singing this relationship is fundamentally altered.

To take the 'operatic' type first, the semiotic resources are formalized (by singing-training) into the tools of an 'objective expressivity' at the composer's command, by which the emotions of the 'I' of the song (it may be supposedly the composer or it may be a character in a song or opera) are expressed; in other words, they become *icons*. But in the case of blues and some other folk song, the expressivity is that of the singer, using those rules and nuances of *enonciation* that he or she already knows from his or her *own* everyday, emotionally heightened speech, and which are familiar to listeners from the same general culture or particular milieu. In both the USA and Britain in the 1950s, most teenagers simply did not listen to operatic arias or lieder. They listened to the various brands of popular singing available, most of which, such as Sinatra or even George Formby, had already assimilated some Afro-American influence. To a small extent, they also listened to Country and Western music. These were then joined by the sounds of blues, soul, rock 'n' roll. This was the singing they knew, and when they began to make music these were the main styles they copied.

We can take this theoretical argument further by employing the terms *significance* and *signifiance*, and also *plaisir* and *jouissance*.[3] Now there is an epistemological gremlin lying in wait here which makes the use of these terms slightly difficult, but I will try to be as clear as possible. For Barthes, *significance* is the denotation and connotation process in language and visual signs. In language, this is done by the subject–predicate structures of rational, scientific, legal and critical discourses. *Signifiance* is then *the rest* of the way signs work, the other aspects and powers they have, their elisions, textures, breaks, traces of old origin, and so on. Barthes thus equates significance with the 'symbolic' realm and signifiance with the 'semiotic'. Unfortunately, Julia Kristeva uses the term signifiance for the whole gamut of meanings, rather than just 'the rest', though she defines *significance* more or less as Barthes does. She tends to use semiotic in this broader way too. I prefer to keep the symmetry of the contrastive pairs, as Barthes does.

If we do so we can then go on to the further stage (again, like Barthes' and Kristeva's work, rooted in Freud), and say that the process of *significance*, working with or in the symbolic realm, produces (for both the maker and the listener) the pleasure of *plaisir*. This is the *pleasure of the ego*, finding affirmation and reassurance in something, and being reproduced as ego by this, complete with the ego's sense of itself, world-sense, and so on. There can be many types of *plaisir*, often occurring together in multilayered experiences such as watching television. I will suggest shortly where musical *plaisir* is to be found. The process of *signifiance*, however, working in the semiotic realm, produces *jouissance* or *jouissant pleasure*. This term is awkward to translate, but means something like thrill, buzz, ecstasy, sudden shivering delight. It is something quite different from *plaisir*. There is only one *jouissance*, it is undifferentiated and largely inexpressible in words. It brings the ego back to the body, it is a loss or deconstruction of the apparent control the ego has over the body, the affects and feelings, and the senses. It also reminds the ego the brain is bigger than it is, and contains other psychic elements. Musical *jouissance* stems from the use of semiotic, non-symbolic resources in song and instrumental playing, particularly when these are not harnessed for iconic effect. Thus listening to 'intensional variety' in jazz, blues and rock and also the 'loss of control' involved in dancing to the beat will produce *jouissant* pleasure, if the listener is open to it and willing to let it happen. My basic argument in this section is that rock 'n' roll and related styles were embraced by young listeners for their high degree of *jouissant* potential, and that *plaisir*-producing elements were relatively marginalized in comparison with most earlier popular styles. This was the *fun* the youth culture responded to, and set out to recreate in Beat music.

I have taken the argument a little beyond singing here, and introduced other ideas, to which I will return later in this chapter and in the next. But first I wish to offer an example in order to clarify my argument about singing, namely the singing of Elvis Presley. This will also lead me on quite inevitably to my next subject, which is 'identification responses'.

The singing of Elvis Presley and the responses he elicited

Elvis Presley's voice gained its impact, in white America and Britain, from being an extreme case, in that cultural context, of the less formalized, more 'direct' type of singing, in which the sort of *enonciation* typical of the oral culture from which Presley came, as a white, working-class Southern boy, entered his singing as a direct source of, and limit on, his style. The immediate cause and condition which enabled Presley to employ this voice more or less 'instinctively' was the familiarity to him of two traditions in which the relationship between singing voice and speech was strong, clear and obvious; namely, Country music and, even more important to the young Presley of the mid-1950s, black blues. He was also familiar with gospel singing of both black and white varieties. These liberated his singing not merely to include direct imitation of gospel, blues and Country singers but also to rely, as they did, directly and unself-consciously on the heightened speech patterns of his own cultural milieu, and of the radio and films which he had been exposed to. The symbolic meanings of many of the lyrics he sang were almost engulfed, in terms of the listening experience, by these (semiotic) resources. How many people, especially older people, reacted to Presley at first more or less as follows: 'You can't make out the words, he just screams, grunts and groans all the time.'

In 'Heartbreak Hotel', 'That's All Right', 'Hound Dog', 'Mystery Train' and many other recordings of the early period (1954–1958 approximately), there was very little musical *significance* (emotions 'objectively expressed'), either in the backing music or the voice. But there was a much greater degree of *signifiance* than had almost ever been heard in white popular singing – at any rate that which was widely mass-disseminated – so much, indeed, as almost to annihilate the lyrical 'sense', particularly for listeners not accustomed to such an assault. To those who did not wholly resist the loss of mainly language-based, constituted subjectivity, of ego, which this singing and listening involved, Presley's voice was at times almost pure thrill, pure *jouissance*. This is the basic character of his singing, and indeed of that of many similar rock, blues and Beat singers of the period, notably Jerry Lee Lewis, Little Richard, Jackie Wilson and others.

It is necessary, however, to go further, and to place this central hypothesis about Presley's singing into a more systematic account of his popularity, and that of others like him, looking at the different types of responses involved. This will necessarily take me beyond the bounds of youth culture, to some extent, since Presley achieved, especially from 1959 to 1960 onwards, much wider acceptance, as we shall see. But to begin with, what was the nature of the extremely enthusiastic and intense responses to Presley found in the white British youth culture of the late 1950s and early 1960s, among both boys and girls? And what, if anything, does it have to do with the description of the singing itself which I have just given? The first and most obvious point is that boys identified in some way with Presley. Of course, the question arises of what this means for girls' responses. And this is not the only problem: it is also by no means a simple task to state what the 'identification' of the boys (and young men) themselves really consisted of. And, of course, it is not made easier by a certain lack of empirical research and oral history in the area of popular listening during those years. None the less, I will make the following rather speculative points.

In the USA, especially the South, it was of course obvious to white male listeners that Presley was one of them in some sense. This was achieved by his strongly speech-derived singing and his visual style. In this respect, he took his place alongside male Country singers who achieved the same familiarity (e.g. Hank Williams). He also used a lot of 'black' sounds in his singing – learnt not from his own speech, but presumably from his listening to black speech, and to blues and gospel music. His case may have been symptomatic of a gathering social change, in that as a working-class Memphis truck-driver, he probably had *more* contact with black speech than his father or mother would have done, due to a certain general progress being made by the black working-class community in those relatively prosperous years.

However, what are we to make of the success of Presley all over the USA, and in Britain, which was achieved within a couple of years of his first recordings in 1954? Most of the songs with which Presley achieved this success did *not* have teen-lyrics: they made no reference to high school, or part-time jobs or coffee bars or driving Daddy's car. So we can make no hasty generalizations about teenagers' 'everyday life' being simply recreated in the lyrics of his songs. On the other hand, they *are* all about sex and courtship, they are all 'love-songs' of a sort, though 'Hound Dog' is an apparently cruel rejection of the lover. Here I will set out the levels of identification responses which I believe were involved in the success of these Presley songs with white British boys and girls, and later with a wider audience.

1 The early records 'All Shook Up', 'Hound Dog', 'Mystery Train', 'Blue Suede Shoes' and to a lesser extent 'Heartbreak Hotel', were all rock 'n' roll records, fairly or very up-tempo, and susceptible of a dance-response; and thus they could elicit, from sympathetic listener-dancers of both sexes, a group identification with the music-making group. This they had in common with most other early rock 'n' roll, with rhythm 'n' blues proper, and with the Beat music which later developed. Swaying, dancing and clapping to the beat, letting the loudness of the sound wash over them, the listeners could truly be 'sent' by this music.

2 The *jouissance* available to the listener, particularly from Presley's singing, as already discussed, offered a 'loss' or release to both male and female listeners. Despite all that was masculine about Presley's singing, lyrics, stage-act and image, the *jouissance* itself stemmed from his *enonciation*, specifically the semiotic resources of 'heightened speech', rather than from anything necessarily or emphatically male. Indeed, a few rock 'n' roll songs by women (Brenda Lee's 'Lets Jump the Broomstick' of 1961 is a good example), a number of Country performances by Loretta Lynn and others, and a whole lot of female soul and rock singing from the 1960s (Aretha

Franklin, Etta James, Mary Wells, Janis Joplin, even Lulu's 'Shout') are full of whoops, shouts, moans, gasps, gurgles and so on, and have the same sort of *jouissant* potential as Presley's performances. Sympathetic listeners of both sexes felt Presley's (and their own) joy, desperation, energy, exuberance and rebelliousness through the *jouissant* thrill; it gave an edge or intensity to these responses.

3 In singing, of course, there is the 'sense' of the words as well as their *enonciation*. In the young Presley's case, this consisted of a set of endearments, pleas, regrets and insults addressed to a female loved one, as well as a few exhortations and threats issued to the listeners at large ('Blue Suede Shoes'), and the rather unclear address of the self-pitying lyric in 'Heartbreak Hotel'. All this in the context of a stage, TV and film image which was a bit wild, 'sullen', 'untamed', with 'sexually suggestive' movements. Clearly, a particular sort of masculinity is being put across here, not quite adolescent (there are no teen-lyrics to speak of in Presley songs), but not exactly fully adult or mature either. There is a desperate, self-pitying, self-proving, insecure undercurrent in the lyrics and his *enonciation* of them.

The young men and boys of Presley's British audience could project themselves quite readily into these 'masculine' lyrics, sung in this way. They became the songs' 'ideal subjects' and 'produced the songs as their own'.[4] American speech patterns were already familiar in Britain, due mainly to the cinema, while the fact that there was little or no gap between the supposedly real Elvis and the conventional 'I' of these songs made the identification a straightforward step for boys and young men to take. In taking it, they gave themselves vicarious access to his lyrical experiences, of success with or even power over girls, the heights of pleasure and depths of despair, and of moving in a world where these experiences crowded thick and fast, seeming to be the real stuff of life, as against the everyday life of growing up in Britain, which only occasionally afforded any hints of such experience.

By a strange and crucial twist, even the highly glamorized world of Presley's films (some of them even set in 'tourist paradise' resorts like Acapulco or Hawaii) could seem to British fans more real, more red-blooded and vivid than the rather boring, 'cocooned' and unfulfilled lives they themselves lived. I myself can recall, at an age not more than eleven, feeling this contradiction: 'this film about sea, sun and sand, with the young hero mingling with dozens of "bathing beauties" and colourful characters, living and working in the middle of plots and significant events which give him opportunities to act, to take risks, seems somehow more *real* than "real life"; somewhere there must be a plane of existence on which all these real things do happen, yet for some reason it never touches here, my "real life".'

Probably the strength of this response can be traced to 'mass cultural' factors once again. The manipulation and organization of peoples' lives 'from cradle to grave', the spread of a 'passive', receptive, domestic leisure style, sitting before the TV or listening to the radio, and the sheer scale of the big states and corporations, the new weaponry and military alliances, all reduce and squeeze the scope for individual or group action on one's own behalf, private initiative with possible public impact, or out-of-the-ordinary adventure, whether at work, in leisure or on the political stage. This applies to both working-class and middle-class people, and it applied with new intensity in Britain in the 1950s, the first TV generation and the first 'bomb culture', the decade of Imperial disengagement and the rise of consumerism on a wholly new scale. Many people inevitably came to feel that life was a series of outside events impinging on them, demanding no more than an adaptation from them. It offered comfort but little risk and little excitement. Even travel became more and more 'tourism' and less and less adventure. Hence the attraction of the spectacle of the Third World and of wars happening elsewhere, and the world of crime, gangsterism, police, detective work and spying. There was also widespread interest in all sorts of 'history', especially the wars and the 'Wild West', as times when events seemed to be more exciting, living more vivid, people and relationships more raw, more intense and more red-blooded. This produced a 'composite dream world', maintained by comics, TV and film, novels, radio-serials and so on, from 'The Lone Ranger' to 'Gone With The Wind', and from the novels of Ian Fleming to those of Hemingway and Graham Greene. Presley's films inherited this wider dream world and connected it to teenagers with a new success, by focusing on a young masculine hero already loved for his singing. In turn, the 'persona' doing the singing was increasingly the he-man, the adventurer, the lover, the unjustly convicted, misunderstood but heroic Elvis of the films.

It was by virtue of the power of Presley's singing that he made a success of these films (despite being a 'mediocre actor'), and the combination of the music and films together gave Presley a uniquely powerful part in the over-all reconstruction of genders going on at the time, with a highly aggressive, tough, sometimes even nasty element being incorporated by him as a legitimate aspect of masculinity. His composite male sexiness, achieved by all these means, was the strongest of its kind, unchallenged in its power over many young listeners and fans, for a period from the late 1950s until the mid-1960s.

4 The early Presley songs also offered a *position* to girl and woman listeners: they were invited to identify with the female objects of desire and long-ing addressed or referred to in the lyrics of the songs. They were given guidance, positive and negative, about what the right sort of boys/men wanted of them. Of course, the sexism of many of these lyrics (and the singing and stage act) did not, by and large, in those non-feminist times, produce a clear response of 'fighting oppression'. Any resentment felt by female listeners had to find more tortuous outlets, such as developing and using the power of 'flirting', and of outwitting the boys and men in collusion with other girls and women – to get the one *I* want, on the best terms I can, and perhaps stay on the look-out for a better one too.

However, there was, in the range of these songs, a type of lyric somewhat gentler, more 'romantic' and 'sentimental' than the rest, suggesting Presley's 'soft-centre', and avoiding the aggression, the self-assertive, self-proving edge of the 'harder' lyrics.[5] The very masculine unpleasantness of the harsh lyrics like 'Hound Dog', or the self-pitying ones like 'Heartbreak Hotel', probably pushed those female listeners who could not easily identify at the lyrical level with those songs towards the 'soft-centred' ones like 'Are You Lonesome Tonight', 'Love Me Tender', etc.; they were free to prefer these while remaining within the male-dominated orbit of 'true fans'. And of course they could still respond to other songs by way of the *jouissance* produced by the voice, the communalizing beat, the rebelliousness of Presley as a singer and a foreground artist, in much the same way as the boys and men did.

It may be as a consequence of identifying not with the *subject* of lyrics but with another *position* either addressed or referred to *in* the lyrics, that female listeners are likely to listen more closely to rock lyrics than male listeners. This may be because, for the males the various levels of identification (from the deep communalizing aspect to the almost conscious 'producing of the lyrics of the song as their own') reinforce each other, pivoting without contradiction on both the singer and the song, whereas for the females, the discerning of the subject-position proffered is a matter of responding particularly to one aspect of the lyrics. This general greater interest in lyrics among girls is confirmed by the first-hand observations of Simon Frith (from a somewhat later period).[6]

5 I must also mention here the workings of the 'star system'. Presley owed his rapid rise mainly to television and radio (the 'Ed Sullivan Show' being the major landmark), and subsequently his coronation as 'king' of the music business to the great international size of his record company, RCA and to films. Along the way, mainly through the efforts of his personal manager 'Colonel' Parker, he was the focus of a great deal of 'hype', as it soon became known; that is, promotion of his name, his face, an image of his personality and (almost incidentally, it sometimes seemed) his records by every available means. Presley is in fact somewhat exceptional in these terms: he did not make numerous non-musical personal appearances, he did not appear much on TV after the first few years, and he made films persistently when few other rock stars did so. A certain grand aloofness from the music business was actually built into his image; he also performed few tours, and none of Britain, despite great success here. This aloofness went along with a 'commercialism' whose crassness was almost breathtaking, in the marketing of Presley memorabilia, a fan club magazine of 'personal' information, letters full of passion and, occasionally, sectarian hate for the non-fan or for other stars – producing an unusual mixture which still holds large numbers in its power long after Presley's death – as evidenced by Gracelands tours and countless books and magazine articles.

What the star treatment of Presley and others like him meant for listening was that a large mass of people were exhorted to identify with and approve of a Presley persona in all sorts of connections other than as a singer.

Presley as a good 'down home' boy, as a white, young, all-American hero, as a soldier doing his duty (a tour of Germany in the US Army), Presley's haircut, his clothes, even his witticisms, his love for his Mum, his becoming a husband and father, his generosity, his religious beliefs. This exhortation was addressed to the public for TV, radio, films and magazines, a far larger and less exclusive public than the young listeners who bought his early records. Many of his later records (from 1959 to 1960 or so onwards) were probably made and promoted with this huge mainstream public in mind, the whole American 'popular culture' constituency, a majority perhaps of Americans. And likewise in other countries.

All this 'hype' generates a highly *deconcentrated* listening pattern. The listener's attention is engaged by the whole set of addresses or exhortations, and the musical responses to the communalizing beat, the *jouissant* voice and the foreground artistry are merely a part of the total ensemble. A whole set of identifications are overlaid on, take over from, and may virtually replace the musical identifications. These overlaying identifications, for the most part (in the case of Presley and many other rock stars, though not all), produce in the listeners *comfortable* affirmations of their sense of themselves (American or would-be American, white or would-be white, attractive to women – this mainly for male listeners – 'straight', normal and healthy, etc.). Elvis Presley thus fits into the ideological world-view which approves all these things, and strengthens and reproduces it. The pleasure derived from such strengthening or affirmation is, of course, *plaisir par excellence*, and it is available in plenty in, for example, a Presley film complete with songs from the early 1960s.[7]

It seems to me that this sort of piling up of essentially non-musical responses is what underlies a lot of the 'commercial-versus-authentic' discussions in books on popular music. The critics, being enthusiasts for music, sense that some listener-responses are 'deeper' than others, but cannot offer more than very vague formulations of this sensing. Nor can they explain why they find some very commercially successful music to be authentic nevertheless, nor why a lot of the 'trash' fails, despite seeming no different to some that succeeds. I believe that the solution to this problem is, very broadly speaking, as follows.

Certain rock music, when listened to sympathetically, offers the articulation of resistant communality, and the pleasure of *jouissance*. This music affects and reproduces the listener at levels which go beyond language and visual impact. In so far as the *ego* is conceived of as the *ego-cogito* of the Cartesian, rationalistic tradition, this means, as we shall see, that the music addresses and reproduces not this 'ego' of the listener but, crucially, the deeper levels we were inclined to think of as more primitive, and more undifferentiated from one person to another. But music which does not (strongly or at all) have these qualities can yet achieve great success on the market, where, as we have just seen, a whole lot of other, less strictly musical, identification-responses are elicited from listeners and buyers. This describes much of the 'commercial rubbish' repeatedly referred to by rock critics and many listeners. It sells by producing *plaisir*, bolstering the egos of listeners, and contains little or no *jouissance* to disrupt the process. I would not go so far as to claim that this is the only way in which 'commercial' music which is 'non-authentic', in the consensus view of many critics, can come into existence. Simply I think it accounts for a lot of it.

6 Presley himself made a large number of records, especially in the 1960s and 1970s, which simply do not display the semiotic resources of heightened speech very much, and which do not have the rock 'n' roll format or rhythmic character. 'Are You Lonesome Tonight' and 'It's Now or Never' are two famous examples of almost 'operatic', certainly very 'white' singing by Presley. These might, for many rock fans, come into the 'commercial, non-authentic' category. However, for Presley fans, not only did all the less strictly musical identification-responses still operate when they heard these records, but also they *remembered* Presley's other songs, and these formed a context for the listening. They listened *for* the little differences which individualized his vocal rendition, in relation to other light-tonal singers, and they incorporated these into the Presley persona. Also, these songs partially turned back the trend which had held sway for a few years in the 1950s, towards the further development of codal fusion, by reinstating the sounds of light-tonal, even semi-operatic singing in the youthful segment of the popular market. This simultaneously broadened Presley's audience (to people for whom codal fusion had not gone so far as it had among teenagers) and it also enabled listeners and critics to claim the legitimation of Presley as 'real music' and as one of the 'great singers of the century'. It made Presley fans feel respectable and proud, within a wider, older popular culture than that of teenagers alone. Of course, the pleasure of being proved right about something, whether music or anything else, is far removed from *jouissance*. It is again *plaisir par excellence*.

This survey of identification-responses to Presley has necessarily been brief and crude. The development in the 1970s and 1980s of 'screen theory' has brought great sophistication to the study of such responses in relation to photographs, film and TV.[8] The challenge of course is to bring the study of listening up to that level. Here I have only sketched the beginnings of such a project.

Most of what is true of Presley holds for other white American rock 'n' rollers, such as Cochran, Gene Vincent, Jerry Lee Lewis, Buddy Holly, and so on. Each artist of course brought something of his own to the basic style: Buddy Holly incorporated a 'little boy' voice into his singing, as in 'Everyday' and 'That'll be the Day', sometimes alternating it with his more adult voice for humorous or sentimental effect. Little Richard had a stylized whoop of excitement or joy, which was widely imitated by other rock and Beat singers, such as John Lennon, until it became almost a new icon. The later 1950s and early 1960s saw the emergence of 'smooth' rock singers, such as Ricky (later Rick) Nelson, Roy Orbison and the British Marty Wilde, who pioneered a 'restrained' type of rock singing, using semiotic resources more sparingly, but without returning to the full-bodied light-tonal style or the 'swinging' lilt of the Sinatra school. This style was very influential on 'middle-of-the-road' singers like (the later) Cliff Richard.

In general, however, the most influential popular singing styles to develop after Presley, and register within rock music, were those of the 'soul' movement, a large body of black American singers and musicians who inherited the market of rhythm 'n' blues, and expanded it to reach large numbers of young white listeners in both America and Britain in the 1960s. These styles were forged in the 1950s and early 1960s by such artists as Bobby Bland, Sam Cooke, Ray Charles, James Brown, Etta James, Screamin' Jay Hawkins and Jackie Wilson. All of them have in common a great, almost overwhelming prominence and dominance of the *voice* over the *backing*, and a lot of use of semiotic singing resources. The influence of black gospel music is added to that of the blues far more than in Presley, and infinitely more than in any of the other early white rockers. There were also black vocal groups, such as The Platters (who performed rock-pop in 'lush' harmonies), The Drifters (who had several lead singers of great 'semiotic' impact who went on to solo successes), The Isley Brothers and The Contours (one of the first acts to score pop success for the Tamla Motown record label, which was to become enormously famous later in the 1960s).[9] During the late 1950s/early 1960s, there were fewer white rock 'n' roll records being made in America in the original styles. Young white (and black) British musicians and listeners alike turned to soul and rhythm 'n' blues records for the qualities (especially qualities of singing) they had first admired in rock 'n' roll. And so these 'black' American singers had a brief period of almost unchallenged influence on white British Beat and rhythm 'n' blues musicians, such as The Rolling Stones and Rod Stewart. The effect was to raise the standards of singing in British Beat and rhythm 'n' blues, as singers gave more thought to their voices and strove for expressive skills which were unusual in early Beat music.

Identification responses and the youth culture: Various aspects

Having outlined, mainly in relation to Presley, different types or levels of listener-response which get mixed up together in the composite decoding process of listening, I now wish to look at the ways these responses actually occurred in youth culture. Again I start from the idea of identification.

Although free to construct a lifestyle more leisure-centred than most, teenagers, both boys and girls, found themselves excluded from adult roles, responsibilities and satisfactions. The job, the mortgage and bills, family needs, the weekly budget – all of these 'restrictions' on adults were also reassurances, offering the certainty and even the self-righteousness of normality. But only to those whose role in relation to these things was clear and compelling. Without ceasing, then, to try to identify with father and mother, teenagers found this identification blocked for several years, even though, especially at the age of 16 and over, they felt themselves to be more or less adults. By a reversal which acquired its power from this blockage, they went away and lived out the blocked options of the adults. Swinging solidly behind the alternative, highly non-parental images of masculinity and femininity on offer, they became the swaggering 'tough guys' and wiggling 'dolls' and 'chicks' of their neighbourhoods.

This view of the 'subject-positions' which made teenagers particularly receptive to rock 'n' roll can also be related to a Freudian view of the transition from childhood to adulthood. Ever since the resolution of the castration-complex and the adoption of gender by the infant, the parents play, in Freud's view, a role as models for the growing child to imitate. Where real parents are absent, or for some reason rejected, other models are found. What he does not go on to say, as far as I know, is that parents can find themselves in ongoing competition with other possible models, whether other adults (e.g. teachers) the child knows, the 'characters' in films, TV shows, comics or novels, or the singers of popular songs. Also the nature of puberty as sexual reawakening may mean that the issue of gender, of 'how to be masculine or feminine', necessarily dominates these imitations during the teenage years. Thus we begin to see a possible explanation of why teenagers in the 1950s – the first TV generation, and the first generation to have almost ubiquitous and ceaseless (in leisure hours) access to recorded music – used these new leisure possibilities to preoccupy themselves with film and TV stars, and especially singing stars, who, like Presley, established strong and even exaggerated gender norms.

Both the film stars and pop stars of the period (James Dean, Brando, Jayne Mansfield, Diana Dors, Presley, Eddie Cochran, Billy Fury, Julie London, Brenda Lee) were marketed and imaged in order to meet what their backers and managers perceived as a demand for extremely strong gender stereotyping. Though this had always been done (Valentino, Sinatra, Harlow and Garbo were striking examples from previous decades), it was done more than ever in the 1950s. The male stars became tougher and more aggressive, even if it meant less attractive in terms of courtesy, charm and grace. The female ones became more 'curvaceous' and more 'sexy'. And these tactics certainly paid off, with big profits and expansion in the music, TV and film industries, fed by an increasingly youthful market.

In the male youth culture itself, the values of toughness, ability to fight, 'hardness', etc., were deeply ingrained, notably in the British working-class sub-culture of the Teds. Not only did the boys pursue this image, but also the girls, in many cases, apparently admired it. And for their own part, though a small minority briefly tried to be 'Teddy-Girls', most girls aimed at a fun-loving, flirtatious, decorative and highly made-up image of femininity. They thus exhibited deep continuities with the parent culture, even when involving themselves in the hard-core youth-cultural activities of supporting their local band. In a passage I have already commented on, Colin Fletcher recalls the division of labour between boys and girlfriends in the forming of an early rock 'n' roll group: 'Girls too assumed a new [*sic*] role – they became the seamstresses'.[10] I think this speaks for itself.

This view of youth-cultural practices (as preoccupied with learning a new version of *genderedness*, a polarized version in which boys and men could be quite aggressive, even a bit violent and sadistic, while girls and women had to be attractive, self-effacing, submissive and supportive), leads to yet another possible account of how and why girls listened to and enjoyed artists like Presley. The girl fan may identify the 'masculine' part of herself with the male rock-star. The 'masculine' qualities which could, if developed, complement and fulfil *her* personality, are out of bounds to her, due to the oppressive prevailing discourse of femininity. The attractiveness of such qualities – and not only the 'nice' qualities – when displayed by Presley, or Eddie Cochran, or Gene Vincent or John Lennon stems from the fact that she *suppresses* or *represses* them in herself. In practice, girl fans probably experienced a mixture of responses, in which this element was often disguised by other less problematical ones.

It is important for an understanding of identification-responses that we see them not just as a *psychological* pattern found severally in individual listeners, but also as a *social* pattern. That is, not only does the same individual pattern occur widely, but also by identifying with a singer or a 'star', a fan necessarily identifies with that star's fans. In the case of youth-cultural groups, this process is intensified to include imitative dressing, talk and behaviour. And, within the youth-cultural group, fans who have actually seen the singer in concert, or have all the records, are identified with by the others as *closer* to him or her in some way. Frith uses the example of female David Cassidy fans who could boast their attendance at his Wembley concert in 1973.[11] But even as deviant a case as Pete Townshend's early 1960s identification with American white jazz pianist/singer/songwriter Mose Allison, was also an instance of his movement into a new friendship and a new milieu:

> I heard my first Mose Allison tune in November 1963 in the 'pad'... of an American friend. This friend turned out to be my ultimate salvation as far as the Blues. I hadn't really heard any until I spent time on the top floor of 35 Sunniside Rd in Ealing where we are [*sic*] at Art School.... The mind-blowing 'Back Country Suite' made up one side, when I heard that I swore he was as black as Cow Cow Davenport.... The man's voice was heaven. So cool, so decisively hip.... My American friend (who has yet to introduce me to pot) grins like his eyeballs are on fire and produces the cover of 'Mose Allison Sings'. 'He's fucking white!' I scream. A real, cool, relaxed, genuine, funky, hipped out WHITE hero.... I was a fairly lame individual with a big nose, a Beatle fringe, and still had time to learn a few Jimmy Reed tunes, but Mose was MY MAN.[12]

Alongside the obvious rebellious individualism reflected here, there are clear indications of Townshend's involvement in a youth-cultural milieu which prized 'blackness' and sought 'authenticity' in music. He had a Beatle fringe and attended art school. And the discovery of Allison was part of an exciting joint listening session with a friend. 'Pot' was soon to follow, a highly social, ritualized drug usually involving sitting around sharing the 'joint', chat and music with a group of others. A tremendously strong identification between individual and musician, then, is still, at the same time, an *entrée* into a somewhat deviant social world, or community of the like-minded, a true youth-cultural group. Later styles of youth culture and sub-culture make the group-forming character of identification-responses even clearer: the 'rockers', 'heavy metal kids', 'Bowie boys' and 'punk rockers' whose very sub-cultural names actually refer to the music they favour.

The place of expressive and iconic meanings in rock 'n' roll and related styles

There is another whole area of responses to rock music, and meanings available in the music, which I have been avoiding up to this point. This is the area of expressive and iconic meanings. Because all this music is music of codal fusion, there is inevitably to be found here the use of the tonal-European conventions for emotional (and abstract) expression. These conventions are to be found in much singing, and also many of the instrumental 'backings' of rock 'n' roll, rock-pop, soul-pop and some Beat music.

Now tonal-European music with its scores, its 'individual composedness' and the consequent objectivism and relative unalterability (from one performance to another) of its effects, is very strong on such meanings, it is fertile ground for 'iconicity'. Afro-American music, on the other hand, by its very nature, is not: it tends to emphasize celebratory, ritual meanings and functions, it is remade radically, through a degree of improvisation, in every performance. The relative freedom of its players and singers, even in 'tight' collective music-making, militates against the calculatedness and repeatability without which iconicity cannot really thrive.[13] An approach to music-making which might be summed up in the slogans 'Do it' and 'process-before-product' (and which is found really only in the *avant-garde* within 'serious' music), is so commonplace as to be normal in Afro-American styles, from the ultra-collectivists of modern jazz to the unrestrained foreground-artistry of much urban blues and soul.

When we turn to rock and Beat music, and also to the 'rock-pop' and 'soul-pop' music which flourished in my chosen period, we find, as we would expect, a complex and confusing set of hybrids and mixtures, ranging from music which is full of icons, and which perhaps even turns Afro-American elements *into* icons (whooping = wildness or blackness, 'raw' saxophone = sexy, etc.), to music which is all communal 'good times', a celebratory ritual of togetherness and very little else. And of course everything between the two poles. The expressive principle (never entirely absent from Afro-American music anyway) is strongly mingled with the celebratory-ritual one in almost all rock and Beat. And of course there is nothing strange about this, it is entirely to be expected in the circumstances. Let me give an example from the very earliest rock 'n' roll – Bill Haley's 'Rock Around the Clock'. Now this is music with a strong, homogeneous beat, music appropriate for 'free' dancing styles. Its song-shape is a simplified twelve-bar blues, the harmonic shape being blurred by the spareness of the instrumentation and the departures from the chordally suggested tones made by the singer, e.g. for the technically minded, in bars five and six, and ten of each twelve-bar verse sung. In all this it is Afro-American, it is 'dance-blues'. Haley's voice, however, is a very 'clean' voice, with little of the growl, the shout or the scream about it, it has little reference to 'emotionally heightened speech' resources. It is closer to the white square-dance 'callers' of Country music than to most blues vocals.

This mixture clearly confirms the codal position of the song as 'fusion'-music 1950s style. It elicits a certain 'takeover' effect via the beat, and the way many people dance to it, not controlling their feet or arms with any exactness, 'moving freely' to the beat. Yet it is done in a lightweight fashion quite distant from most of the black ghetto-music which has influenced it; this is especially apparent in the vocal. Now in some of Haley's other more blues-influenced tracks, notably 'Shake, Rattle and Roll', the melody line of the vocal is almost arbitrary in terms of pitch. For example, the pitch rises an indeterminate number of tones for emphasis on words such as 'Rattle' ('those pots and pans'). It would make little difference if this word were pitched, say, a tone below or two tones above the point Haley actually uses. But if the melody has only an approximate pitch-shape, it is, on the other hand, highly *rhythmicized*, with a string of strong (strongly exhaled) emphases in each line. This is very blues-influenced. In 'Rock Around the Clock', however, the melody line, while it does have something of this quality about it, shows one very important difference: the first phrase of the twelve-bar section (as sung), repeated identically (twice) at each return, describes the I–III–V shape, the ultimate *tonal* convention, according to Cooke, for happy, jolly, merry and joyful.[14] And this beginning constitutes one of the 'hooks' of the song, that is, the very bit (along with 'One Two Three O'Clock') everyone remembers (repeated twice and a third time slightly varied) when asked to sing, hum or whistle it.

Of course, for white audiences who came to blues- and jazz-influenced music already steeped in light-tonal music (hymns, old music-hall and tradit-ional songs, the National Anthem, all the music one could *not* avoid knowing even if one had little or no interest in music), such *raids* on their familiar codal 'given' served as helpful and welcome reference points. And this situation has persisted ever since. Numerous 'hook-lines' can be analysed in these terms, e.g. 'She Loves You' (V–VI–VIII), as if the music were saying 'cheer up' (which is what the lyric is saying!) or 'How do you do it' by Gerry and the Pacemakers, which is a tune almost exclusively composed out of the merry and joyful elements of Cooke's catalogue (major thirds, fifths, octaves, 'perfect' harmonic cadences). The Shadows achieved their own highly popular fusion by setting fairly simple, sometimes more or less light-tonal, always 'catchy', 'whistleable', melodies for the format of a blues/rock band, and using a 'clean', non-bluesy lead guitar to carry the tune. Even artists and groups who aimed at quite a black, blues-based sound, like The Rolling Stones, also made their gestures in the same general direction later in the 1960s: the songs 'As Tears Go By' and 'My Sweet Lady Jane' use rather 'modal' but basically tonal-European melodies, chord patterns and even strings (on the former) to give the sensation of relative repose after the 'wildness' of their rhythm 'n' blues/Beat numbers.

By and large, I think it can be said that the young amateurs and semi-professionals of early Beat music in Britain inhabited much the same musical *world* of codal fusion as the young black and white soul-pop pioneers of around the same time, in Detroit, Memphis or Philadelphia (*c.* 1960–1962), and also the professional writers and performers of slick rock-pop on both sides of the Atlantic: there was a band of possible musical sounds which was fairly similar, though not identical, for all of them – more unified, in fact, than most writing about popular music would lead us to suppose. Differences in style (varying formats of groups, solo singers with session groups, others with big orchestras, artists specializing in dance music, others in ballads), which might seem quite major differences from a contemporary journalist's (or fan's) point of view, are thus set into a historical perspective. It was a fusion not only of techniques but also of fundamental approaches, as I have argued above, and almost everywhere it involved the juxtaposition of some expressive, iconic meanings (used more or less as in tonal-code practice) with the Afro-American codal meanings previously proper to blues, gospel and hot jazz.

I will offer here a few brief descriptions of some recordings, using these categories of description to point out the differences and similarities between different styles of the rock 'n' roll to Beat period.

1 Presley's 'Heartbreak Hotel': An eight-bar structure using the three 'blues chords'; not an uncommon variant in the blues tradition. The 'plodding bass' and 'spare' piano-playing (as the journalist-fan, then or now, might describe them), together with the absence of drums, add up to almost nothing in terms of tonal code 'significance' or expressiveness, they are practically neutral, and, as it were, push the attention away from themselves on to the extraordinary vocal. If they do have an iconic 'feel', it is sad and a bit solemn. But they do not emphasize any of the melodic shapes or harmonic sequences, which would *drive home* this emotional 'feel', to any great extent. It is so *unchanging* on the record, and so dominated by the voice (amplified with echo, of course), that it cannot be thought to have functioned as anything other than a vague affective background. This is 'backing' music for Presley's singing, and the listener is expected to focus almost entirely on the *jouissant* voice and the lyrics.

2 By way of contrast, we can examine any of a large number of recorded examples of early Merseybeat, such as 'Lets Stomp' or 'Do You Love Me' by Faron's Flamingoes, or 'What'd I Say' by The Big Three. Spencer Leigh describes 'Lets Stomp' as 'a raver that was in the repertoire of many Liverpool groups'.[15] The title sums up the spirit of the thing. So incidental is the lyric on this that the group actually gave the job of vocals to the guitarist, Paddy Chambers, while Faron took a breather. The whole impact of the number is in the hell-for-leather quality of the playing, designed to get everyone dancing or clapping and cheering, and begging for more at the end. The sung backing on 'Do You Love Me' ('Mush mush', 'Bow, bow bow, Bow Bow Bow Bow', etc.) is precisely the sort of thing, utterly primitive and banal to listeners who were primarily sympathetic to tonal-

code music, without any 'expressive' or iconic content at all (except to express the idiocy of the singers, these listeners might say), which was ubiquitous in this music, all 'excitement' and 'wildness', performance-music that would be quite impossible (and pointless) to put down on a score. Here again *jouissance* is central, this time not really in the singing-voice but in the beat and the 'stirring up' or 'sending' of the dancing crowd. Such excitement can be very clearly heard on the live Big Three recording.

The lyrics of these songs, celebrating dance, and exhorting the audience to do it, are typical of a whole *genre* of the rock and Beat period: 'dance songs' such as 'Lets Twist Again', 'Let's Dance', 'Twist and Shout', 'Shout' or 'The Locomotion', songs which were almost always accompanied by this kind of music, and which clearly fitted it well. As I have pointed out already, such numbers were/are usually best heard live, because the generation of their chief meanings depends on an interaction between makers and listeners, on 'atmosphere', on the 'stirring up' of a crowd. Dave Laing argues that the success of The Beatles, in their early years, was largely the result of their particular achievement (or that of their producers) in getting the excitement and vigour of live Beat performances on to their records.[16]

3 Yet another pattern which was common in the period, especially in soul music, but also in Beat and rock-pop (which were so often very influenced by soul) is the tonal-European backing, very expressive, obvious and iconic, set against the highly intensional (in rhythm and timbre) performance of a foreground singer. This is a pattern found already in some of that soul music (especially slow ballads) which was aimed at (or at any rate only really registered with) blacks (such as Bobby Bland, Etta James). But more and more often in the late 1950s and 1960s, such records were made by soul-as-pop artists aiming at and reaching a mixed audience, such as Sam Cooke, Ray Charles and Otis Redding. On a hit such as Cooke's 'You Send Me', for example, female vocalists provide a simple chordal background, fully tonal-European in character, while Cooke indulges in tone-bending and melodic improvisation (Wo-wo-oh-oh-oh-oh, etc.) between the lyrical lines. This type of singing comes directly from the gospel tradition. The familiar chords of the setting offer a comfortable sound to white American and European ears, expressing a happy, contented feeling. Ray Charles had great successes in the early 1960s as a singer of ballads with almost no blues influence, except in his voice, and with some Country and Western influence in the chord structures and tunes, to a backing of his own piano and full string orchestra and sometimes a choir too. Following on from earlier artists like Nat King Cole, he allowed the natural 'edge', the *timbre* of his singing voice to do most of the work of making the foreground distinctive and memorable, and used only a limited amount of rhythmic intensionality or improvisation. Examples are 'I Can't Stop Loving You' and 'Take These Chains'. On these recordings, the 'backing' music is full of the 'romantic', 'sad' and 'heroic' icons of the tonal-European tradition. This was later taken further and made more of a *seamless* sound or fusion by artists like Stevie Wonder and Otis Redding (and their producers and arrangers),

again singers who had great success with whites as well as blacks, and influenced Beat music and other pop.

4 Now many British listeners of the early 1960s baulked at such mixtures, especially the use of 'sentimental' icons and 'big finishes'. The white rhythm 'n' blues movement offered them an alternative, as did the American 'folk' recordings of Dylan and others. Even there, however, icons are to be found, such as in the melodic shapes of some of Dylan's sombre or sorrowful lines, falling in pitch and harmonic tension in a manner which exactly fits Deryck Cooke's lexicon for the expression of pain, loss and heartache. Good examples are found in 'With God on Our Side', 'A Hard Rain's Gonna Fall' and 'The Ballad of Hollis Brown'. Of course, the matter is complex; it has also been suggested that these lines are descended via blues from African 'tumbling strains', or that they directly transcribe cries of distress.[17] There can, perhaps, be truth in *all* these views; such coincidences of several possible decodings would then account for the great *power* of certain tunes and sounds.

Meaning and pleasure

Finally, I will look briefly at the nature of the listener-responses to expressive and iconic elements in rock music. The first point is that, here again, an identification is fundamental. The recognition of the element as expressing something (an emotion, a concept) is a meeting of minds with the composer of the song. And the notion that *this* is what the music *means* (and by implication little or nothing else), functions for the listener as an affirmation of an existing conception in him or her of the self and the social world.

As we have seen, a common description of the feeling aroused by the end of a classical symphony or concerto is 'triumph'. The composer has individually succeeded in ordering the raw material expressively, and shaped it into a complex pattern which *resolves* itself at the end, producing a sense of summing up, completion or totality. The interior life has been demonstrated as malleable and controllable. Now Ray Charles's 'Take These Chains' and Presley's 'Its Now or Never' are not symphonies for all their orchestration and expressiveness, but they are heir to that tradition none the less, as it exists in the 'givens' of listeners. The expressiveness of the strings, choirs and 'big finishes' offers a residual, not-very-intense but quite definite measure of affirmation and triumph, in the above sense, to the listener. Listeners who are at home with the tonal-European code, and rather at sea with the Afro-American, will also find a reassurance in these elements, which disposes them to then enjoy any stranger elements, whereas they might otherwise 'switch off'. And when Gerry and the Pacemakers mixed Merseybeat-style drums and bass with a 'big finish' using a crescendo of strings in 'You'll Never Walk Alone', they achieved an expression of triumphalism which has become as familiar to many British people as the National Anthem or 'Land of Hope and Glory'.

We can surmise that widespread music-use that is high in icon-decoding, by reproducing a continuity in, or an existing pattern of, subjectivity (ego structure, self-conception, identifications with a certain type of other person) has, in its broad social impact, what can be called a conformity effect. It works by affirmation and reaffirmation of the listener's identity and sense of self, and it has this general effect across a wide population of listeners. This tends to give some support to the theses of Adorno and others[18] who fear that some sort of mass-conformism might flow from popular music-use. But it suggests that the 'hot' or 'wild' styles, the up-tempo, highly improvised, very 'intensional' styles, are *less* likely to produce it than the styles which perpetuate the icons of 'light music', or turn the isolable elements of jazz and blues into new icons.

A word of warning is appropriate here, however. It is *listening* which is crucial, not the mixing of elements by musicians as though following a recipe. Music which I enjoy for the *jouissance* it brings me may be earnestly enjoyed by another listener without much or any of that thrilling assault. It may remind him or her of a pleasant day out in 1963. Equally, I may be fairly indifferent or hostile to music which is someone else's access to *jouissance*. But broad patterns of preferences and listening styles will, I believe, always occur, corresponding to some extent at least to the potential meanings encoded by music-makers. Thus we may never be able to fully explain or predict the tastes of a given listener, no matter how much we know about him or her. But our understanding of overall trends and patterns of music-use is in no way invalidated by this.

Finally, a mention of 'resistance' again. Significance, the semiotic level and *jouissance* are all descriptions relating to a *deconstruction process* in the listening subject. They subvert certainty, they deny the subject the consolation of recognition, they remind the subject of the fragility of the surface of communication. In relation to dominant ideologies and world-sense, they can only encourage a radical questioning, albeit not an articulate one. The fact that we can detect pleasure in these aspects of rock music-use despite this disturbing aspect, *must* mean that the subject structure which is being deconstructed is itself oppressive to some degree, is frustrating, is susceptible to such questioning. Thus *jouissant* responses to singing-as-semiotic-speech, singing-as-musical-intensionality (foreground-artistry) and backing music which involves both intensional resources and 'beat', are all themselves 'resistances'. They resist the dominant world-sense by virtue of reproducing it differently, producing a knot of insubordination in the ongoing subjectivities of the makers and listeners. I will argue soon that they resist the very subject structure which goes along with that world-sense: 'controlled', highly individualistic, instrumental towards the body and the environment. This deep affinity, as *resistances*, between these various kinds of meanings involved in rock 'n' roll and Beat music-use, is what gives such music its power. These musical meanings all tend the same way, they pull together, and thus they achieve great importance in the lives of dedicated listeners and imitators, as opposed to the much more casual and deconcentrated music-use which tends to accompany 'softer' styles, styles full of icons and styles relying heavily on extra-musical identifications. This set of claims will now be examined more closely in the next chapter, and some historical perspective on it will be provided.

8 Notes Towards a History of Subjectivity: What the Study of Music-use can Contribute

White subjects and black music

One of the problems involved in writing about rock 'n' roll and related styles, which I raised in Chapter 1, is the question of white listeners and musicians taking up styles and techniques of black American origin. If we are dealing with a 'codal fusion' here, then what can it tell us about the black and white people involved? And, conversely, what do we need to understand about the people involved in order to explain the fusion process, and its occurrence at a particular time?

In *Pop Music and the Blues*,[1] Richard Middleton puts these questions at the very centre of an attempt to construct an overview of popular music history in this century. He sees white popular music since the 1950s in Britain and in America as 'the climax of a long attempt' by white people 'to come to terms with non-Western experience through the Negro and his music'.[2] His argument is that, through racist stereotyping, white people have projected on to blacks the quality of expressing and representing 'basic instinctual drives' which whites normally strive to repress. Blacks are believed to be more 'corporeal', more 'at home in their bodies', sexier, less uptight, more spontaneous and more laid-back than whites. And, at the same time, less self-controlled, less intellectual, less disciplined and less hard-working. In its least embarrassed form, this view attributes these supposed differences to a timeless racial character, something innate in body and brain. However, black Americans have achieved emancipation and, in several stages, a degree of social and economic integration. Whites, according to Middleton, have been gradually led to the realization, both conscious and unconscious, that 'black' qualities lurked within themselves, and that a pleasure could be had from relaxing the repressions, and opening up to black cultural expressions such as jazz, blues and certain dancing styles. The particular conjuncture of America in the 1950s (and Britain following closely behind), with the new scale of the music business, black stations on the radio, disaffected teenagers with disposable cash, etc., then provided favourable circumstances for a decisive step forward – at any rate in the areas of music and dance – in this ongoing process of 'coming to terms'.

This argument provides a good starting point for my purpose in this chapter. It draws attention to the centrality of the black Americans in forging this music, and to the importance of distinguishing immediate or *conjunctural* reasons (for a certain style of music doing well commercially) from the deeper underlying significance of what has turned out to be a historic and irreversible change in the sort of music-use practised by masses of white Americans and British people. But for all that, I think Middleton is wrong in some important ways. He argues at too general and abstract a level about whites and blacks, with little attention to factors of class, family life or religion, and, though anti-racist in spirit himself, he uses terms like 'the Negro' and 'Western' and 'non-Western' in over-generalized and unjustifiable ways to construct a dubious overarching thesis about 'basic drives' and the return of a sensual, relaxed subject banished from the white populations of Europe and America since the Renaissance.

Here I set out the basic steps in a reworking of these ideas which tries to avoid such failings:

1 Black American slaves, sharecroppers, wandering labourers and later urban ghetto-dwelling workers, their families, and the unemployed, have always enjoyed a musical life in which music-*making* ranks as an everyday and very widespread activity (more so than most white working- and middle-class people), and in which 'listening' is normally an involved, participatory experience of dancing, singing, playing and clapping along. This music owes something to African traditions, but is also formed by encounters with white American instruments, songs and hymns.[3]

2 The experiences of proletarianization and urbanization, undergone by masses of black men, women and children in the earlier part of this century, especially during the First World War and the 1920s – and followed by a slump which impoverished these urban blacks in the 1930s – were *responded to* in music-making and music-listening practices, and the process altered black American music profoundly, producing the set of styles broadly known as 'urban blues' or 'city blues', which I have described in Chapter 3. These styles achieved articulations of both individual and collective freedom, set against a sense of the socio-physical environment as alienating and oppressive.

3 The ability of white listeners to respond to the potential meanings in urban blues demonstrates that there is no secret racial code involved. The whites who refused to acknowledge the potential meanings of urban blues and rock 'n' roll did so either out of racism or because their musical 'givens' were relatively frozen at an earlier stage of codal fusion, or both. However, the whites who did respond sympathetically to the new music were not, *per se*, any less racist or even any less liable to resort if pressed to discourses of

'primitivism', 'voodoo dancing', black 'corporeality', and so on; merely they had discovered *pleasure* in these things, and felt defiantly ready to embrace and repeat that pleasure. Middleton feels that the stereotyping of blacks by whites had declined by the 1950s.[4] I am not at all sure this is a necessary part of the overall argument, though it may have been a contributory factor.

4 These discourses (of primitivism and corporeality) do *(mis)recognize* real differences between white and black American cultures. They misrepresent these *cultural* variations (rooted in different histories) as physiological, psychic and social differences of a more timeless, 'ontological' kind, constructing a category, 'race', of such transcendent dimensions that it becomes difficult (for white or black people believing some or all of these ideas) to see how it can ever dissolve away or even be altered. It becomes an apparently invariant datum of individual and social life. However, the cultural variations concerned do exist and do, of course, have (changing and complex) psychological and even physiological concomitants. Black American culture bears the marks of extremely intensive and specific oppression and the struggle against it, marks which white culture can never bear. The very prominence of music in black social life has to be seen as one such cultural difference (from whites) which can be historically explained (including reference 'back to Africa' and to the conditions of slave and post-slave black society), and also a *stereotype* used by white people to patronize blacks and to limit their access to other cultural areas. The stereotype then acquires or imbues practical and institutional forms, and thus itself reinforces that prominence.

   Among the so-called 'black qualities' which share this history are a less-repressed, secretive, 'Victorian' attitude to expressing one's physical presence, including sexuality, found in both sexes, and a tendency to be less 'uptight' about 'personal space', and touching – more friendly body-contact between friends, etc. – than is normal among American or British whites, especially if influenced by Puritan and Victorian religious and moral traditions. These things, which often go under the name 'corporeality' – do not add up to very much in themselves: equally noticeable contrasts in such personal and bodily behaviour can almost certainly be discerned between different classes and 'nationalities' within white society, both British and American, e.g. Italian Americans as against 'white Anglo-Saxon Protestants', or Irish workers in Britain in the nineteenth and early twentieth centuries. The so-called black qualities have their origins in a distinctive history, stretching back to Africa certainly, but very distinctive in its American phase too. Of course they inform black music-making and dance, it could not be otherwise. And to commentators and even participants, both black and white, music-making can come to seem like the most archetypal black cultural practice of all.

5 Of course it is at least equally important for a white author like myself to interrogate white working-class and middle-class cultures of the same periods, in America and Britain, and explain why these are like they are. Without such a step, the necessary *dialectical* approach to the music and

significance of codal fusion cannot be expected to develop. In other words, even quite insightful views of one or another 'black characteristic' in musical life, as in other areas, will remain within a *racist* problematic if they continue to be seen as explaining the digression of blacks from a white norm, or the survival of something in blacks which whites have outgrown.

6 It is important to remember what the main articulations of urban blues were, in relation to the social and physical environment. The experience of external, alienating time, and of an alienating, intrusive, oppressive urban soundscape, along with the experience of an impoverished working or non-working existence which afforded little or no access to individual or collective projects in which self-fulfilment or potentiation could be found – these experiences, and the fear, perplexity, boredom and loneliness they brought, were resisted through music-use, both individually and collectively, and a quasi-symbolic victory was won over them, and celebrated. The bitter experiences of boring, unfulfilling work, inadequate income and housing, the high cost of all but the most minimal entertainment and cultural life, the necessity for the individual to 'look out for number one' on the 'mean streets', despite any goodwill, any communal leanings he or she might have, the looseness and relative *distance* of family relationships where people moved around for work, lived in large numbers alone, or in difficult, transitory partnerships – when we list the experiences of the black urban poor (and not so poor, even) like this, we can see that they are a more *intense* and *more inescapable* version of the experiences of all working-class people, and indeed 'new middle-class' people too, in the urbanized, 'massified' environments of the modern Western nations. Certain differential further limitations on blacks *vis-à-vis* access to the labour market, housing, other provisions, 'civil society' and social contact with whites, vicious and vitally important though these have been, are to be understood as over and above (though crucially mediating and influencing) the basic experiences, which are not only universal to working-class blacks, but are known, perhaps less intensely by and large, to all working-class whites too. I believe that the sharing of these experiences, which at root are all consequences of capitalist economic and social relations in their highly developed modern stage of development (state involvement in the economy, monopolies, vast technological infrastructures, little if any survival of non- or pre-capitalist elements), is the true basis for the musical codal fusion of this century and especially since the 1950s. Putting it schematically, black Americans led the way (for reasons growing out of their history and that of whites) in discovering a resistant cultural response, in music-use, to the conditions of their life, and, in so far as those conditions are shared, white Americans, white British, white Europeans, and for that matter Japanese and South Americans, and even black and white Africans in South Africa, learnt to listen to what they did, to decode the pleasure-filled meanings, and to make the same sort of music themselves. They responded 'affectively' to musical meanings they could relate to. Some of them took the further step of a conscious interest in black culture, though many more did not.

However, there is more to the view of 'repressed whites learning to respond to primitive black music', as put forward by Middleton, than just the recognition of an attractive resistant ritual there. As we have seen, rock 'n' roll offered *jouissance* to sympathetic listeners, the 'harder' rock 'n' roll (and Beat and soul) offered more of this than the rock-pop and, no doubt, urban blues offered more still, to many young white listeners and especially imitators. Now *jouissance* is a loss of ego, a thrill of deconstruction of the subject. The ego is constructed by repression. *Jouissance* (whether occasioned by the singing or the dance-beat) is a repression lifted, an inhibition flouted, and thus a subject temporarily transformed, perhaps with lasting after-effects.

White listeners discovering black styles were discovering a music whose articulations went to the heart of the matter: these resistant meanings, in a context of alienating social relations and socio-physical conditions, actually reached deep into their subjectivities, the pre- and sub- and unconscious levels at which *world-sense* exists, and has 'affective' reality, and also, crucially, at which *jouissant* pleasure hits. Because black Americans led the way – for reasons arising out of their own history – there was a lot of easy, unintentionally racist discourse identifying these responses with 'blackness', 'race', 'ethnicity', and so on. The very eagerness and scale of the white take-up of these musical styles ought to have occasioned caution in such generalizing. But it did not. My belief is that there is nothing purely, or timelessly, or ontologically 'black' about this resistance, or about the *jouissance* it brings. Merely it has been easy to imagine that they involve an access of blackness, because of their history, and because we find it so difficult and challenging to think about these matters without mobilizing some time-honoured discourses to help us, by offering us their lexicons of stereotypes and labels.

The most frequently recurring concepts in this sort of discourse are the ideas of black 'corporeality' and 'primitivism'. These occur not only in discussions of music but also, very widely, in comments on popular dancing styles.[5] Thus the labelling of certain dances as 'corporeal', 'primitive', 'tribal' and so on works by denoting a certain dancing style while also connoting (and sometimes explicitly mentioning) the link with black Americans and Africans. Of course such usage does reflect the fact of undeniable black influence on white popular dancing styles, but it also expresses and promotes the assumption that something non-Western, alien and primitive is being imported. It is an easy, apparently obvious way of either damning or praising the new styles of dancing.

Now there may well be continuities of influence stretching right back to African roots, which a historical study of popular dance could establish. But I believe twentieth-century American and British popular dance styles, both black and white, must be seen as responses of the participants to their own contemporary social and physical environment, albeit responses which have made use of the existing dancing styles and traditions which were to hand. I have already put forward the idea of dance as a relaxing of the everyday control, 'instrumentalism' and 'puritanism' that people living and working in modern factories, offices and homes are obliged to practise, and also the idea of dance as a 'letting off of steam' by young people who are healthy yet doing little very strenuous work. To reach too hastily for notions like 'non-Western' and 'primitive' is to blind oneself to these types of explanation. And this is as true for musical styles as it is for dancing. If such grand cultural generalizations are finally to have any value, they must be gradually constructed through patient and sensible examinations of actual practices, and abstraction therefrom, rather than being imported as ready-made and flabby totalizations, vague enough to contain almost anything, and even replete with echoes of their racist origins.

In a recent book, David Hatch and Stephen Millward[6] have assembled a lot of evidence that black and white American musical traditions (both gospel and blues), as well as dancing, are even more intermingled in fact than I have allowed up to now. We must envisage a culture in the USA in which people with 'one eighth or one sixteenth black blood'[7] can be legally segregated, as happened until the 1960s in some states. Many of these none the less did sometimes or always 'pass for white'. It has also been estimated that over 20 per cent of those known as 'white Americans', as a whole, probably have some black ancestry. These facts give a much more confused picture than I have so far assumed. The basic separateness (segregation) of poor rural black communities in the South, and of the urban ghettos of the earlier part of this century, is still apparent. But the existence of inter-racial cultural forms must not be denied or underestimated. A major early example is the nineteenth-century (and early twentieth) religious camp meeting, where African rituals of music and dance often re-emerged in Christianized form as 'ring shouts' involving both black and white participants.[8] It also seems, from Hatch and Millward's study, that a small minority of whites, or more-or-less-whites, took part fully in the development of Country blues, boogie guitar and piano styles, urban blues and soul music. This, of course, in no way invalidates my notion of an 'Afro-American' code, though it emphasizes even more strongly that what distinguishes the code is the deep assumptions involved in and reproduced by it, rather than simply the exclusive listing of recordings by blacks, or songs classifiable in some technical way as blues. We must reject once and for all such ideas as the famous dictum 'White men cannot sing the blues'.

These considerations make it very clear that grand overviews of black and white subjectivities, and personal and cultural qualities, which do not accord proper weight to the realities of various groups, classes, localities, historical movements of population, religious influences, and so on, are likely to be seductive nonsense. 'Race' is a socially constructed category, and it is constructed largely to oppress, to victimize, to excuse, to mystify and to patronize. As such, it is at best a shibboleth, even when employed by well-intentioned, 'anti-racist' writers. It cannot simply be 'used' in the construction of historical overviews, etc.; it must be deconstructed, criticized, problematized. Elements misrecognized in it must be drawn out and closely examined so that they can be better understood.

The 'ego-cogito' and its history

In the past 20 years, in the fields of media studies (especially film), the 'structuralist/Marxist debate' and feminist studies, a new theoretical approach to subjectivity has gradually emerged.[9] This approach, broadly speaking, sees the *subject* as the ever-developing *product and means of an individual's social existence*. In contrast to the traditional philosophical view of an 'ideal' or 'transcendental' subject which stands outside culture and intervenes in it, while remaining an unchanged entity, some authors have gone almost to the opposite extreme, seeing the subject as a mere node in a set of overlapping discursive fields, a spectre at the feast of signs, summoned and exorcized by address and reference, and having no independent, continuous existence of its own. I believe that a middle view is both possible and necessary, grasping that the subject is produced and reproduced by acts of signification (encoding/decoding), but according it also a relative autonomy, a continuity between acts, which influences the orientation of the subject in each new instance. This autonomy is sited in the intersection of the social and the biological, it derives from the particular character of the brain and the body, particularly the existence of *memory*, and the fact that the individual can speak, see and hear. Furthermore, we must not imagine that signifying practices are the *whole* of social reality. It is also produced by labour – the transforming of matter and the consequent production of physical contexts and conditions for other acts. Indeed, it is basically out of such actions that human 'ideas' and 'signs' are themselves generated. The subject must be seen as the subject of actions of all sorts, not just sign-making. The consequence of all this is that subjects, even those in close cultural proximity to each other, and of similar ages, physical needs, etc., do not all respond predictably and identically to a given address. The address 'interpellates' a certain response, certainly, and broad similarities in the way different subjects respond to it can be discerned and related analytically to this interpellation, but deviant, minority, mixed and rogue responses are found to occur in large numbers whenever such situations are studied. Individual subjects vary in countless and complex ways.

Now the 'founding fathers' of this kind of study, such as Freud, Jung, Fromm and Marcuse, were all inclined to argue rather too easily and blandly *from* their view of the subject and the individual (ego and id, etc.) *to* their view of social and cultural history.[10] Often they relied on little more than a rough analogy between the life of an individual from childhood to maturity, in states of sanity or madness, and the life of society, from 'early' times to the maturity of the modern bourgeois world (or the socialist world soon to come), in madness (war, anti-semitism, etc.) and in sanity (full of strong egos and super-egos). But since Lacan and others started off the process in the 1960s, a more sophisticated way of relating psychoanalytic theory to history has been devised, still making use of the concept of the ego as a part or aspect of subjectivity, and analysing how it becomes involved in language and other signs (the *ego-cogito*), and thus in ideology, artistic production and so on, while always remembering that, just as there is more to the Freudian 'psyche' than an ego, so there is more to the cultural subject than the 'ego-cogito' which is expressed in the 'rational' aspects of signifying practice.

Barthes introduces his idea of the 'ego-cogito' in his brief but influential discussions of 'signifiance'.[11] He suggests that the subject of language (and by implication other signs) involves an 'ego-cogito', which is required for, and reproduced by the use and understanding of significant language, it is the 'subject' which can 'predicate' objects and other people, addressing, referring and describing in a 'rational' way which other 'ego-cogitos' can, hopefully, grasp. But signifying practice also involves 'other logics' that 'deconstruct' the ego, and in which the 'ego is lost'. It is implicit in this argument that working-class and middle-class people – women and men, boys and girls, black and white people, Americans and British – in so far as they can all use and understand significant language to and with each other, in speech and writing, and through the new media, all share the 'ego-cogito' aspect of subjectivity. It is a development of their subjectivity, rooted in the 'ego' as posited by Freud, which privileges the use of language as a functional tool for survival and social success, and represses elements which might threaten this. 'Educated' or 'cultured' people will clearly be more confirmed and assured in this development than less educated, less cultured people, but, to a degree, it will be found in virtually everyone in the society. It should not, however, be equated with 'knowledge' or the higher flights of philosophical 'Reason'. It is the thorough-going instrumental approach to language, and to one's own time, body and potential, which defines the 'ego-cogito', rather than any particular excellence in the pursuit of truth. It is the 'rationalizing' of one's personal means to one's social ends, from scientific discovery at one extreme to efficient work at the other, and the ability to dominate and manipulate other people in pursuit of those ends, where applicable. Specifically, it is the mastery of language and other signifying practices involved in achieving all these things.

The 'ego-cogito' aspect of subjectivity can be surmised to exist to some extent in all cultures. It is difficult to imagine any significant degree of human cooperation (let alone domination, exploitation, legitimation) without it. But in the highly organized large societies of the 'capitalist world', with highly technified production methods and complex political spheres, the degree to which people are obliged to develop the 'ego-cogito', and by corollary repress all the other aspects or phases of subjectivity, is probably greater than any-where else in the world, and greater than at any earlier time in history. A suggestion of Marcuse (which is also taken up by Middleton in his discussion of rock 'n' roll and blues) might be helpful here.[12] He considers Freud's notion of the 'reality principle', which is the key component of ego development, being a process by which the human psyche learns to forego immediate gratification in the pursuit of a more satisfying one later. Marcuse suggests that in the highly rationalized and organized societies of the modern West, this principle is intensified into a 'performance-principle', in which peoples' ego development and self-discipline are developed, by competition, to a higher level than the mere 'reality principle', as they struggle not merely to survive and satisfy basic needs but to be 'successful' over the above the social norm, and to 'do down the next man'.

This highly intense and developed ego structure has not arisen out of a mere internal development of the human mind, or even out of a free, context-less development of signifying practices or discourses divorced from other material practices. It stems from adaptations made by people to the social and physical structures, especially central ones such as work, which have surrounded and reproduced them, over a period of three or four centuries of rapid technical, social and political development. We cannot grasp the scope and the limitations of the modern 'ego-cogito' except in relation to structures of social production, reproduction and economic exchange; certainly 'discourses' alone cannot account for it, since they themselves would then be unaccountable.

Let me examine this area a little more closely. The centuries-old archetype of the capitalist or bourgeois is of a man who practises self-discipline, mainly in the forms of saving and hard work, and expects self-discipline of others. He (it is usually a 'he') is willing to impose discipline where it is lacking. He makes production or investment decisions based on an informed assessment of the future, and generally then sticks with the project, if possible, until it shows a profit; but he avoids the sentimentality or obsessiveness which might prevent him from missing the 'main chance' in some other area. The mastering of emotions, the willingness to defer reward, the respect for 'Reason', which in practice means respecting applicable knowledge rather than abstract speculation – not so much Reason as 'reasonable' thinking – all these familiar ideal features of the capitalist can be found again and again in the philosophical and historical writings, the fiction, and the educational practices of the seventeenth century onwards, in Britain and elsewhere in Europe and North America. What is involved is a type of *subject* the bourgeois tries to be, imagines himself to be, and sometimes more or less succeeds in being. If 'Enlightenment' and 'Reason' were the original philosophers' terms (following Descartes and others) for this spirit, the ideas of Rousseau, of Adam Smith, Bentham and Ricardo, and later the nineteenth-century utilitarian thinkers (J.S. Mill, Herbert Spencer, W.S. Jevons, Alfred Marshall) translated it into more pragmatic and popular terms and achieved wide influence in doing so.[13]

What is perhaps more problematical to historians is the hold of these ideas on working-class people; or to be precise, of similar, but differently accented ideas. This partly came about (in Britain, the eighteenth and nineteenth centuries were the years involved) through the reality and the surrounding myth of universal access to the capitalist route to personal 'improvement'. For some working people – craftsmen, sailors, people with a smattering of literacy – this had a degree of truth: the 'self-made man'. However, it was a very attenuated development, as Hobsbawm points out.[14] First, the very development of capitalist enterprises requires that people be proletarianized in larger numbers than they rise to the position of bourgeois – 'hands' are needed for labour; and, secondly, the problem of obtaining some starting capital effectively blocked many ambitious men, with the result that they tended to rise, if at all, not through business or manufacture so much as through certain professions, from the humbler clerks to the clergymen, civil servants and teachers.

Perhaps more important than this in remaking the subjectivities of working people was a process of disciplining them more or less into a simplified, truncated mirror-image of the bourgeois' own self-conception. The process (in Britain) has been traced many times and from different points of view, but one of the most interesting recent studies is that in Zygmunt Bauman's *Memories of Class*, and also a later essay 'Industrialism, consumerism and power'.[15] There he argues that the population explosion of the eighteenth century put a breaking strain on the old institutions of the parish, and led to surplus populations escaping the discipline and surveillance which had been unconsciously built into the old system. New methods of disciplining and controlling the 'dangerous classes' had to be devised, with a degree of deliberation or consciousness of purpose not previously necessary. Specialist institutions were needed.

The factory system was, in Bauman's view, at least as much the consequence of this need as of any grasp of its profit-potential, at any rate in the very early years of its development. Factory labour (men, women and children) was often recruited from the poor-house, and factories had dormitories attached. Petty rules proliferated, with severe punishments for offenders. Grouping together was discouraged, in case it engendered resentments. The end-product was the nearest Britain ever came to having a large supply (indeed a surplus) of unskilled physical labour-power, in more or less equal, interchangeable and mobile units of one body each. The rules of these institutions, and later less draconian ones, extended to the 'labouring poor' the bourgeois prohibitions and restrictions on certain bodily processes, the disciplining of the body's rhythms and needs in relation to time, and the acceptance of working for pay, that is a 'market-orientation' which rested on the notion that the worker selling chunks of labour-power is no different from the trader selling anything else at a price. Bauman then develops his argument into more controversial and original claims, which I need not recap here.

The attitudes and habits which were effectively imposed on the workers by these developments were, of course, to a large degree modelled on the existing bourgeois self-conception. It could not have been otherwise. In many writings of the time, society was conceptualized as a school for the civilizing of the masses[16] whose 'coarse' and 'animal' habits, and unresponsiveness to the chances of great reward, were seen as both obstacles to progress in general and sins of the individual. Many schools were set up to play their part in this civilizing process. Churches, especially Methodist and 'Low' churches, also played a key role, with their revival of puritanism, emphasizing work discipline and sobriety and also the civilizing importance of family-life.[17] As a result of all these efforts (and of the collective and individual 'self-improvements' achieved, often through hard struggle, by the working people themselves), it can be justly said that by the end of the nineteenth century many of the 'refinements' of the upper classes of the seventeenth and eighteenth centuries had become incorporated into the 'decency' or 'respectability' of the working class. Indeed, a 'level' of social behaviour, hygiene, basic knowledge (literacy and numeracy) and Christian moral formation was found widely among working-class people, compared to which the lusty and ignorant hedonism of a part of the land-owning class of only a century or so earlier, would itself have seemed coarse and animal-like.[18]

These habits, moral attitudes and assumptions about society, 'fairness' and so on, add up to a sort of social contract by which working-class people function in a bourgeois world, making of their bodies objects for sale, but dignifying the procedure through ideas of free exchange and duty. Such ideas, habits and assumptions are found in conscious forms, in linguistic and written discourses, but also become deep structures of the individual subject. They become elements of 'world-sense' as well as that narrower ideology which is language and image-bound (see Chapter 2). They 'govern' communication among people, and between the classes, and are reproduced through and by it. They become, in fact, the 'ego-cogito' in each person, and the 'policemen' of its concomitant repressions.

So far in this account I have presented the development of subjectivities not only in a very generalized way but also as though it were mainly a one-way process, whereby outside agencies 'mould the individual', at any rate the working-class individual. In fact, of course, people resist, negotiate and escape this moulding in various ways, as well as exerting their own reciprocal influences on the outside agencies. This is true of individuals, groups and whole classes, and it takes place not only at the level of material practices and more or less consciously articulated ideas, but also at the deeper levels I have referred to. This very broad notion of resistance (including escape, negotiation and the 'expropriation' of meanings) is the wider context in which the modern youth-cultural resistance I have described earlier must be seen. And most particularly the 'resistant' articulations found in music-making and music-listening are to be seen as ways in which the received 'deeper structures' of world-sense and subjectivity itself are resisted, and reproduced in new and different ways.

As a result, then, of the different life-experiences of working-class people, as opposed to the bourgeois, and specifically as a result of the interaction of the pressures and necessities of life in a bourgeois world with the various resistances and negotiations working people make, a working-class way of experiencing and relating to certain aspects of the urban industrial environment has developed. This *way* has shared in the bourgeois assumptions about the body, time, exchange of labour power for money, etc., on the one hand, and yet simultaneously has incorporated a different and distinct response to these constructions. For example, as I have already remarked, both classes have seen *time* as rigid, measured and external, but it has meant something quite different, by virtue of this, to the worker from what it has meant to the bourgeois. To the worker, the externality, linearity and rigidity of time was/is almost wholly a threat and a limitation: 'my time is not my own'. To the bourgeois it is partly this, but it is also the instrument of acquiring interest and wealth, and realizing surplus value on labour-power. Working people have jobs, whereas capitalists and professionals have 'careers'. Therefore, on a basis of agreement about 'how time is' – which has a function in the reproduction of both the means and the social relations of production – two (at least) very different conceptions of 'what this means for me' arise. And the worker is likely to resist the oppressiveness, the alienated-ness of this experience in a unique way arising out of this difference.

An example is provided by some research done into 'streetcorner' black men in Washington DC in the 1960s.[19] The 'fecklessness' of these men, drifting in and out of jobs, blowing a week's pay on a binge, etc., had been seen by various commentators as evidence of a different time-sense from that normal in the society, among 'steady workers' or the middle class. These men were said to 'live for the present' and to be 'unable to defer reward or pleasure'. Elliot Liebow, on the other hand, gathered evidence to suggest that it was the very sense of the 'inevitable future', the 'linear and irreversible progress of time and life' – which these men shared with others in the society – that led them to a sense of futility and despair, since that future held no 'prospects', no progression into affluence, for these unskilled and despised people. The same sense of time, then, in one aspect, but a very different response to it in another. And, incidentally, music-use would probably play a considerable part in the leisure of these men. Washington DC emerged in the 1970s and 1980s as a leading centre of black American musical innovation.

In broader terms, there flourishes in the working and 'new' middle classes an instrumental, disciplined, long-term approach to the *use* of one's body and mind, within a market situation, to achieve a 'livelihood'. The life which is thus guaranteed must itself be adjusted to the need of reproducing one's labour power, or maintaining oneself as an exchange-value. And the individual is likely to be unevenly, intuitively and contradictorily *aware* of this to some extent. This approach functions as a limitation, a mechanism of repression, in relation to all sorts of bodily and other impulses which might threaten the successful reproduction, from wanting to escape the routine in general to drinking too much and being unable to get up in the morning. It involves the 'ego', and perhaps what Freud calls the 'super-ego' within the subject, maintaining constant control over the other processes of the subject, and 'rationalizing' this task in terms of the ideologies of submission, patience and acceptance of the present environment and social relations as permanent and perhaps natural. The expression or realization of *this* sort of ego in language and other signifying practices (including music) is the working-class (and new middle-class) 'ego-cogito'.

To return now to music, if it is true that something like this 'ego-cogito' subject-structure is to be found throughout the working- and middle-class populations of Britain (and indeed America), though with variations of type and degree, then *all* music-use must relate to it in some way, reproducing it, challenging it, bypassing it and so on. This is what I will go on to consider, beginning with some general considerations which are necessary to the argument.

The ears cannot be closed as the eyes can, nor can they be focused in more than a very elementary way. There is thus something imperious, present and unavoidable in sound. Here is what the American composer Aaron Copland says about it:

> You may be sitting in a room reading this book. Imagine one note struck upon the piano. Immediately that one note is enough to change the atmosphere of the room, proving that the sound element in music is a powerful and mysterious agent which it would be foolish to deride or belittle.[20]

Everyone within earshot of a sound hears it, though people may not *listen* intently. On the other hand, several people may all direct their eyes differently on the same street or in the same room, looking at only what they choose. Whereas the eye has become (historically and 'pre-historically') an instrument of, and a function of, individualized, active choice – deliberateness involving consciousness – though it always remains also more than this, the ear has retained a passivity which precludes it from such a function. The eye's movements around the room can be truly called *subjective* (having objects and expressing a subject's relationship to them), the ear's cruder operation can hardly be so called, and hardly expresses anything. The ear has come to seem like an enclave of undifferentiated human stuff, a bit of the ancient suspended in the uneven historicized mix of an individual subject's 'human nature'. The association of music with cult and ritual, the threat which some authors, following Plato, have discerned in it in relation to social order and rationality, the myth of its power over the mentally handicapped: all these discourses can be seen in the framework I am outlining.

I think we must understand that this underdevelopment of the ear persists within a subject-structure which is, in modern times, dominated by an alliance between language and a visual definition of experience and reality.[21] Words correspond to 'things' and things are visible; though words originate as oral-aural sounds they are, in Western literate cultures, given an authoritative visual equivalent in writing and print, which abolish almost totally the semiotic moment of speech as opposed to the symbolic. Only in a minority of written or printed messages (some poems, perhaps) does reading aloud add anything much to the process of decoding. Now the modern 'ego-cogito' is necessarily formed by *this* kind of language, by literacy, and also by a 'literal', visually-dominated approach to 'reality' which sees the environment as an assembly of visible, predicable, usable, exploitable things, and suspects other kinds of perceptions as 'irrational'. Thus language, and an alliance with visuality expressed in print and writing, have come to predominate over other signifying practices, becoming the main signifying practice of the culture. The 'ego-cogito' necessarily embodies this pre-eminence of language in the culture. Musicality is necessarily a marginal aspect of it, even that musicality which largely accepts the 'ego-cogito', the musicality of the tonal-European code.

In this traditional view of the subject, the emotions, bodily processes and affective states are not denied but rationalized; they are given names, and assigned causes and effects. The subject is supposed to intercept his or her own feelings with these tags and explanations, and so to master the 'instinctual and emotional life'. And he or she is supposed to do this alone, as an individual, as a precondition for entering civilized social intercourse. (The supposedly impaired capacity of *women* to do this, according to the traditional discourse, lies at the root of the maleness which this category – subject, Man, human being – normally exhibits.) To people who 'know' themselves through this discursive framework, the unrestrained experiencing of the unsignified, of unwilled bodily and emotional states and changes, feelings and affects, in their 'pre-categorical' reality, is felt as a *threat*, a loss, a deconstruction of that individualized subjectivity whose 'bulwarks' are those of language. It may also be vaguely felt to be 'effeminate'. And of course this goes for not only the experience of 'mysterious' musical affects but *also* the giving up of the symbolic significance of a word or phrase which is involved in experiencing 'signifiance' or the 'semiotic level' in singing.

In the context of a culture which holds up the 'ego-cogito' as the acme of cultured, individualized subjectivity, this sort of experience is seen as a 'loss' of subjectivity or 'ego', to which a 'thrill' attaches. This thrill will be made up of the 'primary' pleasure or stimulus derived from the sounds of the music or the voice, mixed with the excitement of giving up something, of 'letting oneself go', the frisson of guilt, mystery and fear associated with the sense of loss.[22] It is, in both aspects, a thrill of *jouissance*. And, by a crucial, historically produced nexus or association, this loss of subjectivity, of a certain sort, can be seen to be also a loss of individualism. It threatens the individualized subject with a shift (which may seem to him or her and to observers to be a 'regression') into a less individualized, as it were pre-Cartesian, even 'pre-Renaissance' or 'non-Western' state. An element which is held to be shared and undifferentiated in people (the ear, the affects it can bring, imperiously and pre-categorically) is made, for a time, *more prominent* in the structure of the subject, by such listening, while the masterful, controlling, integrating, individually developed intellect, the 'ego-cogito', based as it is on an alliance of language and visuality, is made relatively less prominent.

It is necessary here to be quite clear: I believe the reproduction of the subjectivity of a rock or Beat listener (temporarily, but surely with longer-lasting repercussions) as more communally inclined, less individualistic, less needful of the verbal handle at all times, less uptight about the body, and so on, is *not* a regression, and is not the re-emergence of a '*pre*-anything' state. Neither is it 'non-Western'. The study of the cultures of pre-Renaissance Europe, of the 'Third World' and of various minorities in the First World, may serve the salutary purpose of *reminding* the student of the impermanence, the relativity, the fragility, of aspects of our culture now, which might otherwise seem immutable or natural. They may even offer hints as to *where* to look for resistance, for progress and change, for the hidden springs of future action. But the new young people, making and made by the new music, among other things, are not 'primitives' or 'savages'. To call teenagers a 'tribe', for example, as is often done by music critics and others, can be no more than racist analogy. And analogy is a most dangerous foundation for totalizing theories. Teenagers learning to play and enjoy Beat music, urban blues, soul and jazz, students caught up in a British rhythm 'n' blues boom, and so on, these are all people responding in a new way, to new conditions, and this new way can certainly co-exist with a deep knowledge of, and immersion in, the culture of the European and American past. It is not inherently inimical to the survival of tonal-European music. Nothing is truly 'lost', though everything is criticized from a new vantage point. There is no need to speak of cultural regression, even though we need not feel the need to affirm the development as progress on all fronts.

Of course, when participants in and observers of the new music-use speak of 'loss', they are right up to a point. Certainly, the *jouissance* of the singing voice and the dance-beat poses a challenge to the 'ego-cogito'. To the extent that people do actually produce in themselves a 'self-disciplined', instrumental, 'ego-cogito-in-charge' structure of subjectivity, they experience the new music as loss, and are right to do so. But in so far as they believe this to be entirely negative, and perhaps regressive, they are misrecognizing it. They are missing the exciting communality, and also the potential benefits of release from the 'ego-cogito' which others enjoy in their listening and music-making. The fact that we can use the terms 'loss' and 'release' for the same experience is itself instructive: the sort of subject we are discussing is *both* oppressor and oppressed, *both* gaoler and prisoner, in the sense that the 'ego-cogito' within the subject disciplines and represses the rest of the subject, and the body. The effort and the burden of sustaining this state of affairs takes a toll, so that a person can feel *released* (or relieved) by music which challenges it, and can have his/her 'batteries recharged', can emerge happier, from a listening or music-making experience in which *jouissant* pleasure and a 'free' communality have figured, and perhaps an implicit Utopianism has been affirmed.

We are now in a position to place tonal-European music and Afro-American music as relatively different organizations of the (semiotic) resources used in music and different productions and reproductions of the subjects involved. The former can be seen as a sustained effort to *dam* the tide of semiotic impulses, or to keep 'signifiance' at bay so that a limited type of signifi*cance* can flourish. To achieve these aims, it leans heavily on exegetic and technical language, not only in the training of executants but also in guiding listeners in the 'right' directions, telling them what they are hearing. A point is reached where, as Barthes says,[23] an *adjective* is always on the tip of the tongue, in the listener's response to any piece of this music. This situation not only covers technical description, but (even more so for the 'ordinary' listener) it also applies to 'expression': the music is happy, sad, noble, pastoral, tragic, etc. The musical *icons* I have described at an earlier point acquire their definiteness and repeatability not only from being familiar in themselves to listeners, but also because they can be, and are, *paired off with words*. It is as though music is striving to be like referential language, so as not to endanger, or even so as to reinforce, the 'ego-cogito' produced by such language.

But the tones, rhythms and *timbres* which make up this (instrumental) music remain, ultimately, non-referential. There would be little point in constructing a musical way of making a few very simple statements, or commands or questions, when we already know how to handle millions of more complex ones in words, spoken and written. The pleasure derived from 'proper' listening to this music is primarily *plaisir*, and consists in recognizing and responding to expressive icons in the context of an identification with the composer and his mastery and eventual triumph over his 'materials'. Yet, ironically, it must be the initial reliance on something in the sounds and rhythms chosen by the composer which distinguishes them, and makes them more than just ciphers of expression, which causes a composition, whether vocal or instrumental, to be held to be good or notable or great. For what else can it be? It surely cannot be the mere manipulation of a system of tones, and mere construction of a preconceived 'form' out of them, or the mere success of a simple triumphant statement, such as 'I am happy'.

Thus we have reached the *crux* of the contradiction which lies at the heart of tonal-European music. It relies for much of its power, its ability to *affect* people, on the semiotic reverberations which accompany even its most obvious icons, the signifiance which constantly lurks between tones and rhythms, and refuses to be turned into just another means of 'cold' reference. If tonal music is in the first place an effort to dam the tide of semiotic impulses, then it is also 'the turbine below the dam' – it needs the rush of endless water yet it can only be realized when the water is properly dammed up and limited in its volume and velocity, by the composer, so as to allow the creation of its properly formed and limited products.

Afro-American music, and the music of codal fusion, owe their existence to the arrival on the historical scene of a new kind of human being, or at any rate the beginnings of one. The music can only be grasped in this context. These new people are far from being 'bourgeois' in their class position. Yet they live in a capitalist world, and this has consequences: the labour market at its most brutally atomizing and competitive, the experience of having to migrate to find work, the relative or even total dissolution of the family structure, the overwhelming social odds which weigh on them in the form of wage-slavery or unemployed powerlessness, the repressive rule of the state and even the benevolent interference of its agencies. The archetypes of this position are to be found in many countries. But nowhere more clearly (in the 'First World') than in black America. And, as we have seen, these people *had a music*, and special reasons to cling to it, both making and listening. In their hands and voices, the music mutated into the blues, jazz, rhythm 'n' blues and soul.

The constituencies for these styles, first in black America and later all over the Western world and even beyond, can be described as the 'mass' of people, wage-dependent or unwaged, lacking access to the levers of political or economic power in any degree, organized and manipulated by myriad regulations and laws (policed by agencies of the state), oppressed by formal and informal penalties in the event of their stepping out of line, and possessing only few and weak organizations of their own through which to resist this manipulation and oppression. They are not necessarily always very poor, hungry or hounded. But they are alienated in and out of work, relatively powerless, and subject to the atomization of the labour market, the state and the mass media. And they are not normally in a position to experience first-hand the world-changing projects of the industrialist or the scientist, or to 'fulfil themselves' in paid work which really expresses or develops their creative talents.

These 'masses' of people share the 'ego-cogito' structure of the bourgeois epoch, in the qualified or 'truncated' sense I have outlined, yet they derive little or no benefit from it. Their 'careers', personal lives and destinies express at every turn a stark contrast between potential and fulfilment, between a world 'out there' of endless promises and possibilities and a life 'back here' or 'down here' hemmed in by responsibilities, lack of money, fear and often an utter lack of self-belief outside of the daily round.

Of course this is a deliberately grim picture. There are other less depressing things in working-class (and middle-class) life. But I would argue that all of these flow, in some sense, from *resistance*: in so far as the economic system and its ramifications for social life prescribe the limits, the necessities and the obstacles to freedom for working people, by forming the only basis for continued survival, then all the practices by which they subvert the necessities, bypass or overturn the obstacles and escape the consequences, are *resistant not only in virtue of being defined against* a hostile social and physical environment, but also, crucially, because these practices then enter into the production of the future, so that today's obstacle overcome lays a basis for a greater freedom and a 'higher' level of resistance tomorrow. Not always, or necessarily so, but always *potentially*.

In the new Afro-American-influenced music-use which spreads so fast throughout the West during the 1950s and 1960s, such people discover a new, major means of resistance, one which actually challenges, and offers some relief from, the very 'ego-cogito' itself, its repressiveness, and its highly individualistic character. In the dancing which accompanies the 'beat' of the music, in the small group-based amateurism which spreads dramatically in this period, in a new kind of singing and in the decline of language-about-music which accompanies the new music-use – in all these aspects the new kind of resistance is revealed. Indeed, it is my opinion that these features cannot really be accounted for in any other way.

This, then, is the last of my most central claims for rock 'n' roll and Beat music-use. In making and using such music, and other related styles, young people of the working *and* middle classes in Britain were *transforming themselves*, reproducing their own subjectivities in a new shape. That shape was less individualistic (in the competitive 'performance-orientated' sense) and more communally-inclined. And it was associated with an experience of *jouissant* pleasure arising from the challenge the music mounted to the pre-eminence of the 'ego-cogito' within the subject.

As we have already seen, although mingled with other types of identification which were of a very different order, there was a central identification with the musical group, and with other listeners, involved in this music-use, which was quite simply 'free'. Free in the sense that it was not coerced or institutionalized, and did not involve domination. To claim 'I am a rock 'n' roll fan'

or a 'Beat musician' in 1960 was a gesture against the institutions, a claiming of personal autonomy, cultural rights, space to be different, time to
'potentiate' oneself in a (relatively) new, exciting, deviant and pleasurable
way. To enjoy rock music was to enjoy the shedding of some of the inhibited-
ness, the non-corporeality, the tension, the up-tightness, the cerebral-ness, the
stiffness, of a subjectivity heavily dominated by the 'ego-cogito'. It was a
loosening up which people (still after all having to function and survive in an
alienating socio-physical environment) found pleasurable in a particular way,
and found some compensation or release in, when counterposed to the rest of
their everyday lives.

Conclusions: Taking Popular Music Seriously

In *The Story of Rock*, Carl Belz discusses what he calls the 'folk responses' of the teenage dancers on the 'American Bandstand' TV show of the early and mid-1950s. He writes:

> . . . a panel of three or four teenagers periodically reviewed newly released records. The record was played, the audience danced, and a discussion of the song's merits followed. The discussion invariably contained remarks such as 'It's got a great beat . . . I'll give it 85'. The panellists never talked about the artistic properties of the record: the way the song was structured, the relation between its structure and meaning, its manipulations of the medium, the implications of its content or any of the kinds of issues that are central to a meaningful statement about a work of fine art.[1]

Now I do not think Belz's fine art/folk art distinction is really very useful. But he certainly points to something important here, which I have commented on at several points myself. It is true that in abandoning the discourses of training and criticism even more so than in jazz practice or jazz-influenced pop, rock 'n' roll listeners and makers alike move close to folk-music practice – the closest ancestor here, as in the music-making itself, is probably that quasi-folk-music, the urban blues.

The youth culture, however, is not a true *community*. It only exists in small groups, mainly in leisure hours, and forming at most a *layer* of society, mingled in everyday life with other layers. Such a 'layer' cannot have its own folk music in the traditional sense of the term. Even the black American ghettos of the 1930s and 1940s were not true communities in every sense, but they were far more nearly so than the fragile groups of the youth culture. The conditions for any cultural practice to flourish in the youth culture are only ever present in a fragile, embattled and fleeting way, continually destroyed and recreated over quite short periods. There is no such thing as a long teenage career, and youth culture provides neither the time nor the resources to its participants for central binding institutions to develop, training schemes or refresher courses. This very fragility tends to reinforce the characteristic retreat from verbalization of musical meanings and responses, all the more so since the routes to verbalization available in the received discourses of the parent culture (through school, the press, TV and radio) are of the sort which (in the 1950s especially) habitually undervalue and/or patronize popular and folk musics. Why however does music-use *survive* this fragility, and this turn-over of participants, which necessarily characterize the youth culture? Why indeed should music play a *more* central part in this fragile youth culture than in more established and slowly changing cultures?

The very unverbalizability of musical meanings, *especially* of *jouissant* pleasures and world-sense articulations, their very intractability as objects of study, their mystery, must be seen as part of the attraction, as it were, of music as a central constitutive practice of youth culture. In the same way as blues and other music have formed the *unpoliceable core* of American black culture, from before the Emancipation right through to the urban ghettos, so the youth culture has crystallized and reproduced itself around the mystery of rock 'n' roll. Male teenagers have made of this music the core of their lifestyle and the chief component of the social cement which has held it together. Its very incomprehensibility to others, its secret character, have made it precious. The distrust and rejection of 'pseudish' criticism and scholarly treatises, which have always characterized both the artists and audiences of rock 'n' roll, can thus be quite clearly related to this new centrality of music within the youth culture and especially its sub-cultures such as Teds, Mods and Rockers.

In the 1950s and early 1960s, there was a virtually total *ignoring* of rock, Beat, soul and rhythm 'n' blues music in the schools, in the press, on the radio and even in some of the specialist 'popular music' papers. The defenders of the elitist discourse of 'musicality as a rare gift', and the rest of the assumptions of the tonal code, did not really enter the battle for the hearts and minds of the young with much vigour. They condemned from *outside*, betraying their ignorance even while boasting their knowledge, and thus tended only to reach 'like minds'. The kids blissfully ignored them. If there had been a serious and widely read rock press, in which folk, jazz and classical enthusiasts wrote about their doubts and dislikes alongside rock and Beat fans expressing their enjoyment, it might actually have been detrimental to the new music-use in those early years. The culture of rock 'n' roll and British Beat flourished in a Hi-de-Hi-holiday-camp-like atmosphere of cheerful anti-intellectualism and vulgarity, blissfully ignoring what the rest of the world might think.[2]

This most certainly did not mean that incompetence reigned. It is a matter of record that musicians who were competent in other, often more 'acceptable' musical styles (i.e. Country and Western, jazz, rhythm 'n' blues) played and sang on, or produced, the 'crude' records of Presley, Little Richard, etc. In Britain, big-band instrumentalists and jazzmen, whose high skills often did not make them much of a living at the time, doubled anonymously as backing musicians on skiffle and early rock records and on live tours.[3] 'Mainstream' producers and arrangers, like Norry Paramour, helped Cliff Richard and others make their early records. It is also important to point out that the techniques (vocal and instrumental) of rock were, in many respects, fairly new. Bluesmen like T-Bone Walker and B.B. King had pioneered a blues 'lead guitar' style, with loud amplification of mainly 'single-string' playing, as recently as the 1940s. The electric bass guitar was almost unknown in Britain until the mid- or late 1950s, and even the electric organ had only really been a widespread option for a few years. The classical (and folk) musicians who looked down on the rock incompetents would themselves mostly have been lost in trying to cope with the new technology of amps and pick-ups, let alone the resources of the new recording studios. All these things the kids soon picked up *without training.*

The most striking thing about the mistaken contempt of the press, educationalists, etc., in the light of my argument, is that they clearly failed to notice a learning process going on among teenagers and especially musical amateurs, which was highly successful and extremely widespread, despite bypassing almost totally the 'establishment' musical institutions – from schools and local music organizations through to the great academies and the broadcasting efforts of the BBC. This learning process could apparently do without all but the most elementary technical *concepts* and all but the most elementary critical/ descriptive/evaluative vocabulary. It took place in groups, the very existence of which was virtually unknown to music educationalists, the media, and so on – the small peer-group gatherings with guitars, etc., in which exact imitating of records gradually grew over into the composing and performing of original material. It fed the enormous popular music boom of the 1960s with the majority of its artists, yet it was virtually dismissed by almost every commentator – if noticed at all – in its early years. What a hunt I have had to find the Rev. Brian Bird's book on *Skiffle,* virtually the only contemporary book to discuss this development other than to dismiss it![4]

The underlying reason for this incomprehension, this failure to see the obvious, was that the type of 'personality' that accompanied, and was promoted by, the new music-use, was very often not at all impressive to observers from the 'parent culture'; it seemed like stupidity, ignorance, callowness, inarticulacy and faddish gullibility. Yet, precisely, it was *growth*; growth of *musicality* in people who had previously been, and in former times would most probably have remained, considerably less musical. A musicality lacking in a certain kind of sophistication perhaps, but one in which a willingness to try, an intuitive originality, a kind of naive modernism – in sum, a new *creativity* – were to the fore, and one which certainly had no time for the notion that musical life, for the 'untalented' majority, must mean nothing more than listening, perhaps propped up with pre-digested 'appreciation'. It was also growth in another sense: the *communal inclination,* the *solidarity* of the youth culture, greatly boosted by music-use, was a value either missed or dismissed by the outside commentators, with few exceptions.

I believe that our habitual terminology for these matters will have to be substantially cleansed before we can explore very far in language the sort of subjectivity towards which such a development would seem to point. And the task is further hampered, of course, by the existence of tendencies which *go against* the creativity and self-confidence of group amateurism among working-class and middle-class people, the tendencies of atomization and cultural retreat which I have mentioned earlier and the tendencies *within* rock music-use which had more to do with *plaisir* and conformity than resistance and the *jouissant* thrill. But we can say, surely, that it would be a subjectivity formed by music, both listening and making, far more so than has been normal for the mass of people hitherto in Britain, and by an active exploratory musical learning process prefigured by rock, jazz, blues and skiffle amateurism; a subjectivity consequently more communally-inclined, knowing a fellowship in music, and enjoying in good measure the thrill or release of *jouissance* as well as the reassurance of *plaisir*, a subjectivity for which music could thus be *a weapon in a fight* for more wholeness of the self and for more community among people, without being diminished in being so used, since this is, after all, the very heart of what music can do.

Music, as a way of resisting the 'irresistible' social odds of our society and a way of perceiving the 'imperceptible' extra-linguistic dimensions of the social world, and where appropriate resisting these too, can be both a healing balm and a surgeon's knife. It is no accident that so many radical journalists, musicians and so on, from Adorno through to the *NME* columnists of the 1980s, see both *consolation* and *resistance* as popular musical possibilities, often tending to disapprove of the former and seek far and wide for the latter. Yet music *must* do both, they are intertwined in its relationship to language and to the socio-physical environment, and there is no point in trying to abandon the *consoling* function, seeing only bad music where it is evident. One might even say that where the resistant element is best realized, then consolation will be inevitably achieved too – people are made to 'feel good'. But, of course, it is to be hoped that the resistant side of the process, music as a potential weapon for freedom, is developed more and more by the working- and middle-class listeners, amateurs and professional musicians themselves. I am not referring to Politics 'with a capital P' here, but to the *mobilization of the Utopianism* in modern popular music, to show up the alienation and seriality of contemporary everyday life so mercilessly that no-one could still want them.

Notes and References

Chapter 1

1 Gillett 1971.
2 Cohn 1969; Marcus 1977.
3 Gillett 1971: 37.
4 See Hindemith 1961: 35–6; Langer 1960: 238.
5 Robertson 1957: 27, 350.
6 Barthes 1977: 179.
7 Laing 1969.
8 Belz 1972.
9 Middleton 1972.
10 See Gellatt 1977: 272; Newton 1960: 189; Gillett 1971: ch. 1.
11 Gillett 1971; Laing 1969; see also Guralnick 1971: 14–20.
12 Cohn 1969: 11–12; Gillett 1971: 10, 12–14.
13 See Lewis 1978: 9–11, 27, 141; see also Frith 1978: 19–36; Laing 1969: 91–5.
14 Gillett 1971; Laing 1969: 91–5.
15 See Gillett 1974.
16 Cohn 1969: chs 7 and 13–16; Gillett 1971: ch. 11; Laing 1969: ch. 8; Lewis 1978: ch. 6; see also Mabey 1969.
17 See Hebdige 1979.
18 See Leigh 1984.
19 Gillett 1971.
20 See Mellers 1968: passim.
21 Cohn 1969: 24–5.
22 Laing and Taylor 1979; Laing 1985.

Chapter 2

1 See Bradley 1980, 1989.
2 Davies 1978: 25.
3 Nattiez 1976.

4 Barthes 1969: 45–6.
5 See Culler 1976.
6 See Shepherd *et al.* 1977: 69–124.
7 Berger 1972: 7.

Chapter 3

1 See Shepherd *et al.* 1977: chs 1–3; see also Small 1977.
2 Adorno 1978: 289–90.
3 Chester 1970: 78–9.
4 See Cooke 1959.
5 Millett 1971: 23–58; Rowbotham 1972: 28–31.
6 Tagg 1979: 60–61.
7 Adorno 1976: 51; Eisler 1951: 20–21; Shepherd *et al.* 1977: chs 1–3.
8 See Schafer 1967: 6.
9 Langer 1953: 108–113.
10 Ibid., p. 111.
11 See Baumol and Bowen 1973: 445–70; see also Frith 1978: 211.
12 Van der Merwe 1989: 221–86.
13 Ibid.
14 See Harker 1980: passim, 1985: passim; see also Laing 1975: passim.
15 See Southern 1971; see also Roberts 1973.
16 Shepherd 1982; van der Merwe 1989.
17 Middleton 1972: passim.
18 See Collier 1978; Oliver 1970; Schuller 1968.
19 Chester 1970: 78–9.
20 Hatch and Millward 1987: 68–86.
21 See Jones 1967: 183; see also Mellers 1964: 264.
22 Wilmer 1977: 148–9.
23 *Melody Maker*, 26 April 1980, pp. 19–20.
24 Langer 1953: 45–69.
25 See Chambers 1985: 11.
26 Stravinsky 1970: 28–9.
27 Op. cit., note 23.

Chapter 4

1 Rice *et al.* 1989: 118.
2 See Colin 1977: 131–5.
3 See Gillett 1971: 13–16.
4 Ibid., p. 298.
5 Ibid., pp. 299–300.
6 Fletcher 1966: 158.
7 Gillett 1971: 161.
8 See Laing 1969: 69; see also Gillett 1971: 30–31.
9 Gillett 1971: 31.
10 See Cooke 1959: 118.
11 Gillett 1971: 30.
12 See Laing 1971: passim.

13 Ibid., pp. 131–40; see also Gillett 1971: 120.
14 See Gammond and Clayton 1960: 177.
15 Melly 1970: 169.
16 Harker 1980: 146–58.
17 Gammond and Clayton 1960.
18 Rice *et al.* 1989: 118, 206.
19 See Gillett 1971: 21; see also Goldberg 1961: 352; Lewis 1978: 132.
20 Gillett 1971: 37.
21 See Escott and Hawkins 1980.
22 Laing 1969: 68–9.
23 Belz 1972: 42.
24 Barthes 1977: 8–9.
25 Gillett 1971: 315–16, 326.
26 I have obtained information on British rock-pop mainly from the sleeve notes of LPs, such as those by Stuart Colman on '1955–1960 British Rock 'n' Roll', See-for-Miles Records, 1985.
27 Harker 1980: 74.
28 Gillett 1971: 293–4.
29 Ibid., p. 293.
30 Cohn 1969: 72–81, 123–41.
31 Fletcher 1966: 158.
32 See Davies 1968; Leigh 1984.
33 Tremlett 1975: 14.
34 Laing 1969: 115–16.
35 Ibid., pp. 103–118; see also Gillett 1971: 291–332; Leigh 1984: passim.
36 See Small 1977: 213–17; see also Shepherd *et al.* 1977: ch. 5; Schools Council 1968.
37 Lee 1970: 149–79, 220–39.
38 Hirshey 1984: 133 and chs 9–13.
39 Burdon 1986.
40 Melly 1970: 133–5.
41 See Groom 1971.
42 Melly 1970: 173.

Chapter 5

1 Hobsbawm 1969: 249–93.
2 See Williams 1965.
3 See Hall *et al.* 1977.
4 Harker 1980; Hobsbawm 1969: esp. pp. 260–64 and table 50; Williams 1965: passim.
5 Hobsbawm 1969: 285.
6 See Abrams 1959; see also Galbraith 1958.
7 Hobsbawm 1969: 283–4.
8 Ibid., p. 249; see also Chambers 1985: 31–7; Gillett 1971: 294–7.
9 See Gellatt 1977: chs 21–3; Harker 1980: 66.
10 Adorno 1976: 30–31.
11 Chambers 1985; Lewis 1978.
12 Frith 1978: 19.
13 Ibid., pp. 60–63.
14 Abrams 1959: 5–14.
15 Abrams, quoted in Hebdige 1979: 154.

16 Harker 1980: 79.
17 Hoggart 1958: 248–50.
18 Chambers 1985: 28; Mabey 1969: 43–6.
19 See Mead and Wolfenstein 1956.
20 Frith and McRobbie 1978.
21 In Chesser *et al.* 1961.
22 See Friedan 1968.
23 Hoggart 1958: 248.
24 Ibid.
25 Scannell 1981; Harker 1980.
26 Quoted in Vulliamy 1982: 128.
27 Swenson 1982: 73; Chambers 1985: 18–44.
28 Frith 1978: 139–43.
29 Hoggart 1958; Swenson 1982; Hall and Whannell 1964.
30 Chambers 1985: 18–44; Melly 1970: 163–74.
31 See Leonard 1962.
32 Melly 1970: 168.
33 Hoggart 1958: 222–31; Newton 1960: 18–24, 168–76; Routh 1972.
34 See Chapple and Garofalo 1977; see also Garfield 1986.
35 See Abrams 1959.
36 Williams 1961: 344–58.
37 See Burdon 1986.
38 See Willis 1977.
39 See Melly 1970.
40 See all works cited in the Bibliography by Adorno; see also Swingewood 1977;
   Hoggart 1958.
41 See Riesman 1950.
42 Sartre 1976: 256–404, 644–54.
43 Hoggart 1958: 340.
44 Sartre 1976: 644–54.
45 *See Hall and Whannell 1964; see also Thomson 1964.
46 Hall and Jefferson 1976; Hebdige 1979; Willis 1978.
47 See Hall and Jefferson 1976.
48 Hebdige 1979: 73–80, 128–33; see also Cohen 1972.
49 See Bowlby 1965; Spock 1956.
50 Fletcher, C., quoted in Raison 1966: 158.
51 See Rice *et al.* 1989.
52 Laing 1969: 91–5.
53 Lewis 1978: 59.
54 See Kinsey *et al.* 1953.
55 Lewis 1978: 61.
56 Ibid., p. 62.
57 See Chesser *et al.* 1961: 6–7; Kinsey *et al.* 1953; see also Schofield 1976.
58 Melly 1970: 207–216.

Chapter 6

1 Hebdige 1979: passim; Willis 1978.
2 See Laing 1985.
3 Colin 1977: 131–5.
4 Laing 1969: 110.

5 Schafer 1967: 6, passim.
6 Gillett 1971: i.
7 Collier 1985: 51.
8 Laing 1985: 61.
9 Hirshey 1985: 186.
10 Swenson 1982: 72–9.
11 Gorki 1950: 115–17; Lee 1970: 134; Leonard 1962: passim.
12 Townshend, P., quoted in Frith 1978: 172.
13 Mellers 1968: 141.
14 Barthes 1977: 8–11, 179–89; Kristeva 1976: passim; Lacan 1968.
15 Adorno 1978: passim; Small 1977: 170–74; Street 1986: passim.
16 See Harker 1980: passim; see also Street 1986: passim.
17 Willis 1978: passim, but esp. pp. 191–3.
18 Cooke 1982: 196–201; Lee 1970: 174; Middleton 1972: 162–74.
19 Lee 1970: 174.
20 Melly 1970: 168.
21 Leigh 1984: 23–8.
22 Sartre 1976: 345–404, 828.
23 Ibid., pp. 351–63.
24 Small 1977: 170–74.
25 Hoggart 1958: 340.
26 Burdon 1986: 31.
27 Melly 1970: 164–7.
28 Freed, A., quoted in Gillett 1971: 16; see also Gillett 1971: 14–17; Hebdige 1979: 52–4.
29 See Laing 1985: 56–7.

Chapter 7

1 See White 1977; see also Burniston and Weedon 1977: 203–233.
2 White, A., quoted in Hebdige 1979: 164.
3 See Barthes 1977: 8–9; see also Kristeva 1974: passim, 1975: passim.
4 Cubitt, S., quoted in Laing 1985: 80.
5 Chambers 1985: 42–4.
6 Frith 1978: 65.
7 See Fiske 1987: passim.
8 Ibid.; see also Kaplan 1987.
9 Hirshey 1984: passim.
10 Fletcher, C., quoted in Mabey 1969: 48.
11 Frith 1978: 65.
12 Townshend, P., sleeve notes to 'Allison', a double LP from 1972 (RCA 24002).
13 Ballantyne 1984: 108–114, 118–21.
14 Cooke 1959: 115–19.
15 Leigh, S., sleeve notes to 'Let's Stomp: Liverpool Beat 1963', one of several LPs of Merseyside issued by EDSEL (ED 103), on which the first two named songs are to be found. The Big Three recording is available on the 'Liverpool 1963–1964 Volume 2' LP, See-for-Miles Records (CM 125).
16 Laing 1969: 123.
17 Ballantyne 1984: 102; Mellers 1984: passim.
18 See Adorno 1941, 1976, 1978; Mabey 1969; Parker 1975.

Chapter 8

1 See Middleton 1972.
2 Ibid., pp. 127–8.
3 Mellers 1964; Oliver 1970, 1982; Schuller 1968: passim.
4 Middleton 1972: 122.
5 See Leonard 1962; Mellers 1968: 141–2; Swenson 1982: 86–7.
6 Hatch and Millward 1987: 116–29, passim.
7 Ibid., p. 117.
8 Ibid., p. 121.
9 See Barthes 1977; Fiske 1987: chs 3–5; Kristeva 1973, 1974, 1976; see also Kristeva, J., quoted in *Working Papers in Cultural Studies 10: On Ideology.* Centre for Contemporary Cultural Studies, University of Birmingham, 1977.
10 Freud 1953 onwards; Jung 1953–1971; Marcuse 1969.
11 Barthes 1977: 10, passim.
12 See Marcuse 1968; see also MacIntyre 1970: 46; Middleton 1972.
13 Fromm 1963: 78–208; Hobsbawm 1973: 285–92; Williams 1961: 13–84.
14 Hobsbawm 1973: 224–44.
15 Bauman 1982, 1983.
16 Bauman 1982: 59–75.
17 Thompson 1968: 781–3.
18 See Elias 1978.
19 See Liebow 1967.
20 Copland, A., quoted in Giddings 1984: 46.
21 Shepherd *et al.* 1977: passim; Small 1977: passim.
22 Barthes 1977: 179–89.
23 Ibid., pp. 179–81.

Conclusions

1 Belz 1972: 7–8.
2 Gillett 1971: 293–301.
3 Melly 1970: 166.
4 Bird 1958.

Bibliography

Abrams, M. (1959). *The Teenage Consumer*. London, Press Exchange.
Adorno, T.W. (1941). 'On popular music'. *Studies in Philosophy and Social Sciences* IX.
Adorno, T.W. (1945). 'A social critique of radio music'. *Kenyon Review* 8(2).
Adorno, T.W. (1967). *Prisms* (translated by S. Weber and S. Weber). London, Spearman.
Adorno, T.W. (1972). 'Theses on the sociology of art'. *Working Papers in Cultural Studies* 2 (translated by B. Trench). Centre for Contemporary Cultural Studies, University of Birmingham.
Adorno, T.W. (1973a). *Negative Dialectics*. New York, Seabury Press.
Adorno, T.W. (1973b). *Philosophy of Modern Music* (translated by A.G. Mitchell and W.V. Bloomster). New York, Seabury Press.
Adorno, T.W. (1976). *Introduction to the Sociology of Music* (translated by E.B. Ashton). New York, Seabury Press.
Adorno, T.W. (1978). 'On the fetish-character in music and the regression of listening'. In *The Essential Frankfurt School Reader* (edited by A. Arato and E. Gebhardt). New York, Urizen.
Amis, K. (1954). *Lucky Jim*. London, Gollancz.
Ballantyne, C. (1984). *Music and its Social Meanings*. London, Gordon and Breach.
Barthes, R. (1969). *Elements of Semiology*. London, Cape.
Barthes, R. (1972). *Mythologies*. London, Paladin.
Barthes, R. (1977). *Image–Music–Text* (translated by S. Heath). London, Fontana/Collins.
Bauman, Z. (1982). *Memories of Class*. London, Routledge and Kegan Paul.
Bauman, Z. (1983). 'Industrialism, consumerism and power'. *Theory, Culture and Society* 1(3).
Baumol, W.J. and Bowen, W.G. (1973). 'The audience: Some fact-sheet data'. In *Sociology of Literature and Drama* (edited by E. Burns and T. Burns), pp. 445–70. Harmondsworth, Penguin.
Belz, C. (1972). *The Story of Rock*. Oxford, Oxford University Press.
Berger, J. (1972). *Ways of Seeing*. London, BBC/Penguin.
Bird, B. (1958). *Skiffle*. London, Robert Hale.
Bontinck, I. (ed.) (1974). *New Patterns of Musical Behaviour*. Vienna, Universal Editions.
Bowlby, J. (1965). *Childcare and the Growth of Love*. London, Pelican (originally published 1951).

Bradley, D. (1980). *The Cultural Study of Music*. Stencilled Paper No. 61. Centre for Contemporary Studies, University of Birmingham.

Bradley, D. (1989). *From Rock 'n' Roll to Beat in Britain: An Exploration in the Cultural Study of Music*. PhD thesis, University of Birmingham.

Burdon, E. (1986). *I Used to be an Animal but I'm Alright Now*. London, Faber.

Burniston, S. and Weedon, C. (1977). 'Ideology, subjectivity and the artistic text'. In *Working Papers in Cultural Studies 10: On Ideology*, pp. 203–233. Centre for Contemporary Studies, University of Birmingham.

Chambers, I. (1985). *Urban Rhythms*. London, Macmillan.

Chapple, S. and Garofalo, R. (1977). *Rock 'n' Roll is Here to Pay: The History and Politics of the Music Industry*. Chicago, Chicago University Press.

Chesser, E. *et al.* (1961). *Teenage Morals*. London (publisher not given).

Chester, A. (1970). 'Second thoughts on a rock aesthetic: The band'. *New Left Review* 62, 78–9.

Christgau, R. (1973). *Any Old Way You Choose It*. London, Penguin.

Clayson, A. (1985). *The Golden Age of British Beat 1962–67*. Poole, Blandford Press.

Cohen, P. (1972). 'Sub-cultural conflict and working-class community'. In *Working Papers in Cultural Studies 2*. Centre for Contemporary Cultural Studies, University of Birmingham.

Cohn, N. (1969). *Awopbopa loo bop alop bam boom*. London, Weidenfeld and Nicholson.

Colin, S. (1977). *And the Band Played On*. London, Elm Tree Books.

Collier, J.L. (1978). *The Making of Jazz*. New York, Houghton-Mifflin.

Collier, J.L. (1985). *Louis Armstrong*. London, Pan Books.

Cooke, D. (1959). *The Language of Music*. Oxford, Oxford University Press.

Cooke, D. (1982). *Vindications*. London, Faber and Faber.

Culler, J. (1976). *Saussure*. London, Fontana.

Davies, H. (1968). *The Beatles*. London, Heinemann.

Davies, J.B. (1978). *The Psychology of Music*. London, Hutchinson.

Dilthey, W. (1927). *Der Aufbau der geschichtlichen Welt in den Geisteswissenschaften*. Leipzig, Leipzig University.

Dilthey, W. (1933). *Von Deutscher Dichtung und Music: Aus den Studien zur Geschichte des deutschen Geiste*. Leipzig, Leipzig University.

Eisen, J. (ed.) (1969). *The Age of Rock*. New York, Vintage Books.

Eisen, J. (ed.) (1970). *The Age of Rock 2*. New York, Vintage Books.

Eisler, H. (1951). *Composing for the Films*. New York, Denis Dobson.

Elias, N. (1978). *The Civilizing Process*. Oxford, Blackwell.

Escott, C. and Hawkins, M. (1980). *Sun Records: The Brief History of the Legendary Record Label*. London, Quick Fox.

Etzkorn, K.P. (1968). *George Simmel: The Conflict in Modern Culture*. New York, Teachers College Press.

Etzkorn, K.P. (1973). *Music and Society: The Later Writings of Paul Honigsheim*. New York, John Wiley.

Ewen, D. (1977). *All the Years of American Popular Music*. Englewood Cliffs, N.J., Prentice-Hall.

Fiske, J. (1987). *Television Culture*. London, Methuen.

Fletcher, C. (1966). 'Beats and gangs in Merseyside'. In *Youth in New Society* (edited by T. Raison). London, Hart Davis.

Freud, S. (1953 onwards). *Civilization and its Discontents*: Vol. 21 of *Complete Works*. London, Hogarth Press.

Friedan, B. (1968). *The Feminine Mystique*. Harmondsworth, Penguin.

Frith, S. (1978). *The Sociology of Rock*. London, Constable.

Frith, S. and McRobbie, A. (1978). 'Rock and sexuality'. *Screen Education* 29.

Fromm, E. (1963). *The Sane Society*. London, Routledge and Kegan Paul.

Galbraith, J.K. (1958). *The Affluent Society*. London, Hamish Hamilton.

Gammond, P. and Clayton, P. (1960). *A Guide to Popular Music*. London, Phoenix House.

Garfield, S. (1986). *Expensive Habits: The Dark Side of the Music Industry*. London, Faber and Faber.

Gellatt, R. (1977). *The Fabulous Phonograph 1877–1977*. London, Cassell.

Giddings, R. (1984). *Musical Quotes and Anecdotes*. London, Longman.

Gillett, C. (1971). *The Sound of the City*. London, Sphere.

Gillett, C. (ed.) (1972). *Rock File*. London, Pictorial Presentations.

Gillett, C. (1974). *Making Tracks: The History of Atlantic Records*. New York, Sunrise/Dutton.

Goldberg, I. (1961). *Tin Pan Alley: A Chronicle of American Popular Music*. New York, Frederick Ungar.

Gorki, M. (1950). *Articles and Pamphlets*. Moscow, Foreign Languages Publishing House.

Groom, B. (1971). *The Blues Revival*. London, Studio Vista.

Grossman, L. (1976). *A Social History of Rock Music*. New York, David McKay.

Guralnick, P. (1971). *Feel Like Going Home*. London, Omnibus.

Hall, S. and Jefferson, T. (1976). *Resistance through Rituals*. London, Hutchinson.

Hall. S. and Whannel, P. (1964). *The Popular Arts*. London, Hutchinson.

Hall, S. *et al.* (1977). *Policing the Crisis*. London, Macmillan.

Haralambos, M. (1974). *Right On! From Blues to Soul in Black America*. London, Edison.

Harker, D. (1980). *One for the Money: Politics and Popular Song*. London, Hutchinson.

Harker, D. (1985). *Fakesong: The Manufacture of British 'Folksong', 1700 to the Present Day*. Milton Keynes, Open University Press.

Hatch, D. and Millward, S. (1987). *From Blues to Rock: An Analytical History of Pop Music*. Manchester, Manchester University Press.

Hebdige, D. (1979). *Subculture: The Meaning of Style*. London, Methuen.

Hindemith, P. (1961). *A Composer's World*. New York, Doubleday.

Hirshey, G. (1985). *Nowhere to Run: The Story of Soul Music*. London, Pan.

Hobsbawm, E.J. (1969). *Industry and Empire*. Harmondsworth, Pelican.

Hobsbawm, E.J. (1973). *The Age of Revolutions*. London, Cardinal/Sphere.

Hoggart, R. (1958). *The Uses of Literacy*. Harmondsworth, Pelican.

Jones, L. (1967). *Black Music*. New York, Quill.

Jung, K. (1953–71). *Collected Works*. London, Routledge and Kegan Paul.

Kaplan, E.A. (1987). *Rocking Around the Clock: Music, Television, Postmodernism and Consumer Culture*. New York, Methuen.

Kerman, J. (1985). *Musicology*. London, Fontana.

Kinsey, A.C. *et al.* (1953). *Sexual Behaviour in the Human Female*. Philadelphia, W.B. Saunders.

Kristeva, J. (1973). 'The semiotic activity'. *Screen* 14(1 and 2).

Kristeva, J. (1974). *La Revolution du Language Poetique*. Paris, Seuil.

Kristeva, J. (1976). 'Signifying practice and mode of production'. *Edinburgh 76 Magazine* No. 1.

Lacan, J. (1968). 'The mirror phase'. *New Left Review* 51.

Laing, D. (1969). *The Sound of Our Time*. London, Sheed and Ward.

Laing, D. (1971). *Buddy Holly*. London/New York, November Books/Collier Macmillan.

Laing, D. (1985). *One Chord Wonders*. Milton Keynes, Open University Press.

Laing, D. and Taylor, J. (1979). 'Disco–pleasure–discourse'. *Screen Education* 31.

Laing, D., Dallas, K. *et al.* (1975). *The Electric Muse: The Story of Folk into Rock*. London, Methuen.

Langer, S.K. (1953). *Feeling and Form*. London, Routledge and Kegan Paul.

Langer, S.K. (1960). *Philosophy in a New Key*. Cambridge, Mass., Harvard University Press.

Lee, E. (1970). *Music of the People: A Study of Popular Music in Great Britain*. London, Barrie and Jenkins.

Leigh, S. (1984). *Let's Go Down to the Cavern*. London, Vermilion.

Leonard, N. (1962). *Jazz and the White Americans*. Chicago, Chicago University Press.

Lewis, P. (1978). *The Fifties*. London, Heinemann.

Liebow, E. (1967). *Tally's Corner*. Boston, Little, Brown.

McInnes, C. (1959). Absolute Beginners. London, McGibbon and Kee.

Mabey, R. (1969). *The Pop Process*. London, Hutchinson.

MacIntyre, A. (1970). *Marcuse*. London, Fontana.

Marcus, G. (1977). *Mystery Train*. London, Omnibus.

Marcuse, H. (1968). *One-dimensional Man*. London, Sphere.

Marcuse, H. (1969). *Eros and Civilization*. London, Sphere.

Mead, M. and Wolfenstein, M. (eds) (1956). *Childhood in Contemporary Culture*. Chicago, Chicago University Press.

Mellers, W. (1964). *Music in a New Found Land*. London, Barrie and Rockliffe.

Mellers, W. (1968). *Caliban Reborn: Renewal in Twentieth Century Music*. London, Gollancz.

Mellers, W. (1984). *A Darker Shade of Pale: A Backdrop to Bob Dylan*. London, Faber.

Melly, G. (1970). *Owning Up*. Harmondsworth, Penguin.

Meyer, L.B. (1956). *Emotion and Meaning in Music*. Chicago, Chicago University Press.

Meyer, L.B. (1967). *Music, the Arts and Ideas*. Chicago, Chicago University Press.

Middleton, R. (1972). *Pop Music and the Blues*. London, Gollancz.

Millar, B. (1971). *The Drifters*. London, November Books.

Millett, K. (1971). *Sexual Politics*. London, Sphere.

Nattiez, J.J. (1976). *Fondements d'une semiologie de la musique*. Paris, Editions 10/18 (Uge).

Newton, F. (1960). *The Jazz Scene*. London, McGibbon and Kee.

Oliver, P. (1968). *Screening the Blues*. London, Cassell.

Oliver, P. (1970). *Savannah Syncopators: African Retentions in the Blues*. London, Studio Vista.

Oliver, P. (1982). 'Twixt midnight and day: Binarism, blues and black culture'. In *Popular Music 2: Theory and Method* (edited by R. Middleton and D. Horn). Cambridge, Cambridge University Press.

Osbourne, J. (1957). *Look Back in Anger*. London, Faber and Faber.

Palmer, T. (1970). *Born Under a Bad Sign*. London, William Kimber.

Parker, C. (1975). 'Pop song: The manipulated ritual'. In *The Black Rainbow* (edited by P. Abbs). London (publisher not given).

Rice, J., Rice, T. and Gambaccini, P. (1989). *British Hit Singles*. London, GRR/Guiness.

Riesman, D. (1950). *The Lonely Crowd*. New Haven, Conn., Yale University Press.

Roberts, J.S. (1973). *Black Music of Two Worlds*. New York, Allen Lane.

Robertson, A. (1957). *Chamber Music*. Harmondsworth, Pelican.

Rogers, D. (1982). *Rock 'n' Roll*. London, Routledge and Kegan Paul.

Routh, F. (1972). *Contemporary British Music*. London, MacDonald (first published 1964).

Rowbotham, S. (1972). *Women, Resistance and Revolution*. Harmondsworth, Penguin.

Salinger, J.D. (1958). *The Catcher in the Rye*. Harmondsworth, Penguin.

Sartre, J.-P. (1976). *Critique of Dialectical Reason*. London, New Left Books.

Scannell, P. (1981). 'Music for the multitude'. *Media–Culture–Society* 3(3).

Schafer, M.R. (1967). *The New Soundscape*. Canada, Universal Edition BMI.

Schofield, M. (1976). *Promiscuity*. London, Gollancz.

Schools Council (1968). *Enquiry: The Young School Leavers*. London, HMSO.

Schuller, G. (1968). *Early Jazz*. Oxford, Oxford University Press.
Shaw, A. (1969). *The Rock Revolution*. London, Collier Macmillan.
Shaw, A. (1974). *The Rocking Fifties*. New York, Hawthorn.
Shepherd, J. (1982). 'A theoretical model for the sociomusicological analysis of popular music'. In *Popular Music 2: Theory and Method* (edited by R. Middleton and D. Horn). Cambridge, Cambridge University Press.
Shepherd, J. *et al.* (eds) (1977). *Whose Music: A Sociology of Musical Languages*. London, Latimer.
Silbermann, A. (1963). *The Sociology of Music*. London, Routledge and Kegan Paul.
Small, C. (1977). *Music–Society–Education*. London, John Calder.
Southern, E. (1971). *The Music of Black Americans: A History*. New York, W.W. Norton.
Spock, B. (1956). *Baby and Child Care*. New York, Pocket Books.
Stravinsky, I. (1970). *The Poetics of Music*. Cambridge, Mass., Harvard University Press.
Street, J. (1986). *Rebel Rock: The Politics of Popular Music*. Oxford, Blackwell.
Swenson, J. (1982). *Bill Haley*. London, W.H. Allen.
Swingewood, A. (1977). *The Myth of Mass Culture*. London, Macmillan.
Tagg, P. (1979). *Kojak: 50 Seconds of Television Music*. Thesis, University of Gothenburg.
Thompson, E.P. (1968). *The Making of the English Working Class*. Harmondsworth, Pelican.
Thomson, D. (ed.) (1964). *Discrimination and Popular Culture*. Harmondsworth, Penguin.
Tremlett, G. (1975). *The Who*. London, Furure.
Van der Merwe, P. (1989). *Origins of the Popular Style*. Oxford, Clarendon Press.
Vulliamy, G. (1982). *Jazz and Blues*. London, Routledge and Kegan Paul.
Weber, M. (1958). *The Rational and Social Foundations of Music* (translated and edited by D. Martindale). New York, Reidel and Neuwirth.
White, A. (1977). *L'eclatement du sujet: The Theoretical Work of Julia Kristeva*. Paper available from the University of Birmingham.
Williams, R. (1961). *Culture and Society 1780–1950*. Harmondsworth, Penguin.
Williams, R. (1965). *The Long Revolution*. Harmondsworth, Pelican.
Willis, P. (1977). *Learning to Labour*. Farnborough, Saxon House.
Willis, P. (1978). *Profane Culture*. London, Routledge and Kegan Paul.
Wilmer, V. (1977). *Jazz People*. New York, Quartet Books.

Index